Imagining Transgender

An Ethnography of a Category

David Valentine

DUKE UNIVERSITY PRESS DURHAM AND LONDON 2007

© 2007 Duke University Press

All rights reserved

Printed in the United States of America

on acid-free paper ∞

Designed by Katy Clove

Typeset in Sabon by Keystone Typesetting, Inc.

Library of Congress Cataloging-in-Publication Data

appear on the last printed page of this book.

Imagining Transgender

FOR VIANNA-FAYE WILLIAMS,

in place of the chicken soup I never had

the chance to bring you

Contents

List of Illustrations ix
Acknowledgments xi

Part I: Imagining Transgender

Introduction 3

1. Imagining Transgender 29

Part II: Making Community, Conceiving Identity

Introduction to Part II:
Reframing Community and Identity 68

2. Making Community 71

3. "I Know What I Am": Gender, Sexuality, and Identity 105

Part III: Emerging Fields

Introduction to Part III:
The Transexual, the Anthropologist, and the Rabbi 140

4. The Making of a Field:
Anthropology and Transgender Studies 143

5. The Logic of Inclusion: Transgender Activism 173

6. The Calculus of Pain: Violence, Narrative, and the Self 204

Conclusion: Making Ethnography 231

Notes 257
Works Cited 277
Index 299

Illustrations

FIGURES

1. Gender Identity Project Pamphlet (1997) 10
2a and b. Ball Program for the *Great Ball of FIRE* (October 1997) 78–79
3. Crossdressers International Debutante Ball Flyer (March 1997) 86
4. Ruth Messinger's letter of support for *Night of a Thousand Gowns* (March 1997) 92
5. Gender Identity Project Flyer (1997) 107
6a and b. NYC Commission on Human Rights postcard publicizing the "Transgender Rights Bill" 198
7. Postcard advertising the reopening of the Lesbian, Gay, Bisexual, and Transgender Community Center 199

TABLES

1. The organization of performance categories, gender, and sexuality at a Clubhouse ball 82
2. The organization of drag, gender, and sexuality at the Crossdressers International Debutante ball 89
3. The organization of drag, gender, and sexuality at the *Night of a Thousand Gowns* ball 93

Acknowledgments

In my research and writing I have incurred many debts. First among these is to my advisor Bambi Schieffelin, without whose insights and friendship I would never even have started out on this project, and certainly would not have finished it. Bambi is responsible for the length of these acknowledgments, for she taught me, among many other things, that scholarship should never be a lonely endeavor and I have taken her at her word. Among my many other teachers, I need to express special gratitude to Faye Ginsburg and Lila Abu-Lughod for their acute observations and constant encouragement. I am moreover deeply indebted to Don Kulick for turning me into an anthropologist in the first place, and for putting me back on course time after time. My thanks also go to Steven Gregory, Shirley Lindenbaum, Owen Lynch, and Fred Myers for their ongoing interest in and support of this project.

Beyond my graduate school teachers, the list of thanks is long indeed. First, my research could not have taken the form it did without the help of Dr. Barbara Warren of the LGBT Community Center in New York City, who took me on as a staff member, provided me resources, and listened to what I had to say. Rosalyne Blumenstein, who was then director of the Center's Gender Identity Project (GIP), became my friend, my teacher, and a facilitator of my research. I am also indebted to several key participants who shared so much with me during my fieldwork. Without the constant questioning and good humor of Riki Anne Wilchins, this would only be half a book. Riki's querying of the assumptions that inform projects such as mine, and our long conversations, were central to the development of my ideas even though we also disagreed at times. Cindy Shuster, and the entire Tribe of Cindys, was an enormous influence and I can never thank her enough for her friendship and help. Eden Miller has been a stalwart and a reminder of the possibilities for both human resilience and fun. Both Nora Molina and Melissa Sklarz, peer counselors at GIP at the time of my research, shared with me their lives and their expertise, and also became dear friends. A particular debt of gratitude is owed to Nancy Lamar, for providing me with such precise and cheerful sociological observations and facilitating so much of my research. The late Vianna-Faye Williams, to whom this work is dedicated, has my thanks even though I will never be able to tell her.

Literally hundreds more people shared their experiences with me, spent time teaching me, and patiently allowed themselves and their lives to be examined. I cannot thank them all by name, but I must express my gratitude in particular to Alex, Andrew, Anita, Miss Angel and the Alternative Lifestyles Group, the late Penni Ashe, the irrepressible David Barboni, Max Beck, John Capazuca, Cherry, Charity, Cheryl Chase, Chris, Connie, Martha Coventry, Baby Dee, Dallas Denny, Chloe Dzubilo, Diana, Fiona, Caitlin Flowers for her hospitality in Atlanta, Frederique, Glorya Galicki-Gilvary, Nic Gianelli, Antonia Gilligan, Jamison Green, Gwen, Arlene Hoffman, Morgan Holmes, India, Jade, Jamie, Julip, Kerri, Karalyn Kidde, Alison Laing, L'Oreal, Hedda Lettuce, Christopher Leonard, Lisa, Melinda, Tina Melt, Mona, Christian O'Neal, Miss Nina Love, Dana Priesing, Pussy, Rita, Yvonne Ritter, Carla Roldos, Arbert Santana, Mother of the House of Latex, Shantee, Sherry, Renee Smith, Tina Sparkles, Phil Stoehr/Philomena, Sugar, Susan, Sybil, Tamara, Tanya, Tara, Melissa Thunderpussy, Tina, Miss Understood, Velvet and Antonia, Heidi Walcott, Lynn Walker, Bali White, Renee White, and Yolanda. The whole Crossdressers International crowd—Kristine, Carrie, Vicki, Vivian, Karen, Alma, Barbara, Tina, The Lady Lucille, and all the rest—were always welcoming of me and interested in my work, and they have my thanks. I am also grateful to Heino Meyer-Bahlburg and the members of the Working Group on Gender at the NYS Psychiatric Institute for allowing me to participate in their work. My colleagues in the New York Association for Gender Rights Advocacy—Donna Cartwright, Paisley Currah, Carrie Davis, Pauline Park, Joann Prinzivalli, and others who cycled through its board—taught me how to juggle theory and activism, for which I am grateful. I must also thank as facilitators of my research Ed Cheslow, James Grimaldi, Tom Hill, Jay Irwin, Kelly McGowan, Cynthia Rothschild, and Derek Williams. Finally, my fieldwork would not have been possible without the help and friendship of the entire staff of the LGBT Community Center in New York.

In the long stretch between finishing fieldwork and finishing this book, I have developed another set of professional and personal debts. The core members of the Writers' Bloc — Henry Goldschmidt, Ben Chesluk, and Heather Levi — are thanked for their endless readings and rereadings of this work, first as a dissertation, and later as it was being reshaped as a book. I am also grateful to other WB members — Laura Kunreuther, Susan Lepselter, Meg McCullough, Brian Mooney, Amy Paugh, and Angela Torresan — for their help in writing the dissertation which preceded this book. Katherine Frank, Julie Abraham, and Tom Boellstorff all provided wonderful insights and generous readings of various drafts and incarnations. I am further grateful to my colleagues in the department of anthropology at the University of Minnesota for their support, insights, and calming words, and to Hoon Song and Karen Ho especially for their generous readings of my work. Ben Singer, a former "informant," has also become a close collaborator, and I have appreciated his insights, friendship, and help enormously. I must also thank my students Sophie Rogers-Gessert and Guido Sanchez for their research assistance. I am further indebted to Robert Hill, who very generously shared his research on Virginia Prince with me; Lee Brown, who was equally generous in sharing his research into early 1970s gay liberation media; and Richard Ekins, for his willingness to engage in discussions about the origins of the category transgender. I also want to recognize the support and help — in many different ways — throughout this project of Mariette Pathy Allen, Deb Amory, Ellen Benoit, Karl Bryant, Deborah Elliston, Eri Fujieda, Jamison Green, Judith Halberstam, Bill Leap, Ellen Lewin, Martin Manalansan, Jeff Maskovsky, Esther Newton, Shannon Minter, Karen Rader, Shahnaz Rouse, Carole Vance, Beck Young, Carol Zoref, and the 1996 and 1997 SSRC Sexuality Research Fellowship Fellows. Gratitude is also due members of the Society of Lesbian and Gay Anthropologists for providing a supportive context for my research and its presentation. Finally, I should note that my task was immeasurably aided by the diligence and insights of the encyclopedic Susan Stryker, who provided me with historical data and insights at serendipitous moments, and by Joanne Meyerowitz's remarkable book *How Sex Changed,* which was crucial to my understanding of the historical processes I write of in this book.

Of course, all the above are absolved of any responsibility for my idiosyncratic use of their contributions in constructing the arguments in this book.

The research that forms the basis for this study was made possible through a grant from the Social Science Research Council's Sexuality Research Fellowship Program, with funds made available by the Ford Foundation. I (as well as many others) am deeply indebted to Diane di Mauro, the SRFP director, whose vision for a field of sexuality research has had a profound impact. The final preparation of the manuscript was supported by University of Minnesota McKnight and Faculty Summer Research Fellowships. Ken Wissoker, at Duke University Press, has my gratitude for his dogged perseverance in getting this book to print, as do the anonymous reviewers who provided me with both critical and encouraging feedback.

To end, a list of personal thanks: to Diana Boernstein for providing me with a wonderful home before, during, and after fieldwork, and for making it possible for me to go to graduate school in the first place; to Stacey Lutz for friendship, statistical support, and her ongoing contributions to my thinking; and to Dayna Davis and Jerry Jameson, who were beacons for me. Marion and Alistair Boddy-Evans, Lis Duke, Alison Fraser, Raeph Laughingwell, Antigone Nounou, and Michael and Helen West all provided endless encouragement and support in many different ways, from phone calls and gym partnerships to portraits and Greek isle retreats, and they all learned not to ask if I was finished yet. I thank my parents, Marie and Gerald, and my siblings, Joanne, Suzanne, and Anthony, for their love and unwavering support despite not being entirely sure what I was up to. And last, but not least, my thanks to David Landis for seven years of unconditional support, for enduring the writing of this not once, but twice, and for forcing me to explain myself better when I thought I had already done my best. I hope he will read it now.

Part I

Imagining Transgender

Introduction

"I've been gay all my life, been a woman all my life," says Fiona. I am sitting with Fiona and five other people around a table at the semi-monthly support group for transgender-identified people with HIV at New York Hospital in Manhattan. Two of us — myself and James, the group facilitator — identify as non-transgender gay men and are white, male-bodied, middle-class professionals. The other five, including Fiona, though born male, present themselves and live their lives as feminine people and are either African American or Latina.[1]

However, although the group is billed as a transgender support group, none of the participants routinely refer to themselves as transgender. More often, they talk about themselves as girls, sometimes as fem queens, every now and then as women, but also very often as gay, this category being one I share with them in talking about myself. Most of the group members work in poorly paying service jobs, many have had some experience of sex work, and all have experienced some kind of harassment or violence directed at them because of their feminine presentation. At least two rely on some form of public assistance, and all of them have traveled to the wealthy Upper East Side from the Bronx, Brooklyn, New Jersey, and the East Village to be at the group. Finally, it is worth noting that while "transgender" is conventionally seen to incorporate both male-to-female (MTF) and female-to-male (FTM) identified people, the group has never had an FTM participant.

Since the early 1990s when the term was coined,[2] the category trans-gender has come to be understood as a *collective* category of identity which incorporates a diverse array of male- and female-bodied gender variant people who had previously been understood as distinct kinds of persons, including self-identified transexuals and transvestites, but also many others such as Fiona and her peers. In its collectivity, the capacity of transgender to incorporate all gender variance has become a powerful tool of activism and personal identification. And, even more remarkably, in the period since the early 1990s it has already become institutionalized in a vast range of contexts, from grassroots activism, social service provision, and individual identification, to journalistic accounts and the way that this book itself is categorized. Most importantly, transgender identification is understood across these domains to be explicitly and fundamentally dif-ferent in origin and being from homosexual identification, a distinction referred to in the social sciences as *ontological*. This distinction, in turn, has been made possible through another that developed in social theory and activism over the past thirty years: that between sexed body, social gender, and sexuality. In this ordering of human experience, gender iden-tity is not causally related to sexual desire, and both are conceptualized as independent of sexed bodies. In short, "transgender" has changed the terms by which U.S. Americans understand and differentiate between gen-dered and sexual variance.

As such, Fiona's claim seems to confound this distinction. As a male-bodied person, by claiming to be both a woman (understandable in con-temporary terms as "transgender") but also as "gay" (indexing her attrac-tion to other male-bodied people), her statement can be read as a claim to occupy the categories of *both* transgender *and* homosexual as equivalent categories of personhood. While many self-identified transgender people do indeed also identify as gay or lesbian, for these individuals gay or lesbian identity is understood as a separate issue, a matter of *sexuality*, and distinct from the *gender* identity which is expressed through their identi-ties as transgender. But Fiona makes no ontological distinction between her "gendered" life as a woman and her "sexual" desire as gay. The fact that she and her peers do not use transgender to talk about themselves highlights this alternative understanding and organization of their gen-dered and sexual lives.

For many of the social service providers and activists who were my colleagues, however, Fiona's view of gendered and sexual identity was not merely an alternative categorization but a false one. In their view, Fiona was using an outmoded view of gendered and sexual identity which conflates or confuses her transgender identity with homosexual desire. This is a result, they argue, of class, racial, or cultural inequalities which have left Fiona and her peers outside the conversations and historical developments which have made this distinction possible. Likewise, my presence in this group, doing research on transgender communities, points to the same set of orderings: I was there because it seemed to me that Fiona and her peers were clearly transgender, an understanding framed by the name of the support group itself. By their presence, it was obvious that they must recognize this term as being at least somewhat relevant to them, but Fiona's use of the term "gay" to describe herself confounded the distinctions I understood to be relevant at the beginning of my research.

This is not to say that Fiona and her peers did not make distinctions between themselves and other kinds of people, though. This became apparent when I turned up for the next meeting two weeks later. With great sensitivity for my feelings, the participants told me that it might be best if I didn't attend the group anymore. Not everyone felt this way: Diana said she didn't mind if I attended because "we're all gay." However, Frederique, speaking for the majority, said: "You aren't a girl, you don't have boobs and this figure," motioning down her body with her hands. "With you here, there's another man in the room." Even though Diana, Frederique, and other members of the group had spent much time jesting with me about our common identification as "gay," it was clear that being "gay" meant something different for me and them.

People everywhere categorize themselves and others; this is one of the most fundamental aspects of human language and meaningmaking. But the ways in which these categorizations are made, and which categories come to have effects in the world, are never neutral. If Frederique saw me and herself as different, it is for reasons other than those proposed by the social service providers I worked with. The difference between these categorical systems, the value attached to them, and the differential impact that they have in U.S. American society is the central story of this book. The questions that underpin this story emerge from this brief ethnographic snapshot: How is it that these five people have come together in a "transgender" group when they rarely use the term about themselves? If to be gay indexes her male embodiment, how can Fiona also claim to be a woman? How have group members been included in a notion of a "transgender community" as a broad collectivity defined against homosexual identification when that distinction is not entirely relevant to them? In turn, what does it mean that the group members refer to themselves as "gay" when homosexual identification is routinely seen as radically separate from "transgender" in many institutional contexts? Yet again, why is it that the way the girls understand themselves as "gay" is clearly different from the way they — and I — conceptualize *my* "gayness"? Why do my colleagues see Fiona's claims about herself as, essentially, invalid? And why have I — an anthropologist interested in transgender communities — found my way into a context where people don't use this category about themselves? Moreover, why are there only male-born people in the room and why was I able to talk to and work with so few FTM participants over the course of my study? Why are all the group members poor and people of color, and how might the structure of identity categories described above resonate with — or create anew — racial and class inequalities? On a broader terrain, what is the reason for the incredibly rapid dissemination of "transgender" in the United States since the early 1990s which has cemented the distinction between gender variance and sexual orientation? And what do these questions tell us about the broader politics of gender and sexuality (or, as I will more often write, "gender" and "sexuality") in the contemporary United States?

These are all questions that I take up in this book which is a critical ethnographic exploration of the origins, meanings, and consequences of the emergence and institutionalization of the category transgender in the United States since the early 1990s. The reason these questions are important, I will argue, is that for all the power of transgender as a category of identity and social justice activism, my fear is that people like Fiona — poor, black, and disenfranchised — may be left out of an imagined future of justice and freedom frequently understood as enabled by this category.

The New York Hospital support group was just one of many sites I worked in over the eighteen months of my fieldwork in New York City, and I spent much time bicycling from one field site to another that appeared to me and my social service provider colleagues to be part of a transgender community. But I was often confused by just the kinds of categorical complications I describe above and how they upset the terms of a stable transgender community I was attempting to study. These complications — and my confusions about them — ended up shaping this ethnography and the theoretical and political questions that underpin it. To best understand how these questions emerged, then, I want to start with an ethnographic amalgam of a Saturday in the summer of 1997, to show how these categorical complications arose out of the contexts of my own imagining of a transgender community.

MAPPING THE TERRITORY

The first thing to tell you about is my bicycle. A bicycle can take you from the semi-industrial, semi-dangerous Meat Market of the far West Village to a community center for residents of low-income housing in the East Village in about ten minutes; from a cross-dresser bar on a littered stretch of 10th Avenue to an activist's apartment in the leafy calm of Greenwich Village in about fifteen; or from a splendid drag ball at the Hilton in midtown to a subterranean club near Tribeca on the same evening, with a stop at your apartment for a quick and necessary change of clothing. I use the metaphors of my cycling and of mapping because they describe how social practices, discourses, sites, and people became part of the conceptual field of my research, shaped by an imaginary of a transgender community, but how, simultaneously, the people that I and my colleagues mapped into this imaginary confounded its terms.[3]

So, to the mapping: on the fourth Saturday of every month, the Transgender Health and Education Clinic (THE Clinic) holds hours at the Community Health Project (CHP) on the second floor of the Lesbian and Gay Community Services Center on 13th Street in Manhattan.[4] On one such Saturday in the summer of 1997, I cycle to the Center from my apartment in the Village and walk upstairs through the Saturday morning crush to meet Melissa. Melissa is a Jewish transexual woman who has recently transitioned and who volunteers at THE Clinic as a counselor.[5] Melissa also works as a peer counselor at the Gender Identity Project (GIP), located on the third floor of the Center, where I have a staff position for the duration of my research as both researcher and safer-sex outreach worker, and where, just a few years before, she had herself been a client. At THE Clinic, clients receive inexpensive medical care, and once they have had their blood monitored for three months, the attending doctors may agree to prescribe hormones in order for the client to pursue transition.

Today I see Andrew and Cindy, both friends I have made during my research, and I catch up with them in the cramped waiting area, eating pizza. Melissa tells us about her most recent visit home to California, and of the victory of having her nieces introduced to their Aunt Melissa. Cindy shows me a pamphlet from a clinic in Montreal where she has an appointment for sex reassignment surgery in January. Later, Cherry walks in and after saying our hellos she sits down to read the autobiography of the Lady Chablis, a famous drag performer. The talk is of hormones, transition, coming out at work, taunting endured, a recent murder of a fem queen who was turning tricks — doing sex work — in the nearby Meat Market district.

THE Clinic brings together a range of people who would otherwise be unlikely to meet: Cherry is a young African American self-identified transsexual woman. Unlike many of her peers such as Fiona, Cherry does not understand herself as "gay" and she despises the term "fem queen." Cindy is a white, working-class, transexual woman who lives with her former spouse and their two children. Andrew is a white, gay-identified transexual man who travels in from out of town once a month for his appointment.[6] While they and others are gathered here under the category "transgender," they have different attitudes toward it. Cherry likes the term, though she uses it interchangeably with "transexual," while Cindy dismisses it as "tranny crap." But outside bars and clubs, THE Clinic is one of few places that I can sit and talk with a variety of people who could be identified as transgender. In my early field notes, I note with some relief that THE Clinic is a "site of community."

Later that afternoon, I make the short ride from the Center to Riki Anne Wilchins's apartment. Riki is the founder of Transexual Menace and the executive director of the Gender Public Advocacy Coalition (GenderPAC), a coalition of groups dedicated to "racial, gender, and affectional equality" founded in November of 1996.[7] I have come to help hir[8] make lobby kits for GenderPAC's Gender Lobby Days in Washington, D.C. The aim of Lobby Days is to bring to Congress members' attention the plight of those who experience violence and discrimination because of their gender-variant identities or expression. These include transgender-identified people, though Riki believes "transgender" limits the terms of hir politics.

We sit on the floor collating press releases about the same murder that was under discussion at THE Clinic, but our talk is of the Human Rights Campaign (HRC), the preeminent gay and lesbian political and lobbying organization in the United States. Riki is concerned about HRC's reaction to GenderPAC's demand for language that would accommodate gender-variant people in the Employment Non Discrimination Act (ENDA). ENDA is a federal bill which aims to outlaw discrimination in employment on the basis of sexual orientation but which excluded "gender identity or expression" as a category of protection. This means, effectively, that it would not apply to transgender-identified people.[9] This exclusion is interpreted by most transgender-identified activists as political expediency on the part of HRC as the bill's already-slim chance of passage would almost certainly be thwarted by language which would extend protections to cross-dressers and transexual men and women. Transactivists also see this as a rejection of the historical roles transgender-identified people claim in the gay and lesbian civil rights movement. But Riki and others argue that the bill would also not cover effeminate gay men or butch lesbians, for they could be denied employment because of their gender-variant behaviors.

After a few hours and much talk I leave to get some xeroxing done for the press kit and then head home for a nap. Fieldwork for me is primarily a late-night endeavor, and I have miles to cycle before I sleep.

Around eleven that night I ride up to Karalyn's, a narrow, poorly lit bar on a barren stretch of 10th Avenue in the 50s.[10] I walk in to see Nancy at the bar with some friends. Nancy is the New York president of Crossdressers International (CDI), which has an apartment in midtown where its membership meets weekly to dress and socialize. Like CDI, Karalyn's is frequented mainly by transvestites or cross-dressers who, in psychiatric diagnostic terms, are heterosexual (and, from my experience, usually white, middle-class) men who cross-dress for erotic pleasure. But of course, Nancy tells me, it's not that simple. She points out Clara, who is attracted to men when she is cross-dressed, and Irene, who only likes women. She explains the differences between those who are "autoerotics," and people like herself, a bisexual transvestite.[11] And it's not all about eroticism, she says. Cross-dressing started out as a sexual activity for Nancy but nowadays, when she changes back into men's clothes, she feels like she is putting a part of herself away. The question for Nancy is: is there a transgender community, or is it more like a "scatter chart"?

I hand out safer-sex kits containing condoms, lubricant, and a GIP pamphlet which places cross-dressers on the "transgender spectrum." But I am beginning to wonder about how Nancy and her friends fit into "transgender" alongside Andrew, Riki, Cindy, or Cherry, each of whom has their own way of mapping differences and similarities between themselves and others. Nancy herself rarely uses the term and frequently talks about the differences between transexuals and "a TV like me," a statement which

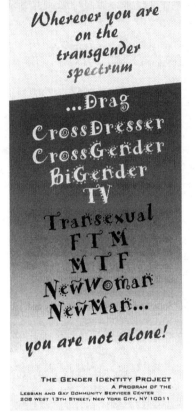

FIGURE 1:
Gender Identity Project
Pamphlet (1997)

seems to undercut the collective description of transgender in the GIP pamphlet.

Around midnight, the crowd begins to thin and I bid Nancy goodnight. I have several more stops to make before I can go home tonight. I cycle forty blocks south from Karalyn's to the Meat Market, a rapidly gentrifying, semi-industrial neighborhood incongruously positioned on the Hudson River between the expensive residential areas of Greenwich Village and Chelsea. On weekends, the dark and dirty cobblestoned streets are filled with truckers, dominatrixes, gay leather men, the occasional film crew, and party-goers. Amid the crowds are dozens of sex workers—intelligible in the late 1990s as transgender—who try to catch the eye of potential clients, cruising by slowly in their cars.

It is still early—at least, it's late for Nancy and the Karalyn's crowd, but in the Meat Market midnight is early and many of the girls (a category they take for themselves) will not be out until around one o'clock. So I take a seat in the twenty-four-hour neon-lit clamor of Dizzy Izzy's Bagel Store on 14th Street and drink tea. Sooner or later someone I know will come in, be it one of the girls or someone who, like me, has condoms to give out from one of various social service agencies around the city. Like me, they come to find "transgender sex workers," despite the fact that the girls rarely if ever refer to themselves as transgender or, in many cases, have never even heard the term.

Rita is the first person I see. Rita is Latina, in her late twenties, and one of the more successful girls—she has an apartment, a dog, and a boyfriend who paid for her surgeries. Like most of the girls out here, Rita has had breast augmentation and facial surgeries, but not sex reassignment surgery (SRS); that is, she has male genitalia. Far from being a hindrance, such an embodied state is a selling point in the sexual marketplace of the Meat Market. But it can also be dangerous: thrown bottles, insults, and, more seriously, beatings and murder are a fact of life on the stroll.

We talk about the cops who had, this month, been very active in rounding up sex workers in the latest "quality of life" sweeps. Rita is very angry that they "don't care about gay people." Surprised, I ask her if she thinks of herself as "gay." She looks at me as if I had asked a very stupid question and says: "Yes, I know what I am." She's not a woman, nor does she want to be a woman, and she would *never*, she says, have SRS.[12] Like most of the Meat Market girls, Rita refers to herself as a fem queen, a drag queen, a girl, or as just "gay," and while a few may say they are transexual, the same people may also refer to themselves as "gay." At the same time that she "knows what she is," however, Rita doesn't want other people reminding her of it and resents people saying "You're a boy." It's none of their business.

Rita knows "what I am," but it defies my social-service and ethnographic categories. Is she "transgender"? Undoubtedly, in the language and vision of transgender activists. But at the same time, she sees herself indisputably as "gay," something Cindy, Cherry, or Melissa would fiercely reject. When I write up this evening's field notes, I ponder this question again: who is "gay" and who is "transgender"? And whose definition comes to stand as the truth about Rita?

I have one more stop tonight, even though it's going on for two o'clock, and I am very tired. A five-minute bike ride from the Meat Market brings me to Tranny Chaser, a fun, heaving, downtown party on Thursday and Saturday nights at a basement-level bar in the Village. Tranny Chaser attracts people of all gendered and sexual identities and expressions: gay men in drag, straight male cross-dressers, transexual men and women, drag kings and queens, wannabes, their friends, admirers, partners — straight, gay, lesbian, bisexual — and generally at least one or two photographers, filmmakers, reporters, or ethnographers. Around two in the morning, a drag show draws a big crowd, with performers like the guitar-playing cross-dresser Stacey or Baby Dee, a transexual performer who plays the harp and accordion. In other words, at Tranny Chaser, no one can be quite sure of how another may identify from their appearance.

I scan the crowd, mouthing hellos to those I know over the grinding beat of DJ Fabian's club music and the one-note hubbub of shouted conversations. Melissa is here tonight, in quite a different outfit from her professional turnout at THE Clinic. Like many white, middle-class transexual women, Melissa had transitioned later in life and has had the associated problems with employment faced by many transexual women and men, so she works as a waitress and in the coat check at Tranny Chaser to make ends meet. I make a face of surprise and admiration at her new wig.

"You look like Barbra Streisand!" I yell above the noise, thinking this — naively — to be a compliment. Melissa's face falls. She shrugs, grins ruefully, and takes off to serve someone a drink as I try to figure out what has gone wrong. I know Barbra isn't everyone's cup of tea (certainly not mine), but I had figured Melissa would take it as a compliment.

Later, we are standing together by the coat check, watching Tina Sparkles, a well-known drag performer, dancing with a couple of patrons.

"Do you really like it?" she asks, pushing back a piece of stray hair.

"Yes, I really do . . . it really suits you," I answer truthfully.

"My biggest fear is that people will think I'm a drag queen," she says, looking down and straightening her bodysuit.

Several things occur to me from this interaction. Melissa's fear of being thought of as "a drag queen" indicates some central issues around the category transgender (not to mention the diva status of Barbra as a figure frequently appropriated as a persona by gay male drag queens). Melissa's struggle to attain the identity of woman has been long and hard, and she is constantly required to defend it against other definitions of herself which are potentially (and continuously) possible. Because of the variety of people at Tranny Chaser, and indeed, because of the overarching collectivity of "transgender," Melissa's fear is understandable. A casual glance or comment which implies she may be a gay man in drag has deep significance for an individual who resists such a reading, though she might be unable to counter it. Not surprisingly, Melissa (like Cindy) doesn't always like the indeterminacy of transgender and the way it can include the drag queens and cross-dressers with whom she does not want to be identified, even as she recognizes its political effectiveness. Like Rita, she is caught in a system of signification, power, and meaning over which she has little control. And, by her inclusion (and the inclusion of Riki, everyone at Tranny Chaser, Karalyn's, and THE Clinic) into my Saturday mapping of "transgender," her self-definitions become further blurred.

This dynamic has multiple implications, though. A few nights earlier Shequida, another well-known drag performer, had told me in no uncertain terms that she was explicitly "not transgender." "I don't have *any* sort of gender problem. I'm a man! I know what I am." Her drag persona was just that, she insisted: a stage performance. For Shequida, identification as "transgender" denies her primary identity as "gay man." While she may be confused with Melissa at Tranny Chaser, and while she may say the same thing about herself as Rita ("I know what I am"), all three of them have different relationships to the category transgender.

Four o'clock is closing time and I gratefully say my goodbyes to Melissa and the others I know. I unlock my bike for the final time to head home. Bleecker Street is packed with bar-goers from the suburbs, obeying the same closing time as I. But at Thompson Street, I hear my name being called.

"David Valentine!" It's Ed, looking for a parking space for his/her truck. I had originally met Ed, a female-born, male-identifying person, at a GIP support group at the Center. Ed doesn't have a gender — at least some people may gender him/her as a butch-looking woman, but s/he often gets taken for a man, and his/her own sense of her/his gender is contextual, s/he tells me. Ed is among the very few people I have met during my fieldwork whose identity and experience of gender truly is as fluid as some theoretical accounts of gender-variant people propose that they are. Such a chance meeting is reason for celebration, so we go to a nearby diner and have what is, I suppose, breakfast. For me, this evening, it seems that the whole of New York is a transgender community. By the time I bid Ed goodnight, go home, scribble down a few field notes, and get to bed, it's well after six o'clock.

To reiterate, this book is not an ethnography of clubs, transgender sex workers, social service agencies, transgender activists, transgender identity, or even of something called the transgender community. Rather, it is best understood as an ethnography of how, in the last decade of the twentieth century, these sites, places, and people became comprehensible to activists, social service providers, journalists, public policy makers, anthropologists, and others through the category transgender. Put another way, this book is a critical ethnography of the *category* "transgender" itself as it has become institutionalized in a broad range of political, social, medical, and other contexts in the United States since the early 1990s. As a term which describes a community and the identities of those who are its members, it has also served as the analytic tool for my research. But as the above stories make clear, "transgender" contracts and expands in particular situated contexts. In other words, the map I set out above is not the territory: rather, it is the practice of mapping—by myself, social service providers, activists, scholars, legislators, journalists, and many others—which is my concern because those gathered into it confound its imagined topography.

The work of this mapping revolves around four broad themes which I will now describe and explain how they are approached in the chapters that follow.

MAPPING THE BOOK

The primary theme of this book is that the recent (and spectacular) rise and institutionalization of transgender as a collective term to incorporate all and any variance from imagined gender norms is both a product of, and contributes to, a broad and ongoing shift in U.S. American understandings of those human experiences we call "gender" and "sexuality." I want to argue that "transgender," rather than being an index of marginality or "an out of the way category" (to paraphrase Tsing 1993) is in fact a central cultural site where meanings about gender and sexuality are being worked out. Despite the collectivity and inclusivity implied by this use of "transgender," I will argue that its employment in institutionalized contexts cannot account for the experiences of the most socially vulnerable gender-variant people. Drawing on a Foucauldian methodology I want to ask, then: in what ways does transgender not only *explain* non-normative genders but also *produce the effect* of those differences by effacing others? It is this complex social and political process that I refer to as "imagining transgender."

Related to this process is another category, one which stands as the implicit Other to transgender: homosexuality. One of the oft-told progressivist stories of the late twentieth century is that of the depathologization of homosexuality. This story rests not only on the social validation of homosexual identity but centrally on the assertion that homosexual identity is not rooted in a gendered inversion. That is, if in the contemporary United States "transgender" describes a deviation from gender norms, then "homosexuality" indexes same-sex eroticism between *gender-normative* people.

But this understanding presents us with a puzzle, for as recently as the early 1970s, homosexuality was popularly imagined as a *gendered* inversion, and those who are understood as transgender today were frequently classified as part of a "gay community," both by insiders and outsiders (though disputes and disagreements over this classification abounded). There has therefore been a radical transformation in the past thirty years in the possibilities of gender and sexual identification in the United States. I take up these histories of transgender and homosexuality in the first part of chapter 1.

The second theme of this book, then, is an ethnographic exploration of what "gender" and "sexuality" *themselves* mean in the contemporary United States, a discussion which takes up the rest of chapter 1. In much contemporary social theory and grassroots political activism, it is a matter of faith and theory that "gender" and "sexuality" are distinct—if related—arenas of human experience, experiences which are neither reducible to one another nor which can be explained by the other. Less often explored is how the two terms are related, and it is even rarer to see an explanation of what people might mean by these terms. By putting those two terms in quotation marks I am suggesting that "gender" and "sexuality" are neither self-evident experiences nor natural explanatory frameworks. Rather, they are *also* categories with complicated histories and politics, and which therefore deserve critical attention. I will argue that the emergence of transgender is central to the ongoing working-out of what "gender" and "sexuality" can mean in contemporary U.S. American activism and social theory.

The separation of gender and sexuality is often represented in scholarly and activist accounts as a progressive move enabling more accurate self-identity. But as we have already seen, not everyone has come to understand homosexual and transgender identification as so radically separate. Indeed, many of my study participants who were labeled "transgender" by social service agencies or activists did not even know this term or, if they did, were fiercely resistant to its use. And, like Fiona, these people usually referred to themselves as "gay," confounding this distinction between same-sex desire and gender-variant expression. The sexuality/gender distinction is further complicated by different histories and experiences of those born male and female, and the relationship between the categories "gay" and "lesbian" (I use "gay" as the unmarked category of homosexual identification, rather than "gay and lesbian," for reasons that will become clearer in chapter 1). These points raise further questions: why do some people who appear to be "transgender" to others call themselves "gay"? Why do others resist any identification at all even as others attempt to categorize them? What are the politics of this disagreement? How are embodiment, gender difference, race, class, and other social differences implicated in it? And, again, what does it tell us about "gender" and "sexuality"? These alternative modes of conceiving gender and sexuality — and the different values given to them in public discourse — are the topics of chapters 2 and 3. In these chapters I look at institutional imaginaries of transgender identity and community and examine how they are confounded by the daily practices of those understood as transgender by activists and scholars.

It is important to note that I am not interested in making claims about what transgender-identified people can tell us about "binary gender" (which is the object of many authors who take on this kind of topic). Nor do I intend to engage in the fruitless debate over whether transgender-identified people "uphold" or "contest" gender norms. That is, this book is not strictly about transgender identity, transgender community, or performativity, even though I engage these topics. Rather, I am interested in why it is that transgender-identified people — and transgender identity, transgender community, etc. — are seen to be figures which *can* tell us something about a category of experience we call "gender," but not about other kinds of human experiences, that we call "race," "class," or most importantly, "sexuality."

This observation leads me to the third broad theme of this book, activism, identity politics, and social theory in the United States, a theme that spans chapters 4, 5, and 6. In these chapters I look at the production of knowledge about transgender-identified people and communities in the context of the emerging field of transgender studies (chapter 4) and transgender activism as it developed in the 1990s (chapters 5 and 6). My goal here is to examine how in both scholarly and activist work the use of transgender as a category of analysis and action restricts the possibilities of explaining gender variance as much as it enables it. My central question here is: by identifying transgender people as experiencing discrimination or violence along the axis of gender identity, or describing gender-variant people through the framework of transgender, how are other kinds of social experiences elided? This is not to say that scholars and activists do not recognize the significance of those things we call race, class, and so on in the lives of transgender-identified people. Indeed, social theorists and progressive grassroots activists have come to describe this phenomenon as "intersectionality," a way of recognizing that, for example, being a social woman must necessarily be configured by intersections of race, class position, cultural background, or location in a stratified global economy (Crenshaw 1991). Arising as a critical response by feminists of color to the unitary nature of the categories "woman" and "gender" in second-wave feminism, intersectionality has evolved into a diverse set of methodologies, broadly distributed throughout the social sciences, with the shared goal of drawing attention to the inequalities produced in these intersections (Alarcón 1990, McCall 2005). But an intersectional analysis might not always capture the lived dynamics that intersectional analyses aim to describe. My concern is that while scholars who use intersectional theories and methodologies have complicated the assumed clarity of analytic categories ("gender," "race," and so forth), in the emerging fields of transgender activism and transgender studies there is a heavy reliance on the distinction between an unproblematized "gender" and "sexuality" which undercuts the critical impulse of intersectional analyses.

For those like Fiona, who work with alternative meanings of what gender and sexuality themselves signify, this very difference from activists' understandings of the terms could indeed be ascribed by those activists to intersections of racial and class inequalities in their experience. As we will see in chapter 4, claims such as Fiona's are ascribed to a lack of "education," a lack which indexes her and her peers' racial and class otherness. In turn, though, these intersections can — and do — stand as an explanation for activists of why Fiona is unable or unwilling to access more "accurate" meanings of gendered and sexual identification. That is, if we as scholars and activists already assume we know what is signified by "gender" or "sexuality" in this field, then alternative readings of the meanings of those terms may be erased by an intersectional reading which presupposes the character of the domains which are said to intersect.

While I use an intersectional approach in this book, I will argue that the very description and categorization of experience as "sexual" or "gendered" — however intersecting — in this field has the potential to produce the difference it claims merely to describe by assuming the ontological difference between the terms. Rather, I want to suggest that the contours of racial or class experiences can shape and reshape what gender or sexuality themselves can mean. That is, I argue that, rather than assuming categories of social analysis (gender, race, class, etc.) to be self-evidently descriptive of (intersecting) experiences, we could more profitably see them as tools for actively extracting certain aspects of daily lived experience but not others. To see analytic categories as merely descriptive draws our attention away from the work of activists and scholars in identifying what is "gendered" about a particular life or moment, and what might be "sexual" (or "racial" or "cultural"). This third theme, then, is about the labor of scholars, activists, social service providers, legislators, and others in producing accounts of difference and their intersections that may in fact erase the complexity of those differences. I will argue that, in effect, the erasure of Fiona's understanding of gender and sexuality as a false account is itself connected to a series of broader inequalities structured along the lines of what we call race, class, and culture, the very phenomena that activist and scholarly intersectional accounts are concerned with. That I must use the very categories I critique in order to name these inequalities is a central tension in this book.

These inequalities, in turn, have been compounded by the restructuring of global economic, political, and social systems through what are generally referred to as neoliberal ideologies and practices. In a time frame that maps onto the ascendence of identity-based politics in the United States, since the early 1970s a broad (and sometimes contradictory) range of neoliberal policies have asserted business rights over public life, increasingly privatized public services and public space, undercut labor and class-based progressive alliances, and reframed "rights" in terms of a framework of consumption in the United States and beyond. The intensification of inequalities that have attended neoliberal regimes in the United States and globally are thus part of the broader historical context wherein the politics of transgender have developed in the latter part of the twentieth century. In these chapters, I will argue that the restructuring of gay and lesbian political organizing around civil rights and privacy claims, and the emergence of transgender, is intimately bound to these political economic developments. On a broader terrain, I hope to push past this observation to make a larger claim about gender, sexuality, and U.S. American politics of identity and personhood. The processes I describe are not necessarily about transgender identification itself but are part of a broader reshaping of self-making with deep roots in U.S. American culture and history, and which are linked in turn to recent neoliberal reorderings of political, economic, and social life.

Fourth, and finally, this book is also about the complicity of social scientists and social theorists in producing the objects they are investigating, and the politics of this process (Marcus 1998). Anthropologists — as much as political activists, social service providers, politicians, journalists, and others — have come to use the idea of transgender as a useful shorthand in describing non-normative genders and as a way of describing a group of diverse people both in the United States and beyond its borders. If this book is entitled *Imagining Transgender,* it is also about the ways in which this formation is part of an anthropological and epistemological imaginary too. I elaborate on this theme below, and more fully in chapter 4.

In summary, this book is an ethnography of the production of a field of knowledge. It is an argument about, and a critical ethnography of, the conceptual space of gender and sexuality in the United States as they have become reshaped through the historical development of institutionalized understandings of transgender and homosexuality. It is simultaneously about shifts in mainstream U.S. culture and political economy, and how political, activist, and scholarly description and action are conceptualized in the context of contemporary political economic orders. Finally, it is also about how this analytic and political space has been shaped by ethnography and other modes of scientific and popular knowing. This book is therefore a call to think about gender and sexuality as political formations: not simply in terms of the politics that attach to gendered and sexual systems, experiences, bodies, and identities but in the very constitution of gender and sexuality *as social and analytic categories.* Above all, I am concerned that the unquestioned use of "transgender" in activist, academic, and other contexts, while progressive in intent, actually reproduces, in novel and intensified forms, class and racial hierarchies. Thus, my concern is to open up what "transgender" might mean in order to think about both its possibilities *and* its political, theoretical, and ethical limits. In the conclusion, I will argue that the kinds of questions I raise in this book are central to careful, thoughtful, and effective political action.

In the rest of this chapter, I develop the fourth theme discussed above and place this research in the context of anthropological approaches to culture and meaning making. I do so in order to clarify my own stakes in this research, but also to highlight the politics of writing a book such as this.

THE ANTHROPOLOGICAL IMAGINARY

While this is an ethnography of a series of categories, like any ethnography it is located in specific social spaces and at a historical moment—primarily New York City, mostly among male-to-female (MTF) transgender-identified people, in the late 1990s. As such, the specific people and organizations with whom I worked shaped the kinds of questions at the heart of this book. Despite this locatedness, though, my eventual framing of this project drew on a broader anthropological dissatisfaction with traditional ethnographic frames of analysis. In contrast to foundational anthropological models which imagined "culture" as an object attaching to a homogenous community of (usually non-Western) people with a coherent cosmology, for contemporary anthropologists, "culture," "community," and "cosmology" no longer have this solidity. Whether they are working in the United States or outside its borders, the facts of U.S.-dominated globalization and unequal transnational flows of people, information, and capital make such a conception of culture impossible to sustain.[13]

At the same time, my project was initially conceptualized very much in the traditional "research imaginary" of anthropology (Marcus 1998). I proposed to study what I understood to be two distinct "transgender communities" in New York City: a group of activists called Transexual Menace, and a group of (as I then understood them) transgender sex workers who work in the Meat Market of Greenwich Village. My aim was to consider, from a linguistic and cultural anthropological perspective, how race, class, and other social differences "intersected" with social identities which were, in the mid-1990s, increasingly written about in queer and feminist scholarship as "transgender" or under the rubric of "drag."

But the week I started fieldwork, an article on the national transgender activist movement was published in the *New York Times* (Goldberg 1996).

The large amount of space and the generally favorable coverage of a national movement that only five years previously did not have a name indicates the growth of a "transgender community" in the popular imagination, and one that was far more diffuse than my project proposal had implied. The first weeks of my eighteen months of fieldwork also challenged me to think about the terms of my project. My research was facilitated by a staff position in the Gender Identity Project (GIP) at what was then called the Lesbian and Gay Community Services Center in Manhattan. The GIP operated out of cramped offices on the third floor as a part of the Center's Mental Health and Social Services program, with a staff of a director, Rosalyne Blumenstein, and a number of hardworking volunteer peer counselors and outreach workers. The staff counseled the transgender-identified people who came in for help and simultaneously sent out news of its programs and services to those spaces it identified as constituting part of a transgender community. Within weeks, I was part of this process, traveling around New York on my bicycle and going to drag balls, sex work strolls, support groups, meetings of a cross-dresser organization, clinics, bars, clubs, and a host of other settings where I identified myself as both an anthropologist and a GIP safer-sex outreach worker.[14] At the same time, with the help of activists, I traded my bicycle for airplane tickets and went to conferences, demonstrations, vigils for murdered transgender-identified people, and even to the U.S. Congress to lobby representatives on issues facing transgender-identified people. I was startled by the range of contexts my research pulled me into, and as I spent time in these different spaces, even more so by the different kinds of people I met there.

Yet, as I wrote above, I was struck by the observation that a large number of the people I met and talked to did not know the term "transgender" or were resistant to its use to describe them. From the outset, then, faced with a far more varied set of fieldwork contexts and a larger set of research questions than I had first presumed, I began to rethink my project in terms of examining the idea of transgender itself and how it is setting the terms by which people come to identify themselves and others.

Simultaneously, however, especially at the vigils for those who had been murdered because of their gender-variant expression, or in the Meat Market when I saw bottles thrown at the girls walking the streets, I also came to see that transgender was potentially transformative and powerful. It became clear to me that it could have (and was beginning to have) social and political efficacy by drawing attention to a group which was subject to violence, danger, and discrimination. Despite the nature of my research questions, I also felt that I could contribute to this change.

At the same time, in many field sites I discovered that the practice I was engaged in — ethnographic research — was not always welcome. "So," said one activist at our first meeting, "are you planning to write *Transexuals in the Mist?*" For many like this activist, my presence was unwelcome and representative of a broader violation of their lives by non-transgender-identified social scientists. I was, in many people's view, simply another researcher bent on the exoticization of "natives." In these encounters, I was challenged to be accountable to those I studied and to use my data to argue for legislative protections and for interventions in political and social contexts (a challenge I take up in chapter 6 and the conclusion). I was taken to task for a range of issues: for engaging in this research in the first place, for the lack of attention I paid to transexual men and female-bodied masculine people, for simply the task of taking notes. For these people, "transgender" had enabled them to know themselves without the intervention of an anthropologist. The fact that I was raising questions about the very category which enabled this empowerment led, at the very least, to some complicated discussions.

In short, the *category* transgender became both the ethnographic object and central dilemma of my research, for if it was potentially socially and politically transformative, my research showed that it was not equally so for all people gathered into its purview. More complexly, though, as I described above, the practice of gathering all these subjects into my fieldwork imaginary was complicit with the very cultural process I was concerned with.[15]

These observations thus requires me to place myself and my research practices in relationship to the field I was both studying and helping construct, and first of all in relationship to transgender itself. In a field where those who are transgender-identified have historically been the subject of pathologization, ridicule, and barely disguised disgust, the position of the author (both political and personal) is deeply significant. In the first paragraph of this chapter, I identified myself as a non-transgender-identified male-bodied gay man, and therefore (according to the system of identification I have laid out) presumably outside the category of transgender. I read myself as "gender normative" in my daily presentation (and I imagine — perhaps incorrectly — that most people read me as such). I was ascribed male at birth and have that constellation of genitalia, secondary sex characteristics, and gender identity that are conventionally understood as male and masculine.

But I am erotically drawn to men rather than women. This fact is usually explained as my "sexuality," something distinct from the way I understand myself as "man," which is my "gender," and "male," which is my "sex." And, indeed, this is on the whole how I understand myself. In this book, though, I want to look at how this possibility has become available, because it has not always been so. How is it that my erotic desires, in the present day, do not (necessarily) implicate me as feminine? I put "necessarily" in parentheses because for many U.S. Americans, homosexuals *are* evidence of a gendered inversion (as well as of the sinful state of the human race or of mental illness). My argument is that the idea of the gender-normative gay man is not a natural fact that has slowly gained credibility over 150 years but rather that the replacement of earlier models of gender-variant homosexuality has been a historical achievement. So, when I write that I am "non-transgender," I do so to position myself in terms of contemporary understandings of what that term means (to me and others) while, at the same time, I am critically investigating how it is possible for me to make this claim in the first place.

Second, I consider myself as a political ally of people who identify as transgender or who express their gender/sexuality in non-normative ways. I recognize the usefulness of transgender as a category of social action and social justice activism and I see my study as contributing to, not detracting from, this work. The title of this book — *Imagining Transgender* — should in no way be seen to imply that I believe the realities of transgender experience and identity, or the violence and discrimination faced by transgender-identified people, to be imaginary. Rather, I use this framework to draw attention to the way that transgender has *enabled* certain people to see themselves and others as being part of this category in order to bring about social change. Again, central to this dynamic is to query how it is that I, as a gay man, can understand myself as "ally" and not as a member of the class "transgender." My aim, in taking a critical view of this process, is to suggest other ways that a progressive politics of gender variance could be conceptualized and utilized in promoting social justice.

Third, like all ethnography, this book is characterized by its own absences, situatedness, and location in a historical moment. The most significant of these absences is that of female-to-male (FTM) transgender- and transexual-identified and female-bodied masculine people. As several readers of earlier drafts pointed out, my work reiterates the broader absence of female-born people in the literature about gender-variant and transgender-identified people, with the result that claims about transgender experience are usually, and implicitly, made from the perspective of MTF people (see Meyerowitz 2002: 94). Moreover, this absence ignores vital developments in the history and meanings of transgender such as those which have taken place in the "border wars" between butches and FTMs, developments I write about in chapter 4, but which were not part of my research experience. While I talked to, interviewed, and spent time with FTMs and female-bodied masculine people, the vast majority of my research was conducted with MTF transexual- and transgender-identified people and male-bodied feminine people.[16] At the same time, the observation that FTMs and female-bodied masculine people are elided in the literature on transgender is one of the things that I am interested in exploring in this book. I will ask: if it is true that broader cultural models of "transgender" are being formulated around the experiences of those who were born male, what does this say about the category itself? Indeed, the meanings of transgender I focus on — its institutionalization as a collective category of difference — cannot account for many gendered and sexual identificatory possibilities. But it is precisely because the model I describe here has gained momentum in public health, social service, academic, and legislative contexts that it is important to lay bare the logics of these institutional maneuvers which elide these understandings of self.

These issues of representation and identity also shaped the choice of illustrations for this book. There are no pictures of people — transgender-identified or otherwise — in the pages that follow, only images of organizational pamphlets, programs, and fliers. I have made this choice in order to remind the reader that the focus of this book is on how people come to be understood through certain categories, and the effects of those orderings.

Another obvious absence in this book is a sustained analysis of the category "queer," which resonates with "transgender" in many ways. Queer theory, and the activism organized by this term, arose at almost the same moment as "transgender" in the early 1990s. Like transgender, queer has a range of different meanings and can also be understood as a collective.[17] On the other hand, by drawing on poststructuralist understandings of a shifting and contingent subject, queer theory is suspicious of categorization and is attentive to the process of categorization itself. Indeed, the distinction between transgender and homosexual identification is only one of many kinds of productive distinctions queer theory aims to interrogate in its exploration of intersecting oppressions and expressions. However, "queer" has not been institutionalized in the same ways or the same contexts that "transgender" has outside the academy. Thus, since I am concerned here with categories that are the focus of queer theory — gay, lesbian, transgender — I draw on a queer theoretical perspective. At the same time, my primary concern is with the institutionalization of political organizing, legislation, social service provision, and so on, and "queer" does not figure in these contexts in the same way as the categories it critically examines.[18]

A final, but vital, point to make is about the language I use, as language is a central site — theoretically, practically, politically, and ethically — for the negotiation of meanings in any field. Moreover, language use and debates over categories were major concerns for my study participants and have become increasingly so for those (non-transgender-identified) scholars who work in this area (e.g., Broad 2002: 242, Meyerowitz 2002: 12–13).

First, when I refer to someone as a transgender- or transexual-identified man or woman, I am referring to their gender of identification, not their ascribed birth gender. Further, use of the unmarked categories "man" and "woman" should not be seen to imply non-transgender identification. I will use the term "non-transgender" to talk about people who do not identify, or are not identified, as transgender. This is both a political and theoretical move, partly as an attempt to mark the unmarked categories of gender normativity, but also to highlight the understanding that all identities are discursively produced. However, I also use my informants' descriptions of themselves as butches, fem queens, transvestites (and even as gay or homosexual) without collapsing them into or replacing them with "transgender." This is necessary both to respect individuals' senses of themselves but also to highlight the complications emerging from the institutionalization of transgender as a collectivity.

Second, I spell "transexual" with one "s," a usage of activist informants who employed this spelling to resist the pathologizing implications of the medicalized two "s" "transsexual." However, I make no claims to the value of either spelling and retain the two "s" spelling in quoting sources. My usage may seem like a conceit, but if nothing else it marks the historical moment and the context within which I worked (see Wilchins 1997: 15, Cromwell 1999: 3 n. 1 and 19–20, Meyerowitz 2002: 234). Likewise, I use "transgender" both as a noun and adjective (as opposed to "transgendered") following the usage of some informants who objected to the "ed" suffix, arguing that "transgendered" carries a similar (and negative) connotation to the construction "colored" in speaking about people of color. I also tend to use "transgender" rather than "transgenderism" in referring to a more abstract social phenomenon.

Perhaps most importantly, I will use the construction "transgender-identified" (as I have above) rather than simply "transgender" as an identity qualifier to emphasize a central tension in this book. On the one hand, it validates those people who adopt transgender as a meaningful category of self-identity; but it also draws attention to how people are identified by others as being transgender even though they may not necessarily use this term in talking about themselves. This phrasing thus highlights how self-identity and one's identification by others are complexly intertwined and shaped by relationships of social power (Foucault 1983, West and Zimmerman 1987, see Boellstorff 2004: 161, Kulick 2003). Thus, while I do not focus on transgender identity formation per se, this textual move draws attention to the tensions and politics of self- and other-identification that lie at the heart of my arguments.

These tensions are apparent throughout this book, but nowhere more so than in my use of "transgender" itself. Because "transgender" is under investigation as a category, when I use it in this sense I have often included it in quotation marks. However, even as I investigate its origins and meanings I also use it as an unmarked descriptive term in order to recognize the social facts of transgender identity and community. In other words, I will write of a transgender community or of transgender-identified men and women, because this describes a social reality; while at the same time I am investigating how it has become possible to call a community or a person "transgender." I am not so much interested in resolving this tension as I am in using it as a productive node through which the workings of "transgender"/transgender become apparent, even if only for a moment.

Some other brief notes on language. First, some readers may struggle with the unexpected third-person pronouns *ze* and *s/he* (rather than "he" or "she") and *hir* (rather than "his," "him," or "her") that appear in places. While *s/he* has gained currency as a textual tactic to avoid sexist language, it is usually regarded as unpronounceable. However, some of my study participants use it freely in speech, and it can be pronounced something like "shu-he." *Ze* can be pronounced like the letter "zee," while *hir* can be pronounced without difficulty as "here." Others prefer the third-person plural (they/them). Most of my study participants, however, tend to stick to standard gendered pronouns. Second, much of what I will quote or draw from in the following chapters will reflect the language of national activism and social services which cater to transgender-identified people. The use of contractions and neologisms such as "transcommunities," "transpolitics," "transpeople," and the like are common, and I employ them without comment, but with a similar caveat that I am curious about their origins, histories, meanings, and consequences.[19]

Finally, I also use other terms at times to avoid using "transgender," such as "gender variance" or "crossgender," or to account for subjectivities that do not easily fit into the homosexual/transgender distinction, such as "gender/sexual variance." However, these constructions do not solve the problem of naming, nor are they any more devoid of historical and cultural meanings than "transgender." Similarly, my use of "male-bodied/ born feminine people" or "female-bodied/born masculine people" is an attempt to assert the specificity of different embodiments and their social consequences for located social actors, but also to avoid the specificity of identity categories, especially in talking about non-Western or historical subjects. Yet this is also problematic, because — especially for many transsexual men and women — the invocation of some kind of originary embodiment denies and effaces their own senses of self as female or male, whatever their bodies are like. Moreover, shorthand like "FTM" or "MTF," which index both transsexuality and birth gender, can also conflate directionality with identity (see Rubin 2003). The assertion of the sexed body at the heart of such formations, and the implication of a definite movement across a stable gender/sex border, erases the specificity of certain identities and the complexity of such transitions. These points highlight a central problem with language and naming: there are simply no neutral terms (see Wieringa and Blackwood 1999:7).

In short, I do not want to assert that any of the language, categories, or divisions I use in this book lie outside history or culture. Like "transgender," or any other category, they simultaneously carry, enable, and restrict meaning. Moreover, this highlights a vital point: I don't think that people shouldn't use "transgender." I simply think we need to be careful about what we mean by it (or by any category), what meanings it can bring with it, and what the consequences of these might be.

The result of these usages, neologisms, and careful phrasings is, in places, a tendency toward apparent redundancy and overcomplexity. But complicated topics require complicated language, and when a particular linguistic structure seems overly complex, I would ask that the reader pay attention to why I might have chosen a particular phrasing. My concern is with the power of categories — their power to enable action in the world, to describe ourselves to ourselves and others, but also their power to restrict possibilities. If the categories we use to talk about our worlds contribute, at least in part, to how we shape our action in the world, then we must think about how they impact on those whose categories might be different from ours.

In the following chapters, I move through many contexts, lives, and spaces. My mapping traverses (and produces) disjunctures and fractured points, but it also draws in moments of humor, love, and remarkable courage mounted in the face of violence, pain, and ostracism. This work is aimed at contributing to the struggle against such culturally institutionalized violence and is written in honor of friends who lost their lives even as I have been engaged in the process of writing. It is the hope that this work will contribute, even in a minimal way, to the lives of my friends, study participants, and colleagues that has made its writing worthwhile.

1

Imagining Transgender

Since no one had ever seen the diversity of the lesbian, gay, and bi populations, most people assumed that being gay meant being transgendered. We thought so, too. — LESLIE FEINBERG, *Transgender Warriors*

Nearly a hundred years since homosexuality was formally defined, news reports and gay and lesbian activists still routinely claim both historical and contemporary transgendered people as lesbian and gay. — AARON DEVOR AND NICHOLAS MATTE, "One Inc. and Reed Erickson: The Uneasy Collaboration of Gay and Trans Activism"

Leslie Feinberg's *Transgender Warriors* focuses on reclaiming a specifically transgender history and demands attention to a long history of transgender people from antiquity to the present. Simultaneously, ze and Devor and Matte imply that transgender people have, for a long time, been misrecognized — or misclaimed — as homosexual. The reclamation of "transgender warriors," and their distinction from homosexuals, is a central feature of contemporary transgender activism and history making, but by creating a distinct transgender history, transgender-identified writers are not acting without precedent. From the 1970s on, gay and lesbian writers and scholars have made similar kinds of claims about those they perceived to be their ancestors and who were misrecognized as heterosexual (e.g., Katz 1976), including some who, in Feinberg's and Devor's and Matte's view, are more accurately understood as transgender.

Another approach to history, however, problematizes these kinds of simple reclamations (Altman 1993 [1971], Foucault 1990 [1978], D'Emilio 1983b, 2002, Halperin 1990, Weeks 1981). Most famously, Foucault has argued that "homosexuality" was not even a category of personhood until the mid-nineteenth century. At the root of this social constructionist view of history is the contention that the organization of contemporary gay and lesbian (and by extension, transgender) identity cannot make sense of historical modes of non-normative gendered and sexual identities or of romantic and affective relationships between people of the same sex/gender. From this viewpoint, to imagine historical subjects as "gay," "lesbian," or as "transgender" ignores the radically different understandings of self and the contexts that underpinned the practices and lives of historical subjects. How then is Feinberg able not only to claim specifically *transgender* warriors from antiquity to the present day but also to distinguish them from distinctly *homosexual* forebears? And how are Devor and Matte able to posit a (misrecognized) historical distinction between homosexual and transgender subjectivities? These questions are particularly important in the light of opposing claims of who fits in what category but also because of the apparent merging of these categories in the common contemporary acronym LGBT (lesbian, gay, bisexual, and transgender).

In this chapter, I approach history from a social constructionist perspective, but not simply to contest the reclamation of historical figures as homosexual or transgender. Rather, I aim to examine the history of "transgender" and "homosexuality" as *categories,* the history of their relationship, and the theoretical and political implications of seeing them as discrete throughout history. Following Foucault, I take a genealogical approach, one which examines the meanings, values, and investments of naming and labeling. Like Foucault, I am interested in how these categories do not simply *describe* discrete histories but rather are *productive of* the very phenomena they seem to describe. Put another way (in James Ferguson's Foucauldian terms), rather than simply asking " 'What does this concept *mean;* what does it really refer to?' " I want to ask " 'How and to what effect is this concept deployed; what does it *do?*' " (Ferguson 1999: 205, emphasis in original). If, as I noted in the introduction, transgender as a category itself only emerged in a collective, institutionalized way in the early 1990s, what histories, politics, and practices have enabled this kind of historical claim? Moreover, if "homosexuality" is also a relatively new concept, and if it has been used to describe transgender forebears, how do we account for what Feinberg and Devor and Matte see as this conflation? In short, how is it possible to extract certain actors from the categorical embrace of "homosexuality" and into "transgender"? What has this historical reorganization *done?*

A crucial corollary to these questions is: how else could those people described as transgender or homosexual at different historical periods be described? By this I mean, what other forms of social identification — racial, class, national — cross-cut these sexual and gendered categories of being and knowing, and how might those identifications disrupt the easy assertion of homosexual or transgender identification? How does race, class, or geographical location figure into the naming of people as transgender and/or homosexual? These latter questions are engaged in the analysis below, but I take them on most fully in chapters 2, 3, and 4.

Underpinning the historical reclamation of certain homosexual forebears as transgender is a distinction between two other categories: gender and sexuality. To invoke Foucault again, how might the claim that gender and sexuality are distinct be *productive* of that distinction rather than simply a description of the way things are? Such a question is vital to ask if we are to make sense of contemporary, historical, and cross-cultural evidence of (what we call) gender and sexual variance, and the racial and class dynamics that underpin it.

I am working here with an assumption that is central to anthropology: that language shapes how we make sense of our worlds (Whorf 1956 [1939]). In this view, "gender" and "sexuality" are not self-evident experiences or domains outside language. Rather, they are linguistic tools which extract certain information, experiences, and feelings about ourselves and others from the stream of daily life for the purposes of making meaning about, and representing, ourselves and others. But the absorption of certain meanings by these terms is not a natural fact: it is the product of a constant, social reiteration (and contestation) of those meanings in a range of contexts — from the day-to-day assertions of gay, lesbian, and transgender identities and the activist strategies of LGBT movements, to the intellectual labor of scholars.

This chapter is thus a genealogical and critical review of these categories — transgender, homosexuality, gender, and sexuality. First, we must examine the category of transgender itself.

Let me start with a somewhat standard account of the history of "transgender" in the United States.

Most authors give credit to the activist Virginia Prince for her coinage of the term "transgenderist" in the United States sometime in the 1970s (e.g., Docter 1988, Frye 2000, G. MacKenzie 1994), though its actual origin in Prince's writing is less than clear and a more complicated history of its origin has been suggested by Robert Hill (2007).[1] Though she more frequently used other terms, Prince is represented as using this concept — or variations of it — to describe those who, like her, lived full time in a gender other than that to which they were ascribed at birth, but without surgical intervention. By doing so, she and others differentiated themselves from transexual men and women on the one hand, and fetishistic cross-dressers on the other, which was (for Prince at least) a moral claim to (implicitly white, middle-class) normality and a rejection of deviant sexuality (Califia 2003 [1997]: 199, Meyerowitz 2002: 181) though others explicitly saw such a "third way" in more politicized terms (Hill 2007; see also Ekins and King 2005, 2006).

With the advent of early 1990s activism and scholarship in the United States, "transgender" gained a new meaning as the "radical edge" (Ekins and King 1999) of gender variance by people such as Holly Boswell (1991) who advocated for a position of crossgender identification which embraced an androgynous style and mode of identification, a position which also drew on more radical 1970s conceptions of gender-variant identity. Unlike Prince's assertions of normality, Boswell challenged the notion of "normal" itself, claiming a space for transgender not simply as a category between "transexual" and "transvestite" but as an alternative to binary gender. Boswell's call resonated with the radical call to embrace (specifically) transexual experience by Sandy Stone in her classic essay "The Empire Strikes Back" (1991), though Stone did not herself use "transgender" as a category (see Stryker 2006).

However, the idea of transgender as a radical alternative or as a "third way" between transexuality and transvestism, both of which had developed unevenly through the previous two decades, was quickly overtaken in the early 1990s by a third usage of transgender as a *collective* (often spoken of as a *spectrum* or *umbrella*), inclusive of all and any gender variance (Bolin 1994, Califia 2003 [1997]). Leslie Feinberg's early call for "transgender liberation" in 1992 is among the first published uses of the collective form of transgender which explicitly politicized transgender identification beyond individual radical acts and called for a social movement organized around its terms. This collective sense is that which most activists and social service providers adopted in the early 1990s.

Contemporary activists, providers, and scholars include different kinds of people in this collective/spectrum/umbrella, and a relatively modest list would include at least some of the following identity categories: transexuals, transvestites, cross-dressers, men or women of transgender or transexual experience, drag queens, drag kings, female or male impersonators, genderqueers, intersexuals, hermaphrodites, fem queens, girls, boys, trannies, feminine gay men, butch lesbians, male-to-female, female-to-male, female embodied masculine persons, and even, simply, men or women. The inclusion of certain kinds of people — and the absence of others — from lists of this sort is, as we will see shortly, a significant feature of definitions of transgender.

"Transgender" in this collective sense, then, arose in the United States in uneven, often contested ways, primarily in white, middle-class activist contexts in New York and California in the 1990s, though it appears to have had earlier manifestations in California in the 1980s, and in independent, if resonant, developments in the UK around the same time.[2] In the context of activism and social service settings, "transgender" was seen as a way of wresting control over the meanings and definitions of gender variance from medical and mental health professionals to replace an assumption of individual pathology with a series of claims about citizenship, self-determination, and freedom from violence and discrimination (see Stryker 1998, 2006). Just as importantly, it was seen as a way of organizing a politics of gender variance that differentiated it from homosexuality.

In the years since then, particularly since the mid-1990s, "transgender" has become ubiquitous in progressive community-based organizations, identity-based political movements, popular media accounts, international human rights discourses, academic debates, anthropological descriptions of gender variance cross-culturally, and, astonishingly, it is even finding its way into the medical establishment, the very institution to which transgender was originally opposed. Transgender Studies is becoming an acknowledged field of inquiry (see chapter 4), and in popular culture, transgender is being used in TV shows, newspapers, magazines, movies, cartoons, personal ads, and on the World Wide Web. Transgender-identified activists are lobbying federal, state, and local legislators around issues of hate crimes and discrimination, and the right wing has discovered in "transgender" the latest enemy of American Family Values. It has been used on the floor of the U.S. Senate and was already included in the Merriam-Webster dictionary by 1998 (see note 2). Currently in the United States there are several national and dozens of statewide and local organizations which are dedicated to transgender issues. Web sites, newsletters, sections in bookstores, funding proposals, magazines, meetings, conferences, and social services focused on or incorporating trans-gender issues are springing up all across the United States (and the world) or are using "transgender" as part of organizational schema. This is all the more remarkable as the earliest use of transgender (in its institutionalized, collective sense) in U.S. activism dates back no further than 1991 or 1992, and therefore marks a significant shift in discourses, practices, and personal identities around gender variance in an astonishingly short period of time.

At the same time, "transgender" has already come under critique by many who are seen to fall under its purview in institutional terms. FTMs, transgender-identified butches, and female-bodied masculine people have argued that it is formed implicitly on a male-to-female model that cannot account for the complexity of butch/FTM experience (e.g., Halberstam 1998b, Hale 1998). Some, who adopt a more radical view of gender-variant identification, argue that "transgender" has either become a synonym for "transexual" or renders the specificity of transexual experience invisible (e.g., Valerio n.d.). And a younger generation of self-proclaimed gender-queers explicitly reject "transgender" as an identifier at least in part because of its institutionalization (e.g., Nestle, Howell, and Wilchins 2002, Wilchins 2002). However, despite these and other critiques from among those who are seen to occupy the category, "transgender" has been phenomenally successful in becoming institutionalized in an enormous range of contexts, and attempts to deconstruct the category have themselves been critiqued by activists who see value in institutionalization (Park 2003).

This potted history, though, requires asking four interrelated questions: first, why did the collective sense of "transgender" emerge in the way it did only in the 1990s? Second, what do different people mean by "trans-gender" and which meanings have gained traction in institutional settings?

Third, given the move to the acronym "LGBT," what is the relationship between transgender and gay and lesbian identities and politics? And finally, what role do class, race, and geographical location play in these dynamics? To answer these questions we need to look first at the development of "transgender" in the 1990s.

THE RISE OF TRANSGENDER-AS-COLLECTIVE IN THE 1990S

Califia (2003 [1997]), Cromwell (1999), and Bolin (1994) all discuss the rise of transgender activism in the 1990s, implicitly pointing to qualitatively new forms of social organizing around gender-variant identities in that period. Meyerowitz (2002: 208ff.) notes, however, that activism by transexuals and transvestites — and other people we might refer to today as transgender — is not new. After Christine Jorgensen's highly publicized sex reassignment surgery in 1952, people who were coming to understand themselves through the new medical category of transexual began organizing themselves through social and activist networks (see also Frye 2000, Members 1998, Silverman and Stryker 2005, Stryker 2006). Transexuality in the United States was both celebrated and contested from the 1950s in popular culture, medical, and scholarly contexts, but claims and counterclaims over this subject position also emerged among those who saw themselves framed by its terms. That is, many of the features associated with contemporary *transgender* activism — the rejection of pathologization, social and political networking, the celebration of the possibilities of shifting genders — were evident in specifically *transexual* activism of earlier decades of the twentieth century.

Yet it is also clear that for various reasons the 1990s saw qualitative and quantitative shifts in these kinds of activism, theory making, and contestations (Broad 2002). Bolin (1994), for example, argues that the closure of university-based gender identity clinics in the early 1980s allowed for the possibility of client-centered, private clinics to offer services, enabling surgeries for people who had been turned down by the more research-oriented university centers. Califia (2003 [1997]: 223ff.) suggests several other specific reasons, including the anger at poor surgical results in university clinics, the growing visibility of people who were unable to "pass" in their chosen gender, and the politicization of transexual women because of their negative experiences with lesbian-feminists. Califia also sees the emergence of FTMS as a strong and vocal group in the 1990s, and the increasing visibility of FTMs and transmen as another important impetus for the coalescing transgender movement (see also G. Rubin 2002, Broad 2002, Cameron 1996). This activism has further been facilitated by communication technologies such as the Internet and the World Wide Web which radically transformed communicative possibilities from the early 1990s on (see Stryker 2006 for a broader historical contextualization of the emergence of transgender activism and scholarship).

These different factors enabled a groundswell in activism, publications, and a radically different intellectual and political project around gender variance through the category of transgender. At the same time, the "new" transgender politics of the 1990s has also been characterized by debate and contestation over methods, theory, identity, and indeed the very boundaries of the category itself (Broad 2002). These debates, as we will see, are central to the constitution of what "transgender" can mean in different contexts. However, in this early period, the sense that something new had emerged was powerful indeed (Broad 2002: 44ff.). Sandy Stone's essay "The Empire Strikes Back" (1991), the early 1990s battles over the exclusion of transexual women from the Michigan Womyn's Music Festival, and the vigils at the trial of Brandon Teena's murderers in Falls City, Nebraska, in 1993 are all early moments in the consolidation of the meanings of transgender in the 1990s, despite differences and contestations about those meanings.

The emergence of transgender must also be seen, however, in the context of broader changes in U.S. American understandings of identity politics, the body, and embodied identities in the late twentieth century. These understandings have, in turn, been shaped by shifts in neoliberal capitalist modes of production and consumption where "difference" can be exploited as a market niche as much as enabling new forms of subjectivity (Chasin 2001, Martin 1994, Sender 2004). "Transgender" has thus entered public discourse in the context of a vast range of concerns and activisms around normative and non-normative embodiment, including the emphasis on exercise and health promotion (Conrad 1994); the representation of both male and female bodies in mass media (Bordo 1999); claims of people with disabilities (Ingstad and Whyte 1995); the increasing popularity of tattooing and other body modifications (DeMello 2000); the demands of intersex activists who reject surgical interventions on infants with anomalous physiognomies (Chase 1998); overweight people who claim fatness as an identity (Goldberg 1999, Kulick and Meneley 2005); the debates over abortion

(Ginsberg 1989); the possibilities enabled by genetic testing (Rapp 1999); and a broad range of grassroots health activism.

These developments must in turn be seen in the light of emerging social movements in the past thirty years in the United States where "identity" has become a primary mode of politics — from grassroots organizations to federal legislation. The civil rights movement, feminism and the women's movement, and the gay and lesbian rights movement have all provided language, precedents, and models for the burgeoning transgender movement. The collectivity of transgender, then, is in some senses no different from the collective identity of other groups who have engaged in such politics. What is different in this case, though, is that transgender has arisen out of a realignment — contested as it may be — of the kinds of individuals who see themselves or are seen as being part of the collectivity, and who were previously accounted for by other terms including "homosexuality," "transexuality," and "transvestism."

I will discuss the broader context of identity politics and the history of transgender activism in chapter 5, but next we must consider the second question I raised above.

WHAT "TRANSGENDER" CONTAINS

The collective mode of transgender, for all its potential to reshape understandings of gender variance, yet poses several questions. While the conventional definition — an "umbrella" term that includes all people who are in some ways gender-variant — seems self evident, the question remains: what counts as gender-variant and who is included in "transgender"? The answer to this question is not clear and is sometimes contradictory. A few examples of definitions provided by transgender- and non-transgender-identified scholars and activists will demonstrate this point.

Meyerowitz gives one of the broadest definitions of transgender. She writes that transgender is "an umbrella term used for those with various forms and degrees of cross gender practices and identifications. 'Transgendered' includes, among others, some people who identify as 'butch' or masculine lesbians, as 'fairies,' 'queens,' or feminine gay men, and as heterosexual cross-dressers as well as those who identify as transsexual. The categories are not hermetically sealed, and to a certain extent the boundaries are permeable" (2002: 10). Califia (2003 [1997]) makes a similar claim about the collectivity and recency of the category, though his definition is somewhat hazier. While he notes that transgender is an "umbrella" term, at different points in his book he is ambivalent about what the category includes. So, for example, at some points he argues implicitly that male transvestites are not part of the category transgender ("their [i.e., male transvestites'] cultural history overlaps and is linked with the politics of the transgendered community but is not identical to it" [198]), though in other places he implicitly includes male transvestites within "transgender" (e.g., 256). Bolin (1994), writing earlier in the history of the emergence of this category, provides another criterion for collectivity. She writes: "While there is not universal agreement on the term *transgendered,* there is an emerging generic semantic space that is inclusive of all people who cross-dress" (465, emphasis in original). For Bolin, cross-dressing rather than gender identification seems to be the primary criterion of membership in "transgender."

Finally, Namaste (2000), writing at the decade's end, also focuses on transgender as a collective term. She writes that

> [a] variety of different identities are included within the "transgender" label: cross dressers, or individuals who wear clothes associated with the "opposite" sex, often for erotic gratification; drag queens, or men who usually live and identify as gay men but who perform as female impersonators in gay male bars and leisure spaces; and transsexuals, or individuals who take hormones and who may undergo surgery to align their biological sexes with their genders. (1)

Most of these authors recognize that these definitions are tentative and shifting, precisely because the meanings of the term are still being negotiated. Yet, such definitions and lists abound in spite of the difficulty of pinning down the category. Indeed, earlier in this chapter, I provided my own (qualified) list, even more extensive in its inclusiveness than Meyerowitz's.

Let us examine three broad features of these definitions. First, the minimal definition of "transgender" includes transsexuals and (male) transvestites (though Califia is hazy even on this point). However, some definitions also include gay male drag queens (though none of those quoted explicitly include drag kings or male impersonators), and Meyerowitz goes so far as to include feminine gay men and butch lesbians, as does Henry Rubin (2003: 18). This raises a central question: does "transgender" include (some) self-identified male-born gay men and female-born lesbians who themselves do not identify as transgender? As we will see in chapter 2, many gay male drag queens are insistent that they are not part of this category as are many butch lesbians (see G. Rubin 1992, H. Rubin 2003). The second point to note is the implicit absence of FTMs/female-bodied masculine people (or at least the absence of an explicit naming). Definitions like Namaste's which include the unmarked "transexual" and "cross-dresser" alongside gay male drag queens unintentionally reassert the MTF experience.[3]

Third, though, what is most interesting about these definitions is the way that they can shift within a text, and the resulting flexibility that transgender has for explaining and describing phenomena, people, and practices across time and space. The flexibility of transgender can result in the listing of people at the edges of the boundaries, like feminine gay men or butch lesbians, while omitting others, whether male transvestites or FTMs. Alternately, it enables one group — frequently transsexuals — to stand in for others while giving the impression of collectivity. And very often it is used to encapsulate a range of historical figures on the basis of their gender variance. The very flexibility of transgender, its strength as a tool of political organizing, thus makes it possible to use without specifying who is being invoked in particular instances. So Califia can define transgender as an "umbrella term" while at the same time that which he describes is specific to transsexual experience. Similarly, Meyerowitz, while she is clear that "transgender" is a historically recent term, sometimes also finds it useful in writing about the collectivity of transexuals, transvestites, butches, queens, and fairies of an earlier point in history (2002: 36, 95).

The capacity to stand in for an unspecified group of people is, indeed, one of the seductive things about "transgender" in trying to describe a wide range of people, both historical and contemporary, Western and non-Western. Even using "transgender" as a descriptor for historical or cross-cultural behaviors or practices rather than identity (as, for example, Cromwell [1999: 17] does) still enables an author to avoid these definitional difficulties. Indeed, that "transgender" can stand both as a description of individual identity and simultaneously as a general term for gendered transgressions of many kinds makes it almost infinitely elastic.

These slippages embody a central tension of the collective mode of "transgender." This is not simply a theoretical point either, since, as I will show in part II, these definitional issues have political effects too. Attention to those places where "transgender" enables a certain haziness is important precisely because the boundaries of the category are inhabited by not only historical and anthropological subjects (such as those Feinberg or Meyerowitz discuss) but also by many contemporary Western individuals who also contest this boundary through their particular professions of selfhood.

It should be clear that I am moving toward an examination of the boundaries between "homosexuality" and "transgender." But before I do so, I want to propose that another reason transgender emerged in the 1990s is precisely the historically recent redefinition of what "homosexuality" means. The clue here is the inclusion of feminine gay men, butch lesbians, drag kings, and drag queens in some definitions of transgender, but not in others. To develop this argument I must turn next to the category of homosexuality itself.

HOMOSEXUALITY

A central tenet of contemporary transgender theory, activism, and identification is that transgender identity is distinct — in some accounts, radically so — from homosexuality (some important exceptions are Halberstam [1998b] and Hale [1998]). While this distinction is important to and descriptive of many contemporary transgender, as well as gay and lesbian, people, it is in fact a remarkably recent distinction. As such, it is important to talk about the history of homosexuality as a category in relation to what has come to be understood as transgender (see Halberstam 1998a: 142–43).

Foucault (1990 [1978]), D'Emilio (1983a), Weeks (1981), and others have argued that "homosexuality" only emerged as a possibility for identification (in both senses of that term) in Europe in the latter part of the nineteenth century. Foucault argues that in the context of urbanization, changing forms of state organization, and the reshaping of kin and labor relations, same-sex erotic practices were de-linked from a broader set of non-normative non-procreative practices (broadly understood as "sodomy" and as sinful) and were reorganized into a form of pathological *personhood* that we would today call "homosexuality." In Foucault's oft-quoted words, "The sodomite had been a temporary aberration; the homosexual was now a species" (1990 [1978]: 43). But, once a species, how was he (or more rarely, she) identified by nineteenth-century scientists, legislators, and others?

First, the implicit pathology of homosexuality was seen to be evident in what contemporary social theorists would deem visibly physical and behavioral markers of non-normative *gender* expression. Late-nineteenth-century and early-twentieth-century sexologists such as Havelock Ellis and Magnus Hirschfeld argued for (primarily male) homosexuality as an intermediate or third sex, evident in the adoption of feminine practices and behaviors to which erotic attraction to other men was intimately bound. While Hirschfeld (1991 [1910]) distinguished between (primarily hetero-sexual) male transvestism and male homosexuality, his commitment to the third-sex model implicitly drew on the idea of a certain femininity travel-ing with male homosexuality. In *Die Transvestiten,* Hirschfeld wrote: "One can understand all too well that most of them [his male *transvestite* subjects] wish they had been born female, a wish that is certainly expressed in great measure by [male] homosexuals" (129).[4]

Likewise, Karl Ulrichs, the nineteenth-century German lawyer who is touted as "the first gay activist" (Lombardi-Nash n.d.), saw the male Ura-nian (his term for those who felt same-sex desire) as having an innate femininity (Ulrichs 1994: 55ff.). The body, for Ulrichs and later sexologists such as Hirschfeld, was the evidence of a spiritual inversion in male Ura-nians manifested simultaneously in embodied gendered inversion and sex-ual and romantic desire for people of the same sex. "Ulrichs took it for granted that the male [Uranian] body also showed some feminine quali-ties; his successor, Magnus Hirschfeld, believed this more firmly" (Hekma 1994: 220). Moreover, "for Ulrichs, the most important sign of gender inversion was sexual preference" (220).

If Ulrichs saw a spiritual etiology to Uranianism, other models located homosexuality more directly in the body itself, drawing on nineteenth- and twentieth-century concerns to define the implicit deficiencies of all bodies which were not white, male, and procreatively inclined. Here, too, the *physical* evidence of "femininity" in male people and "masculinity" in female people was linked to homosexual desire.[5] In the United States, Terry (1995) notes the attempts by the mid-twentieth-century Committee for the Study of Sex Variants (CSSV) to identify visible evidence of homo-sexuality in the body, manifested (as the researchers believed) in the geni-tals, skeletal structures, musculature, and voices of their subjects. Kinsey's work in the 1940s temporarily decentered the focus on homosexual bodies by arguing for a model of natural sexual variation. However, the publicity surrounding Christine Jorgensen's SRS just four years after the publication of *Sexual Behavior in the Human Male* (Kinsey et al. 1948) reanimated the push for a stable and embodied diagnostics of homosexuality both to differentiate it from transexuality but also as part of the ongoing work of delineating homosexuality as a dangerous condition (Freedman 1989, Meyerowitz 2002: 172). The search for clearly definable and primarily *visual* evidence of homosexual bodies was certainly complicated by the contradictory and uncertain results of these various researches. But three central themes emerge from this history: first, the ways in which these researches focused on practices that would likely be understood as "gendered" by contemporary theorists; second, the almost exclusive focus on male bodies and/or psyches; and third, the emphasis on the visible. These are all points I will return to.

However, it is also clear that the link between same-sex desire and inverted gender identification was contested from early on by those who were the subjects of such research. Hekma's (1994) analysis of late-nineteenth- and early-twentieth-century sexual rights movements shows that the sex/gender-inverted model of homosexuality did not stand unchallenged, at least among European male homosexuals. In Germany, Ulrichs's model of the trapped female soul and Hirschfeld's championing of the third-sex model of male homosexuality met opposition in the person of Adolf Brand and his organization Die Gemeinschaft der Eigenen (The Community of Self-Owners), which "defended a virile, pederastic form of homosexuality, which was far removed from Hirschfeld's third gender and sexual intermediaries. The split between the two movements concerned for the most part the different contents and meanings given to homosexuality" (1994: 228–29). Well-known, self-identified homosexual men of the period such as André Gide also spoke out for a " 'movement for masculine culture' " (228), rejecting the characterization of homosexuality as a form of gendered inversion and claiming that homosexuality was morally and physically normal (Rosario 1996: 41). Likewise Chauncey (1994) describes how some early-twentieth-century U.S. homosexual subjectivities were formed in opposition to medical and popular discourses linking (male) homosexuality to (feminine) gender. He notes how "fairies" were spurned by mainly white, middle-class homosexual men who were developing gender-normative understanding of their same-sex desire (see also D'Emilio 1983b).

Thus, by the mid-twentieth century, various kinds of self-named fairies, queens, butches, femmes, homosexuals, transvestites, and latterly, transexuals were coming to understand themselves through scientific and judicial categories but were also generating distinctions for and among themselves: "People who decades earlier might have been grouped together as 'inverts' were now sorting themselves out" (Meyerowitz 2002: 184) in what amounted to a "taxonomic revolution" (169; see also Newton 1979 [1972]: 51–52, Weeks 1985: 61–95). In the United States, many now-gay-and-lesbian-identified people (mostly white and middle class), insisted on gender-normative presentation as the hallmark of homosexual identification and rejected other sexual/gender subcultures as "deviants." The rejection of gender variance was, moreover, a rejection of class and racial otherness. For example, in the 1950s, the membership of the Mattachine Society (a post–World War II homosexual rights group) put pressure on the society's left-leaning (and in some cases communist-party-member) founders to abandon their radical class politics, while simultaneously rejecting "overtness," "flamboyance," and gender-transgressive models of homosexuality (Duberman 1993). As Gayle Rubin (2002) notes, being "overt" was not only a marker of homosexuality but also of class, since "overt" homosexuality was not compatible with middle-class employment (see also Faderman 1991: 178, Meyerowitz 2002: 178, Newton 1979 [1972]: 7–19, Newton 1993: 275). Gender/sexual non-normative desires and practices among communities of color were doubly complicated by the experience of racism and the facts of segregation (Mumford 1997).

At the same time, though, police, judicial, and legislative restrictions on sexual/gender non-normative practices (including bar raids and imprisonment), as well as informal practices of policing in broader society, contained those differences. By this I mean that while distinctions within sexual/gendered urban subcultures were recognized and internally maintained, opprobrium against any kind of gender/sexual non-normativity prevented a broader social elaboration of those differences. This is apparent in the autobiographical account of Jayne County, a self-identified transsexual woman and musician, writing of Atlanta in the 1960s: "There were certain divisions in the gay world even then, but we didn't have the words for them. Everyone was just gay as far as we were concerned; that was the word we used. . . . It didn't matter whether you were a very straight gay man, or a screaming street queen, or a full-time drag queen, or a transsexual who wanted to have a sex change: you were gay" (1995: 29–30).

These identificatory, class, and racial tensions coalesce in the iconic moment of gay/lesbian (and, as we will see, transgender) history, the Stonewall riots. The story in its broad outline has been told frequently: On the night of June 27, 1969, a routine police raid on the Stonewall Inn, an unlicensed gay bar in Greenwich Village, New York, turned into a melee and then a riot that resulted in several days of street protests and clashes with police. The riots catalyzed a massive activist reaction and is today usually represented as the originary event of the gay/lesbian (and/or transgender) movement.

However, how it happened — and what happened — is a contested story. For contemporary transgender-identified people, the story goes that it was drag queens and butches of color who led the resistance against the police and that it was in fact (also) the beginning of a transgender rights movement (e.g., Feinberg 1996: 97–99, Frye 2000: 457, Wilchins 1997: 70). On the other hand, some contemporary gay male writers contest the idea that any drag queens, transvestites, or butches were significant actors (e.g., Marcus 1999). Duberman's (1993) social history of the pre- and post-Stonewall era claims that Stonewall habitués were a complex mix of people, and that the stories of that night point to several different protagonists as the spark that lit the fuse. He argues that the Stonewall Inn was not generally welcoming to drag queens or even effeminate gay men who wore androgynous clothing, and that women — butch or femme — were rarely to be found there (see also Bravmann 1995). These debates, moreover, are structured by claims about race and class, a point I return to below.

Duberman and others note that despite its iconic status, Stonewall was not the origin of gay and lesbian (or, we might add, transgender) resistance to agents of the state (see also D'Emilio 2002: 146ff., Rechy 2000, Silverman and Stryker 2006).[6] Yet Stonewall brought to a head tensions between East Coast postwar accommodationist homophile leaders and a more radical group of youthful activists who were inspired by the Black Panthers, the civil rights and anti–Vietnam War movements, and early second-wave feminism. For activists in organizations like the Gay Liberation Front (GLF) which emerged in the post-Stonewall era, the radical politics of social transformation were evinced by and consciously claimed through the adoption of unisex hair and clothing styles, a challenge to gender norms as much as to broader political institutions. " 'Many of us in GLF,' one publication proclaimed, 'are traitors to our sex, and to this sexist society. We reject 'manhood,' 'masculinity,' and all that' " (quoted in Meyerowitz 2002: 235; see also Brake 1976 for a Brititsh perspective on these politics). At the same time, drag queens and what we may call today transgender people did not have an uncomplicated relationship with GLF or other new organizations on either the East or West Coast. Thus, in the period immediately following Stonewall, the adoption of non-normative gendered clothing and identities by radical gay male activists further muddied the identificatory possibilities of the moment.

Current debates over who started the riots at Stonewall, then, are complicated by the ways in which the social actors of the time understood themselves in relationship to the historically available ways of identifying and the politics of gender and sexual transgression in the opening days of the 1970s. Eric Marcus (1999), in his refutation of the "seven feet tall (in platform shoes)," Stonewall-led-by-drag-queens version of events, claims that it was a diverse group of "fluffy sweater boys, dykes, sissies, college students, boys in chinos and penny loafers" who led the charge against the police. Yet the point he misses is that for contemporary transgender activists, the (implicitly white) sissies, fluffy sweater boys, and (at least some of) the dykes are interpretable through the category of transgender as much as the self-identified drag/transgender (Latina and African American) actors like Sylvia Rivera and Marsha P. Johnson who claimed to have been at Stonewall and who have asserted the centrality of transgender-identified people in the events. Likewise, for early 1970s radical gay and lesbian activists, the "sorting out" of differences within the gender/sexual subcultures of the urban United States was, if for a brief time, roiled by the assertion of a conscious politics of transgressive gender by some of their number. In short, it makes equal sense to view Stonewall as a central moment in both what we understand as a gay and lesbian movement on the one hand, and a transgender movement on the other, if only because those distinctions were not operative in 1969 as they are today. Moreover, these debates over Stonewall speak to the racial and class politics of these various historiographies. Marcus's gay "boys in chinos and penny loafers" assert not only a non-transgender but an implicitly white history to Stonewall, just as Rivera's and Johnson's claims put poor people of color at its center.

In order to fully understand these processes, we must look next at a different genealogy of "homosexuality."

PARSING WOMEN

The history related above is virtually entirely told in terms of the experiences of male-bodied people. The experience of female-bodied people who transgressed gender/sexual norms converges with this account in many points. For example, Terry's (1995) discussion of the CSSV studies into homosexual bodies in the mid-twentieth century cited above shows how both male- and female-bodied "deviants" became the object of scientific investigation. Meyerowitz (2002), Duberman (1993), Newton (1993), and others detail the social and activist connections between male- and female-bodied people in the gender/sexual subcultures of the twentieth-century urban United States. And, as with Chauncey's account of primarily male gender/sexual subcultures, Kennedy and Davis (1993) and Faderman (1991) argue that class and race became central to the different kinds of identificatory possibilities for female-bodied people. Social history (Faderman 1991, Kennedy and Davis 1993, Meyerowitz 2002), sociological accounts (H. Rubin 2003), and fiction (Feinberg 1993) all indicate that the distinctions between gender-normative same-sex desiring female-bodied people (whom we might gloss as lesbians) and gender-transgressive female-bodied people (or "passing women" and butches) developed across the span of the twentieth century. As with feminine identities and gender-inflected sexual relationships among male-bodied people, the solidification of butch/femme roles and communities in urban settings in the post–World War II period was marked as primarily a working-class form of identification. Likewise, as with the male homophile movement, mid-twentieth-century white, middle-class lesbian activists in the lesbian rights group the Daughters of Bilitis stressed the importance of gender-normative, respectable presentation for its members. For example, in the 1950s, the Daughters of Bilitis had already decried butch styles among lesbians, seeing them as "the worst publicity we can get" (quoted in Faderman 1991: 180), an explicit appeal by its white, middle-class leadership and members for gender-appropriate behavior. And finally, as with the emergence of transexual women, the possibilities (however restricted) for SRS and hormonal reassignment of female bodies in the postwar period heightened the stakes in both activism and personal identification (H. Rubin 2003).

The crucial point, though, is that the history of non-normative gender/sexual identities and practices for female-bodied people cannot be separated from the history of women's struggles for full citizenship in the United States in the twentieth century. While male-bodied people who adopted feminine practices/identities or who desired other men were contravening one set of norms, the desire of a female-bodied person for another female-bodied person, and/or their adoption of masculine behaviors, occupations, and so forth was simultaneously refracted through claims about women's status (and vice versa). This context set the stage for both the negotiation of identificatory possibilities in the 1970s and also for the movement of debates about the meanings and politics of lesbianism into the women's movement.

The Lavender Menace zap at the Second Congress to Unite Women in 1970 changed both the relationship between lesbianism and the women's movement as well as the politics of identification within lesbian, butch/femme, and female-bodied gender-variant communities. The zap, led by Rita Mae Brown and the Radicalesbians, was one of the many moments when lesbians attempted to confront the implicitly heterosexist bias of the women's movement, but, like Stonewall (less than a year before), it has achieved iconic status as a turning point. The response of the Congress was to pass lesbian-inclusive resolutions, making lesbianism part of (or even central to) the women's movement, but also bringing to a head debates about the status of "male-identified" female-bodied people. The resulting embrace of lesbianism as central to the women's movement resulted in the de facto figure of the (non-role-playing, woman-born-woman) politicized lesbian-feminist as the most valid form of lesbian identification in the 1970s. Lesbian-feminism both embraced an essentialist claim for the category of "woman" and simultaneously asserted lesbianism as "elective," a "conscious political choice to leave heterosexuality and embrace lesbianism" (Faderman 1991: 207). Henry Rubin argues that it was this event, rather than Stonewall, that is understood as the beginning of a specifically lesbian feminist movement, clearly distinguished from the politics of sexual liberationist gay and lesbian activism (2003: 67).

This shift within the women's movement had several radical consequences. First, lesbianism came to be framed institutionally within feminism as primarily a political (rather than only or necessarily erotic) identification. Indeed, in the rejection of association with gay male activists and of the "old gay" forms of working-class lesbian identification, lesbian-feminism was organized around a rejection of "homosexuality" as a framing category for their experiences (Seidman 1993: 112). While not all lesbian-identified women subscribed to these politics or forms of identification, as Faderman and Duberman make clear, lesbian-feminism had a profound effect on public discourses and personal identification.

Moreover, the new lesbian-feminism, while far more radical than the "old gay" politics of homophile organizations, carried with it the earlier distaste of masculine identification and practices in female-bodied people. In this context, then, "gender" came to index both gendered inequalities in the distribution of power *and* the radical discrepancy between (naturalized) masculine and feminine identification. The butch, her femme girlfriend, and FTMs became representative of the "false consciousness" produced by patriarchal systems of oppression, adherents to the "old gay" way of life. Once again, these issues shaped and were shaped by other kinds of social differences, for where the newly politicized lesbian-feminists were primarily white and middle class, the butch/femme subculture they condemned was essentially a feature of bar culture whose members were primarily working class (H. Rubin 2003).

INSCRIBING HOMOSEXUALITY AND GENDER VARIANCE

The radical moment of 1969–70 is also evident in the nascent gay liberation and lesbian-feminist press of the time, and both provide insight into the politics, claims, and orderings of identities that pertained in the immediate post-Stonewall era.[7] For example, in the summer 1972 issue of *Fag Rag,* an anonymous author wrote the following under the heading "Transvestites":

> We transvestites have to take care of ourselves because, as past history shows, no other homosexual is going to do it. . . . Most gays either hate us, are scared of us or, at the very most, see us as entertaining or amusing. They should be proud that we are members of the gay community. Looking back on the events of the last two years, it was half-sisters and upfront faggots who started the Stonewall riots which heralded the birth of the gay liberation movement. It wasn't the butch numbers but the screaming queens. . . . "Revolutionary" gay men mock transvestites. Their rhetoric tells men to wear a dress to smash manhood—"Be a fiery femme." You can't make yourself into something which you are not. This mockery oppresses us. They can flaunt revolutionary drag for theatrical effect and wear their "man" drag to be safe. (Anonymous 1972c: 4)

In the same issue, an advertisement for gay pride week of 1972 includes a listing for a film called "*I WANT WHAT I WANT a film about the changes of a transsexual.*"[8] The description underneath reads: "TRANSVESTITES AND TRANSSEXUALS getting together to talk about our uniquely beautiful life and the problems we face. Other gay people interested will be getting together at the same time to talk about our relationships, gender roles, etc." (Anonymous 1972b, emphasis in original).

Evident in these two brief examples are some of the primary tensions — political and categorical — that underpinned the early gay liberation movement. First, it is clear that there were already clearly developed lines between "transvestites," "transexuals," and "other gay people." In the first quote there is also a further complication of the idea of "drag," with the anonymous author deriding radical gay activists who played with gender roles by "be[ing] a fiery femme," implying that cross-dressing by gay men for political purposes was at best mockery.

Yet, at the same time, it is also clear from the above that "transvestites" and "transexuals" were seen as part of a "gay community" both by themselves and by others. This is most clearly spelled out at the level of ontological unity in "sexual orientation" in a manifesto published in the *Gay Liberator* in October 1972. In calling for "Full Civil Rights for Gays!" the (once again anonymous) author writes: "Gay people must be included in civil rights guarantees. There must be no discrimination on the basis of sexual orientation in employment, housing, or any other area. 'Sexual orientation' includes male and female homosexuality, transsexuality and transvestism, etc." (Anonymous 1972a).

Yet once again, resistance to these claims is also evident from other media at the time. In the pages of *The Advocate*, letters to the editor expressed explicit claims over what "gay" should contain as a category, an issue that also drew on class and racial anxieties. For example, Donald Currante, who identifies himself as a "senior Gay — conservative and well connected socially and actively in the straight and gay world," complains that his gay identity is "prejudiced by screaming exhibitionists who usually have nothing to lose by their tantrums" and attributes to "flouncing, screaming 'fags' " the endangerment of civil rights gains by the gay community. "It is time," Currante claims, "we drew a line just what [*sic*] is embraced in the Gay Lib Movement — what it supports and what it doesn't. You can't make a blanket coverage of every type of homosexual. The movement will dissolve into weakness unless it takes a definite stand and let it be known whom it includes and ex-es" (1973: 36, 40). It is not clear whether Currante is referring to what contemporary readers might distinguish as transgender people and "overt" effeminate gay men, but he identifies precisely the categorical concerns over (class and racially inflected) gender non-normative behavior in the gay liberation movement. His reference to "whom it includes and ex-es" points to the active processes of differentiation that were underway even as these differences were still subsumed by "gay."

These concerns were further elaborated, in different ways, by lesbian-feminists who were invested in claiming a unity to womanhood based on biological sex at birth and by a politicized lesbian identification. In 1973 the *Gay Liberator* printed a debate over the denunciation of drag queens, transvestites, and transexuals by a spokeswoman for Lesbian Feminist Liberation at the 1973 Stonewall commemoration march. A letter writer, Jeff, demanded to know where the *Liberator* stood on this issue, and in reply the editors claimed that while drag could be mocking and offensive, they saw no necessary relationship between male drag or MTF transexuality and ridicule of women (Editors 1973). These debates played out in different ways in the specifically lesbian media of the time, as Henry Rubin (2003: 75–84) notes in his analysis of articles and letters in *The Ladder* and *The Tide*. The debates over butch/femme relationships and roles were also about who should be included in and excluded from the category of lesbian. These debates became especially heated as more FTMs explicitly identified as men in the early 1970s. Rubin cites a letter written in *The Ladder* by Karl Ericsen, a transexual man who attempted to distinguish between FTMs and butches. Rubin notes that "Ericsen's 'The Transsexual Experience' represents a transition from a single deviant identity, the invert, to multiple deviant subjects, now determined by either sexual or sex/gender inversion. . . . By the 1970s, FTMs had become much more clearly distinct from lesbians" (85).

These accounts are compelling because they point to the opposing agendas, positions, and identifications of the people engaged in them: clear boundaries are hard to define. The editors of the *Gay Liberator* in their response to Jeff's letter, and the lesbian feminists who decried drag and transexuality, both claimed a feminist perspective; likewise, writers in these publications made claims about inclusions and exclusions of various orders. Moreover, the categories that are used in these accounts — transvestite, transexual, gay, FTM, lesbian, butch, femme, "flouncing, screaming 'fags' " — speak to the complex ways in which, while differences were recognized and policed, at the same time this was a debate over whether or not this variety could be encapsulated by "gay" or "lesbian." Even as heterosexual cross-dressers and transexuals were distancing themselves from homosexuality, as Meyerowitz (2002) shows, transexuals, transvestites, drag queens, effeminate gay men, butches, and others who were marked by "flamboyance" or " blatantness" were trying to assert their place within gay and lesbian activism, politics, and social life.

How then do we account for male-bodied feminine people and female-bodied masculine people in the pre-Stonewall era who may be identified at a historical remove as either homosexual or transgender in the contemporary United States?

For some contemporary gay male scholars, historical male-bodied feminine people are seen as having been forced into feminine roles and dress because of public opprobrium and expectations about the feminine nature of homosexual men. Hekma, for example, speculates that "perhaps sodomites adopted feminine styles, habits and clothes as an expression of their deep desires, but it is more likely that it was either a pose to attract the sexual attention of men from outside the subculture or a mimicry of male-female relations" (1994: 236). This analysis is shared by Cole, who argues, in his history of gay male dress, that homosexual men wore certain clothing primarily to attract male sexual partners. In considering the cross-dressing of the late nineteenth century and early twentieth century, he argues, "it is important to view effeminacy as often a symbol of availability rather than of the object of desire" (2000: 20). Like Hekma, Cole sees cross-dressing, feminine behavior, and feminine style among male-bodied people as purely situational, and, above all, to signal sexual availability rather than an index of an internal feminine gender identity.

Hekma and Cole are arguing, therefore, that same-sex activity between two male-bodied people that involved cross-dressing or feminine expression was somehow false, a function of circumstance in historical and social contexts where homosexual men could not easily find gender-normative partners who would desire them as men. Ken Plummer implies the same thing when he writes of Ulrichs's third-sex model of homosexuality that it "embraced the *mistaken* idea of a third sex with a woman's mind in a man's body, and vice versa — an idea which *misleadingly* pervades much contemporary sexology" (1992: 5, my emphasis). In a more overtly political mode, Andrew Sullivan (1995) also characterizes the gender variance associated with homosexuality as a product of homophobia, and an unnatural state for gay men. In all these accounts — historical, sociological, and polemic — gay male effeminacy is thus an unnatural product of inequality, homophobia, and oppression (see Phelan 2001: 121ff.).[9]

There is also a convergence between representations of male-bodied people and female-bodied people who engaged in cross-gender practices and behaviors in the early- and mid-twentieth century. As with the characterization of femininity in male-bodied people by some contemporary gay male scholars as merely strategic, the characterization of the "false consciousness" of butches and FTMs in lesbian-feminism implicitly marks these subjectivities as unnatural products of social and hegemonic forces. In historical scholarship too, butches and "passing women" tend to be seen as having engaged in masculine behaviors in order to achieve independence and/or to develop forms of erotic relationships with other female-bodied people (Kennedy and Davis 1993: 3–4; see Califia 2003 [1997]: 150). In other words, underpinning these different accounts is an assumption that the gender-normativity of male homosexuality and the woman-identified-woman of lesbian-feminism are natural. At the same time, the gender variance of historical butches, queens, transexuals, and transvestites is understood variously as the product of circumstance, oppression, or false consciousness.

Thus, by the mid-1970s the "sorting out" of gendered and sexual identities — though for different reasons and with different outcomes — had produced a field in which gender transgressions were increasingly seen as being outside the bounds of what "gay" or "lesbian" could mean. Likewise, the development of transexual identities and others that resonated with these under the rubrics of "drag" or "transvestism" provided a nascent space for the negotiation of categorical orderings, which was reformulated through the possibilities of "transgender" in the 1990s.

Before I continue with this analysis, I want to summarize three themes in the above accounts. The first is to note that there has been an inordinate amount of work done to distinguish gender-normative homosexuality from transgressively gendered identities and practices. I am interested in the political implications of and theoretical possibilities generated by these kinds of claims. To argue that the feminine practices of male-bodied people were simply oriented toward sexual liaisons dismisses the possibility that (at least) some may have had more at stake than simply attracting sexual partners. Likewise, for female-bodied people, it is not enough to assume that passing as men was simply for safety or employment opportunities.

The second theme lies in the different ways in which historical male- and female-bodied people who contravened gendered norms are drawn on by contemporary gay men and lesbians (and, more specifically, scholars). Both gay men and lesbians are arguing for a rereading of historical subjects who crossed gender lines to a lesser or greater degree and both see the (gendered) historical antecedents of homosexuality as mistaken, as "false consciousness," or as a hard choice in an unjust world. But while (some) lesbians are interested in reclaiming as butch lesbian icons people like Allen/Lucille Hart or Billy Tipton (female-born people who lived social and personal lives as men), most contemporary gay men appear to be on the whole adamant in their rejection of the historical fairies and queens as models of contemporary gay male homosexuality. Simultaneously, the absorption of all these figures into a transgender history represents both a counterclaim and a reordering of these histories (see chapter 4).

The third theme lies in the mutually constitutive role of class, race, and gender variance in these histories. The tensions between gender-normative homosexual desire and public gender variance is apparent as early as the late nineteenth century, and they were carried over into the earliest homosexual rights movements in debates about strategy, civil rights, and what kinds of gendered/sexual expressions were valid. However, "overtness," "flamboyance," and "male-identification" also indexed a complex condensation of and tensions over racial identification, street life, public sexuality, and implicit antagonism to white, middle-class norms. In the period after the Stonewall riots of 1969 and the Lavender Menace zap at the Second Congress to Unite Women in 1970, these tensions became even more apparent.

THE PLACE OF THE VISIBLE

"By the mid-1970s, like the revolutionary movements on which it modeled itself, the political wing of the gay and lesbian movement was following a far more moderate course, for legal and political legitimacy," argues Urvashi Vaid (1995: 55; see D'Emilio 2002: 83). Vaid further notes, "The major difference between lesbians and gay men in the 1970s was the creation by women of an autonomous lesbian-feminist culture, and the institutionalization, primarily by men, of mainstream gay politics" (64). Levine (1998) points out that for gay men this moderate course was predicated on a rejection of femininity: "Activists rejected the belief that gay men were womanly, claiming that to believe so was a symptom of internalized homophobia. . . . Gay men were simply men who loved men" (57; see also Seidman 1993). Indeed, in a 1978 article in *Christopher Street,* Seymour Kleinberg could ask "Where Have All the Sissies Gone?"

While these politics fell out in different ways in "mainstream gay politics" and in "lesbian-feminist culture," in both cases, the rejection of racially- and class-marked drag, "flamboyance," or "male identification" was a central feature of their institutionalization as movements. These divergent historical developments came together at certain moments, such as the attempt by lesbian-feminists to prevent Sylvia Rivera from speaking at the 1973 Stonewall commemoration (Duberman 1993: 236).[10] Lesbian-feminists objected to Rivera — a Puerto Rican street queen — as "parodying women," but simultaneously, the reassertion of "normality" and "respectability" in mainstream gay and lesbian activism already made Sylvia Rivera undesirable as the public face of homosexuality. Nowhere was the claim on normality more evident than in the then-current attempt to remove homosexuality from the *Diagnostic and Statistical Manual of Mental Disorders,* or DSM (Bayer 1987).

The removal of homosexuality from the DSM was a central goal of early gay liberation activists and is central to the consolidation of contemporary meanings of homosexuality and transgender. The DSM, originally published in 1952, is the central diagnostic and nosological tool of psychiatry and had included homosexuality as a category of mental disorder from its first edition. To post-Stonewall activists, the pathologization of homosexuality was anathema and was seen as central to the broader homophobic structures they aimed to overturn. Gay and lesbian activists adopted a combination of tactics from the radical moment of 1969, disrupting meetings of the American Psychiatric Association (APA), picketing events, and engaging in other protests (Bayer 1987: 388). But at the same time, activists implicitly engaged earlier accommodationist homophile arguments that homosexual desire was simply a natural variation and not pathological, backgrounding the more radical "genderfuck" politics of other gay activism with its roots in the anti-racist, anti-war, and feminist movements.

However, these events coincided with major transformations within psychiatry. First, there was growing dissent from psychiatrists who opposed the pathologization of homosexuality. More importantly, however, within the profession an emphasis on a research-oriented approach and stable diagnostic criteria was being asserted over the psychosocial, clinically based model which had dominated psychiatry in the United States since the end of World War II (Wilson 1993). These transformations were being played out in the development of the third edition of the DSM (or DSM-III) led by Robert Spitzer and the APA's Committee on Nomenclature (APA 1980). Mitchell Wilson argues that DSM-III marked a radical change not only by transforming psychiatric diagnosis but also by asserting "a model of psychopathology that stressed what was *publicly visible* over what was privately inferred" (408, emphasis in original). Wilson's analysis resonates with the arguments made by activists but also with earlier sexological and medical investigations into homosexuality which sought to find visible signs of "inversion." This shift was significant to gay activists since Spitzer and other committee members were persuaded that homosexuality had no stable, visible diagnostic signs. That is, by insisting on "normality" and rejecting visible gender variance, gay activists argued that homosexuals displayed no *publicly visible* evidence of their homosexuality, which was essentially the *private* exercise of sexuality and which was itself neither caused by nor resulted in mental anguish. In short, this was effectively a claim to invisibility — a dense condensation of gendered, sexual, racial, and class normality.

By the end of 1972, the Committee moved to delete homosexuality from the DSM, leading to a contentious debate within psychiatry that continues to the present day (Bayer 1987; see Bieber 1987, Feder 1997, Sedgwick 1993). By the time DSM-III was published in 1980, however, a new diagnostic category had been developed — Gender Identity Disorder (GID). GID created a diagnostic place for people who had not previously been explicitly recognized as such in the pages of DSM, transexuals and others who engaged in *visibly* gender-variant behaviors and who had previously been understood at least partially through the categories of either homosexuality or transvestism. Thus, even as early 1970s sexual/gender subcultures were engaged in naming each other and themselves, developments in psychiatry consolidated a distinction between gender (the realm where transexuals were seen to be "dysphoric") and sexuality (disorders of which affected homosexuals, and others with "paraphilias" such as heterosexual male transvestites). When, in 1973, gay activists succeeded in getting homosexuality removed from the DSM, it was partly through rhetorical appeal to this very distinction, and simultaneously through a denial of the radical possibilities of post-Stonewall gay liberation (see Mass 1990: 213–22).[11]

Another strand in these interwoven histories of visibility lies in developments within feminism in the 1970s and 1980s. The ability of lesbian-feminist claims to define lesbianism — and lesbian sexuality — in the 1970s was never completely hegemonic, but it was a powerful force nonetheless. If gay male activists argued that homosexual desire was a purely natural (and private) variation of sexual nature, then lesbian-feminists argued (from a different perspective) that neither erotic desire nor masculine identification were necessarily defining features of lesbianism. Moreover, with the increasing backlash against feminism as "selfish," and as the resurgent U.S. political right framed abortion in the post–*Roe v. Wade* era as "murder," a range of feminists "thought that rhetoric about privacy and women's health was more respectable and less risky than the language of women's sexual freedom" (Vance 1992: xviii). Vance argues, moreover, that as the anti-pornography movement came to shape much of the debates within feminism in the mid- to late 1970s, the backgrounding of sexuality as the defining feature of lesbian identity in lesbian-feminism was transformed into a demonization of sexuality itself in the feminist sexuality debates of the 1980s (see also Butler 1994). These "sex wars" fractured the feminist movement and led, as Vance (1990) notes, to the hijacking of anti-pornography feminism by social conservatives in their attempts to restrict pornography and other forms of public sexual expression (see also Duggan and Hunter 1995).

My concern with these interwoven histories is to isolate the arguments about *visibility* and how they map onto arguments about the public and the private. As gay male activists argued for the private nature of homosexual activity, so lesbian-feminists and anti-pornography feminists claimed that public representations of women in pornography, or visible signs of gender variance (butch/femme styles, transexuality), negatively impacted the lives of women. Thus by the mid-1970s that which was *visible* among gender/sexual subcultures became newly engaged as the focus of activists, arms of the state, and psychiatry. If the mid-twentieth-century CSSV study attempted to codify the visible signs of homosexuality in the body (Terry 1995), from the 1970s on, different parties — with different motivations — attempted to define homosexuality *against* that which was visible, and in particular evidence of racialized and class-inflected gender-variant behavior and visibly public sexuality.

Given that the bulk of my argument above has invoked the categories "gender" and "sexuality" it is now time to address them directly.

GENDER AND SEXUALITY

To reiterate: the primary categories I've discussed above — "transgender" and "homosexuality" — are only available in their contemporary meanings *as* discrete categories because of a central distinction that developed in the United States in the twentieth century between gender and sexuality (or, remember, "gender" and "sexuality"). The distinctions between biological sex, social gender, and sexual desire were elaborated first by early-twentieth-century European sexologists. This move was precisely to enable them to distinguish between the experiences of people who visibly transgressed conventional expectations of masculinity and femininity in clothing, occupation, or manner (the contemporary realm of "gender"), and those who, despite being content to be social men and women in concordance with their birth ascription, were erotically drawn to people of the same general embodiment ("sexuality"). I employ these roundabout ways of describing what came to be understood as "transvestism" and "homosexuality" in early sexology precisely to point to the work that these researchers had to do in order to separate out these phenomena. Hirschfeld, Ellis, and others did not have this language, for, indeed, the distinction was emerging from their work. In my own account of early sexology earlier in this chapter, the distinction I make between "gender expression" and "erotic attraction" is a contemporary distinction. At the same time, what we now understand as "gender," "sex," and "sexuality" were complexly interwoven in their accounts, for these writers understood homosexuality and transvestism to be properties of the sexed body itself.

As Meyerowitz (2002) details, this distinction was elaborated by mid-twentieth-century psychiatrists and medical practitioners with the advent of transexuality and the possibilities of SRS, for transexuality produced a field in which sexed bodies had to be understood as distinct from social gender role and identity. More work had to be done, however, to distinguish gender from erotic desire/sexuality. While Magnus Hirschfeld had moved toward this distinction in his 1910 *Die Transvestiten,* the separation of gender and sexuality at an epistemological level was only fully elaborated within the medical field by Robert Stoller in the late 1960s, just prior to the Stonewall riots (Stoller 1968). In the early days of transexual medical specialties, many, including the psychiatrist Richard Green, a central figure in these debates, were concerned that the desire for SRS merely masked a repressed homosexual (and thus "sexual") desire (Meyerowitz 2002: 126). The work of Stoller, Green, and others thus enabled the difference between gender and sexuality (and thus transexuality and homosexuality) to be elaborated and institutionalized in medical terms.[12]

The logics of this distinction played out in complex ways. Male-bodied people who clamored for SRS in the period after Christine Jorgensen's surgery in 1952 learned very quickly that doctors expected them to reject homosexual desire and to be horrified by the idea of homosexual sex prior to surgery. To admit to homosexual desire or activity was tantamount to admitting one was not "really" transexual because it indicated an interest in deriving erotic satisfaction from (male) genitals which, in the medical model of transexuality, were supposed to be abhorrent to the transexual patient. In other words, the emerging practices around MTF transexuality themselves framed the *absence* of sexual desire (of any kind) as both a symptom of transexuality and a requirement for SRS (Meyerowitz 2002: 159, Califia 2003 [1997]: 58). Not surprisingly, doctors found themselves presented with a range of patients who professed just such an asexuality and a rejection of homosexual identification.[13] These developments in transexual medicine, in turn, were also central to the dynamics which led to the deletion of homosexuality from and the inclusion of GID in the DSM and to the "sorting out" of identities within gender/sexual subcultures.

This is not only a story of medical and sexological innovations, however. If the distinction between biological sex and social gender (famously proposed by Beauvoir 1989 [1952]) was a central claim of second-wave feminism, then the distinction between gender and sexuality has roots in the feminism of the 1970s as well. Stoller's differentiation of gender and sexuality was drawn on by early second-wave feminists (Jolly and Manderson 1997: 2), though this was not the only or even primary route through which this distinction was developed within feminism. In particular, Gayle Rubin's "Thinking Sex" (1984) stands as an iconic and influential chapter in proposing gender and sexuality/erotics as distinct arenas of social experience that deserved attention as separate, if related, phenomena. Rubin's article, appearing in the context of feminist debates over the place of butch/femme roles, S/M practices, pornography, and the status of sexual desire itself, thus resonated with earlier sexological and medical moves to separate out gender and sexuality as different, if related, aspects of human experience. In many contemporary feminist accounts, then, gender is also understood as connected to, but not the same as, sexuality.

At the same time, "gender" and "sexuality" operate differently in this tradition than they do in psychiatry, sexology, and the critical fields of sexuality and queer theory which have emerged more recently. If feminist and sexological traditions share an understanding of "gender" as "social," and of "gender" as something distinct from "sexuality," the emphasis has also been different. First, the tradition of sex research has not historically adopted the central feminist argument that those gendered as feminine/women bear the negative weight of gendered systems of power, access, and privilege. Indeed, Meyerowitz (2002: 125) argues that "gender" in medical and sexological accounts of transexuality in the 1960s was implicitly tied to a reassertion of traditional gender roles, just as feminists were arguing against precisely these norms. Second, and crucially, "gender" and "sexuality" are more complexly understood against one another within feminist accounts because of the recognition of the importance of sexuality, reproductive rights, and women's sexual agency to the gendered experience of being a woman (Scott 1986: 1057, Vance 1991: 876).

Part of my goal in this book is thus to argue that the "gender" that underpins "transgender" and marks it as distinct from the "sexuality" of mainstream gay and lesbian politics is one rooted in a sexological rather than feminist tradition (see Hausman 2001). This is absolutely *not* to suggest that "transgender" is "anti-feminist," an issue I take up later in this book. But the crucial point is that while in feminism the sexual and the gendered have been (and continue to be) interrogated in terms of one another as systemic and related to inequalities borne by women and female-bodied people, the distinction between "transgender" and "homosexuality" in LGBT activism (and some scholarship) draws its primary meaning from historical discourses which gloss over the different experiences of male- and female-bodied people and which see gender and sexuality in terms of individual and internal identity. This latter understanding of "gender" and "sexuality" thus posits "gender" as just another kind of social difference, one that is structurally equivalent to but ontologically distinct from "sexuality." This observation is also the beginning of an argument in this book as to why MTF and FTM transgender-identified people are differently located vis-à-vis the category of transgender.

Judith Butler makes precisely this point in her essay "Against Proper Objects" (1994) where she analyzes the claim that the "proper object" of lesbian and gay studies is "sexuality" while feminism should be the privileged site for the study of "gender," a claim which rests on a series of methodological sleights of hand. First, it reduces feminism to the study of "gender"; second, it equates "gender" purely with differences between men and women, thereby reducing "gender" to biological sex; and third, it results in a reduction of "sexuality" to "homosexuality." Butler notes that Rubin's "Thinking Sex" was central here. Rubin's intervention in "Thinking Sex" has often been read precisely as a call for the radical separation of gender and sexuality (e.g., Phelan 2001: 131). But, as Butler notes, Rubin's argument in the context of the feminist sexuality debates was not for the establishment of gay/lesbian studies as a field "but for an analysis that might account for the regulation of a wide range of sexual minorities" (8).[14]

Rod Ferguson extends Butler's point, arguing that "sexuality" as a category of knowing is also "constitutive of and constituted by racialized gender and class formations" (2005: 88). As the related histories above indicate, the gendering of sexuality and the sexualization of the gendered is also riven with class and racial origins, dynamics, and processes so that the very constitution of gender or sexuality as objects — proper or not — cannot be dislocated from the broader contexts of daily and institutionalized power in which they come to cohere. That is to say, the competing stories about Stonewall, the claiming of people as transgender or homosexual, and the deletion of homosexuality from the DSM can also be — and must be — seen as implicated in histories of race and class as they are in those of gender and sexuality.

The essential point, then, is that "transgender" has emerged — both as a movement and as an identity category — primarily from within a framework established by a racialized and class-inflected gay and lesbian — and latterly, queer — activism and scholarship. The result is that the distinction between gender and sexuality upon which the transgender/homosexuality divide is based is conceptualized as ontological and cannot account for the complex movements between and reshapings of those analytic and lived domains — "gender" and "sexuality" — which have been the focus of so much feminist theorizing and activism. Moreover, as Ferguson insists, this distinction cannot easily account for how "gender" and "sexuality" take shape in particular racialized and class forms.

Despite these critical (if different) understandings, the assumption that sexed bodies, social gender, and sexual acts/desire *are* intimately connected has remained powerful in U.S. American popular culture and in some (and somewhat questionable) scientific thought (Bailey 2003; see also note 12 to this chapter). In this view, homosexual desire is *necessarily* gender-variant/deviant because sexual desire and sexual acts are, in Western societies (and most others), central features of what it means to be a man or a woman. Likewise, a man or woman who cross-dresses or takes on the roles and behaviors ascribed to another sex/gender is seen to be — or at least suspected to be — homosexual. In such a view, sex/gender/sexuality are interchangeable insofar as sexed body, social gender, and sexual desire are inextricable; and any deviation from this norm is understood as sinful or as a manifestation of mental illness.

These arguments can be — and often are — contested by arguing that this is a *conflation* of different aspects of human lives — gender and sexuality — that do not, ontologically, impact on one another. This, indeed, is at the heart of Feinberg's and Devor's and Matte's claims in this chapter's epigraphs and is frequently and explicitly made in the literature (e.g., Faderman 1991: 45, Cromwell 1999: 46). But *both* of these positions — sexuality and gender as distinct or as part of the same package — rely on the idea that there are domains called "sexuality" and "gender" that have both experiential and ontological status and which can act or not act upon the other. That is, neither of them is "true" insofar as no categorical system fully explains the ways in which those lived experiences we name through "gender" and "sexuality" are lived on a day-to-day basis by particular social actors in particular social contexts (see Gagné and Tewksbury 2002).

Thus, the very idea that gender and sexuality either can be "conflated" or should be seen as "intersecting" relies on a slippage between analytic categories and situated, contextual experience. Claims of conflation rely on an assumption that those things we call sexuality and gender have always been *experienced* as distinct and privilege contemporary theoretical framings as the truth of that experience. Moreover, the argument over the conflation of gender and sexuality obscures other social experiences that we name as class, race, culture, nationality, and so on as equally and vitally constitutive of the lives of those historical subjects whose identities are debated. Thus, the reading back of "conflations" into the historical record is a modernist progress narrative in which contemporary theoretical (and then, implicitly, identitarian) models are taken as the truth of historical and non-Western subjects. Simultaneously, while the separation of gender and sexuality makes sense of many contemporary people's senses of self, there are also contemporary gendered/sexual subjects whose senses of self are not accounted for by this distinction.

I am not proposing a return to a system where self-identified gay men and lesbians are seen as "gender inverts," where transexual- or transgender-identified people are simply dismissed as homosexuals who are too homophobic to accept their homosexuality, or where lesbian sexual practices are policed for their patriarchal content. Clearly, the recognition that "gender" encompasses far more than sexual desire, and, concomitantly, that "sexuality" and sexual desire do not always align in conventional ways with gender identity, is a vital one. But (and this is a big but), the bald assertion of the ontological separateness of gender and sexuality ignores the complexity of lived experience, the historical constructedness of the categories themselves, the racial and class locations of different experiences and theorizations of gender and sexuality, feminist understandings of gender and sexuality as systemic and power-laden, and transforms an analytic distinction into a naturalized, transhistorical, transcultural fact. I am interested in the collective mode of transgender because it is increasingly constitutive of the newly institutionalized uses of gender and sexuality as ontologically separate forms of social difference uninflected by race and class; and, concomitantly, I argue that it has become so rapidly and broadly salient because it both depends on and elaborates this emerging cultural model of gender and sexuality.

INSTITUTIONALIZING PRIVACY

Some readers may argue that the above account denies the complication of "gender" and "sexuality" in scholarship, activism, and even in daily lived experience. Certainly, the histories I have mapped above have not focused on the critique of accommodationist gay and lesbian politics (e.g., Berlant and Warner 1998, Duggan 2003, Joseph 2002b, Seidman 1993, Warner 1999), calls for social constructionist accounts which query the categorical solidity of analytic terms (e.g., Freedman and D'Emilio 1990, Jolly and

Manderson 1997, Sinfield 2004, Wieringa and Blackwood 1999), or feminists who contest a simple reduction of "gender" to an essentialized sexual difference model (e.g., Butler 1994, B. Martin 1994). But these histories point to the fact that, for all these counterdiscourses, public understandings of gender and sexuality (as well as homosexuality, transgender, and feminism) have become institutionalized through a vast set of contexts—from public policy to media representations, and from psychiatry to grassroots activism.

One of the primary sites of such institutionalization has resulted from mainstream gay and lesbian activist claims that homosexual people are essentially the same as heterosexual Americans but for the one fact of privately experienced and conducted sexual desire and practice. Certainly, such an idea is not uniformly accepted, but this line of argumentation has an increasingly powerful rhetorical and explanatory force in U.S. culture. Indeed, in the landmark Supreme Court decision in *Lawrence v. Texas* in 2003, the majority of the justices concurred with Justice Kennedy, who invoked the right to privacy in finding the Texas sodomy law (and by extension, all sodomy laws) unconstitutional. This ruling, however, further reinstantiates the understanding of homosexuality as a *private* concern. As other scholars have argued, the privileges of heterosexuality extend far beyond the boundaries of the bedroom, where gay/lesbian people are expected to conduct themselves as implicitly "straight" members of society (e.g., Knopp 1992).[15]

These concerns about privacy and appropriateness are evident in many contexts. While gay and lesbian organizations celebrate the "diversity" of gay and lesbian communities, it is also clear that the representation of the sober, respectable homosexual is at the forefront of contemporary mainstream gay and lesbian organizations in ways not dissimilar to the claims of the homophile movement of the 1950s and 1960s.[16] As I have argued above, though, "sameness" also operates along multiple axes because other elements of social difference—named through categories such as class, race, and culture—are made invisible through the privatization of gay identity. Indeed, current concerns around gay and lesbian marriage, spousal benefits, and so on, are deeply middle-class concerns and, while important, the focus on such issues has drowned out the insistence by other activists that gay and lesbian organizations also consider issues of poverty, welfare reform, and racism which also have had significant impact on gay- and lesbian-identified people (Jacobs 2004). As we will see in chapter 5, discourses about privacy resonate with a broader assertion of the role of privacy and privatization in U.S. and global neoliberal political, economic, and social orders since the 1970s. Most significantly, the "sameness" argument is intimately bound to repudiating the historical association of homosexuality with publicity, overtness, and gender variance.

I would argue, then, that "transgender," while it has been generated by individuals who so identify, *is also an effect of the historical development of privatized homosexual identity* for it is no longer the case, as Jayne County writes it used to be, that "everyone [is] just gay." Thus, to summarize the logic, "transgender" by its categorical implication of visible gender variance, and its association of "overtness" and the street, confers stability on the gender of (especially white and middle-class) gay men and lesbians. By stressing the otherness of "transgender," its difference as a separate "community" and "identity" from those of "gay/lesbian/homosexual" people, the similarity of the latter to heteronormative models of personhood and citizenship is recognized and demanded. The construction of gender as a public concern, and that of sexuality in the realm of the private, places "transgender" as a category of difference and "gay" as the category of similarity and sameness. I argue, then, that "transgender" has become useful to accommodationist gay and lesbian groups (apart from its usefulness to transgender-identified people) precisely because it has been able to absorb the gender transgression which has doggedly been associated with modern (and especially male) homosexual identities for more than a hundred years.

These effects are not a conscious part of the diverse and liberatory politics framed by transgender. However, my point is that, whatever the political views of particular social actors, the institutionalization of these understandings reproduces these histories or, at the very least, the ontologies of difference that underpin them. To remind the reader, my concern is more than critical or historical. Rather it is political — for again I want to draw attention to those whose understandings of self may fall out of this system, and in turn, what this can tell us about a broader conceptualization of gender and sexuality.

In the end, Feinberg's archaeology of "transgender warriors" with which I started this chapter both opens up a history and closes down another one. In the chapters that follow, I will look at people who have become — in the terms of activists, sociologists, social service providers, public health officials, and journalists — transgender. I will ask what it means to these people — and to us as scholars and activists — that they have been incorporated into this history, and I will look at how my own research, even as it opens up the questions I have asked above, is drawn back into this same dynamic.

Part II

Making Community, Conceiving Identity

Introduction to Part II

Reframing Community and Identity

When I started my fieldwork, "transgender identity" and "transgender community" were the framing ground for this project; I simply assumed that there were such self-evident things as transgender community and identity. But as my research progressed, I increasingly began to wonder about a transgender community and the transgender identities that inhabited it, so that the ideas of "community" and "identity" themselves began to unravel for the same reasons my initial project had. That is, I realized that a transgender community does not exist outside the contexts of those very entities which are concerned to *find* a transgender community: social service organizations, social science accounts, and activist discourses. Likewise, many of those I met who were understood to have transgender identities by social service providers and activists made claims about themselves and others which profoundly contested this understanding.

This does not mean that transgender identity and community are figments of the imagination, but rather that they are *products of an imaginary*. The former position would hold that transgender identity is illusory, and that those who claim such an identity are laboring under false consciousness or are deluded. I would not accept this position. The latter position, though, puts transgender identity and community into a historical and ethnographic framework that requires us to ask a range of questions: How, for all the sociological and observable evidence of transgender identities and communities, did they come to coalesce around this term in the 1990s? Who is seen to occupy this category and who is not? Do all those who are understood through this category see themselves as part of it? And how does the institutionalization of the collective mode of transgender shape the terms in which the previous questions can be answered?

These two issues—identity and community—are the topics of the next two chapters. Given what I have written above, it should be clear that these chapters are neither documentaries of transgender identities or communities nor exhaustive descriptions of the possible categories of selfhood that could be incorporated into "transgender." Rather, they draw on my specific ethnographic experiences with (primarily) MTF transgender-identified people in New York City in the late 1990s in order to see how the collective mode of transgender both succeeds *and* fails to account for the identities and communities so described. I focus on these people partly because they demonstrate the instability of "transgender" even as they are central to an imaginary of what a transgender community is. In these two chapters, the absence of FTM and female-bodied masculine people will be most evident, but apart from the ethnographic context which produced this omission, I want to hold onto the observations I have made in part I: how has the institutionalization of the collective mode of transgender been formed precisely around the same absence? What understandings of gender and sexuality shape this institutionalizing move? And what are its effects?

2

Making Community

The support group meeting I discussed in the introduction is one of several in New York City for transgender-identified people. Several social service agencies run groups focused on transition, HIV status, health care issues, or general support. These kinds of groups gather their members together through the collective power of transgender, and in turn they become enactments of something that participants understand and experience as community.

But ideas about "community" itself are also frequently debated in these spaces. At a Gender Identity Project (GIP) support group in mid-October 1996, Cindy took up this theme as she talked about her experiences online. She noted that some transgender-identified people in online discussion groups frequently questioned the political validity of sex reassignment surgery, arguing for transgender identities and practices which rejected medical interventions. Cindy argued vehemently against these positions, which she saw as invalidating her strong desire to surgically transition and her identity as a woman. Pausing, she shook her head and said: " 'Community!' Where the hell did *that* come from?" This was a pointed question, given that the people in the room had often radically different understandings of their selves and their relationships to one another. Comprising both MTFs and FTMs, cross-dressers and transexuals, those post-surgery and those newly out of the closet, the group was a reiteration both of GIP's understanding of the collective nature of "transgender" and of a trans-gender community, but simultaneously a representation of the tensions within it.

Building—and representing—a transgender community is a central goal of social service and activist organizations which have developed since the early 1990s. The GIP group is one manifestation of this, but the notion and enactment of a transgender community is widely distributed, from the identification of sites for outreach, to the citation of transgender community needs in legislative advocacy. Through my work with the GIP and other social service agencies as a safer-sex outreach worker, I quickly came to realize that the idea of a transgender community was already assumed in these settings. In planning meetings and informal discussions, outreach workers, their supervisors, and ultimately the agencies which funded this work mapped out a community that spanned sex work strolls, middle-class cross-dresser bars, drag balls, and other such sites. This talk turned into a map of New York City that located transgender subjects and the community they were understood to be part of. In turn, this framing shaped the field of my research, taking me to the transgender community I had planned to study.

But even as I cycled between these sites, Cindy's question was also one I had been asking myself. From the beginning of my fieldwork I had been worried that I was unable to perform the traditional ethnographic duty of "living with the natives." There is no neighborhood, building, or area of the city where I could have lived that would have made me any more a part of a transgender community, such as those described by Kulick (1998), Prieur (1998) or Nanda (1990), all of whose subjects are frequently in-cluded under the rubric of "transgender" (see chapter 4). Despite the as-sumption of a transgender community by my co-workers, I came to realize that rather than a pre-existing community, there are a variety of dispersed places which are brought together *by* "transgender" into an idea of com-munity (cf. Boellstorff 2005).

Here, anthropological models come up against—and intersect with—identitarian notions of community. Like the imagined unity of such move-ments, anthropologists have traditionally assumed "community" as the base line of investigation, facilitated by the ways in which anthropologists' objects of study have been located historically in small, geographically bounded groups. As more recent ethnographic studies have shown, how-ever, anthropology's traditional concern with social coherence and eufunctional models of culture elides the ways in which community is rarely as coherent as anthropologists have suggested (e.g., Gregory 1998, Gupta and Ferguson 1997, Ferguson 1999, Ortner 1996). A concern within anthropology with resistance, contestation, transnational processes, border crossings, and difference has highlighted the extent to which "community" — and "culture" — is more contingent than traditional anthropological models would have it. Whether geographically bounded or not, community is not a natural fact but an achievement, a process that does not happen without the exercise of agency and power (Anderson 1991 [1983]).

My concern is thus not identical to that posed by Cindy in her rhetorical question. Cindy was questioning why those seen to be part of her community would negatively judge her desire to transition. My question was focused on an ethnographic dilemma, revolving around the classic imaginary of anthropology which posits a coherent and homogenous community in which one can gather data. However, for both of us the underpinning concern was: how is it that people with different life goals, understandings of their gendered and sexual beings, and different social positions come to be gathered under "transgender"? In this chapter, I draw on these briefly sketched anthropological understandings of community to see how they provide insights into the idea of a transgender community. I do so not to contest the realities of a transgender community but to highlight this community as an achievement. Moreover, I do so in order to consider how the achievement of a transgender community fails to account for all its imagined members. Finally, I want to consider how, in looking at "communities," anthropologists — including myself — and others can become implicated in the production of that very object of investigation.

In order to address these concerns, I will discuss three drag balls that were conceptualized by my co-workers at GIP as being part of New York's transgender community. I do so for two reasons. First, drag as a trope has come to dominate much of what is written under the rubric of transgender, a term to describe both cross-gender dressing but also, more broadly (and most famously by Judith Butler in *Gender Trouble*) the performativity and constructedness of gender itself. Butler (1990) herself invokes Esther Newton's (1979 [1972]) classic ethnography of urban U.S. gay male drag queens and female impersonators from the 1960s to make her point, and its citation there shapes much of how "drag" has come to operate as a trope in scholarly analysis since the 1990s. However, in this book, rather than being a trope for understanding the constructedness of binary gender, drag is more usefully understood in terms of the constructedness of a transgender community and how it is contrasted to a gay community. While gay men and lesbians recognize drag as a feature of their histories and communities, increasingly "drag" is understood through the framework of "transgender." As with the other categories I examine, I will also ask what meanings attach to "drag" and how they might complicate the distinction between a gay and a transgender community.

The second and related reason for choosing "drag" as a framing device is that it helps me explore the edges of the inclusivity of transgender, the places where it fails to fully explain the experiences of some people included under its purview. Rather than focusing on the implicit center of transgender — transexual women and men — I want to look at its boundaries, the places where, as Mary Douglas (1992 [1966]) reminds us, categories become dangerous. The first of these boundaries is an embodied one. Virtually all the drag I discuss below is engaged in by male-bodied people. While there is a history of male impersonation in the United States (see Boyd 2003) and while there has been an explosion of drag king practices and performances in the United States and elsewhere since the 1990s (Halberstam 1997, Halberstam and Volcano 1999), the focus on male-bodied people in this chapter reflects the historical U.S. American (and European) conception of what drag is (see Baker 1994). As such, it is important to note that this chapter is not a comprehensive review of drag practices nor of the meanings of drag, but rather an exploration of what three drag balls can tell us about institutionalized understandings of transgender. This framing thus also enables us to consider the frequent absence of female-bodied masculine-identified people and drag kings from popular cultural conceptions of drag and how this absence is also enacted in the institutionalized form of transgender-as-collectivity. Second, since drag in the sense that I use it here indexes theatrical performance, its inclusion as part of "transgender" highlights the complexity of transgender-as-collective for transexual men and women who reject the metaphor of literal performance to describe their selves. The historical association of drag with male homosexuality complicates the inclusion of "drag" in transgender for these same people. Finally, this framing serves to carry forward the argument that transgender not only describes a set of practices and discourse about identity and community but also implicates and is productive of particular ideas about gender and sexuality. I want to show how "drag" is a category which should attract analytic attention not so much for what it can tell us about gendered categories such as man or woman but about the analytic categories of gender and sexuality themselves.

AT THE CLUBHOUSE

Mid-March in New York is cold and wet, and not a good season for a cyclist, and so this week I resort to the subway and cabs. There is a lot of traveling to do as I have three balls to attend. The first is the weekly Wednesday night ball at the Clubhouse in Hell's Kitchen, frequented primarily by young African American and Latina/o people who usually describe themselves as gay. The second is the annual Crossdressers International (CDI) Debutante Ball at a small piano bar called Judy's in midtown, an event in which ostensibly straight (mostly white and middle-class) male cross-dressers get together for their most formal annual event. The third and final is the grand *Night of a Thousand Gowns* ball at the New York Hilton Ballroom hosted by the Imperial Court of New York City, a philanthropic and social group of mostly white and well-off gay male drag performers. Though there are only three balls, it feels rather like a thousand, and the contrasts are striking.

The weekly Wednesday night mini-drag ball at the Clubhouse on 28th Street is my most challenging field site, for the music is loud, the hour is late, and I am confused. At the Clubhouse, where virtually everyone except me is either a person of African descent or Latina/o,[1] the way people talk about themselves is not what I had expected. For a start, while I have come here to do research on the transgender community, I and most of those present share the term "gay" in talking about ourselves. Why, then, am I here?

These balls have become well known through one of the most watched documentary films of the 1990s, Jennie Livingstone's *Paris Is Burning*.[2] Dorian Corey, who provides much of the commentary during the film, notes that the balls started in the 1960s in Harlem as sites for the achievement of status (and just plain fun) for black and Latino gay men. People compete — vogue — in different categories in the balls for trophies, and the competition is fierce (see Jackson 2002). Individual participants are usually affiliated with — or are trying to get into — groups called Houses, many of which are named after fashion designers, and each of which is headed by a Mother or a Father (or both). Houses often serve as alternative families and support networks for their members or children, as well as forming competing teams during balls (McCarthy Brown 2001). While the balls took place in Harlem as late as the early 1990s, some have subsequently moved downtown, at least in part because of the impact of the film. Such balls have a long history in New York's gay communities (Chauncey 1994), but the specific demographic of African American and Latina/o participants mark it as different from other such balls, as I will show below.

Chris, who is the party promoter, lets me in ahead of the lineup and without charge as he knows I have GIP safer-sex materials to give out. My presence here has been made possible by the network of social service agencies which do outreach to different aspects of the transgender community. However, not everyone at the ball is deemed to be a part of this community, as we will see.

Inside, about seventy or eighty people have already arrived, some twenty of them vogueing to the deafening music between the rough and ready barriers which define the performative space, preparing for the ball like athletes prior to a meet. I greet those I know — girls from the Meat Market, outreach workers from other social service organizations — and then take up my usual spot against the wall on the left-hand side of the narrow club. I look at my watch. It's only half past midnight. It could be two hours until the first category is called, and even if anyone would talk to me, we wouldn't be able to converse over the staccato clamor of *Din Da Da,* a popular ball track.

So, while I wait, I'm going to map this space into the field of the transgender community I am trying to make sense of. The Clubhouse is about fifteen city blocks directly north of the Lesbian and Gay Community Services Center (less than a mile), and perhaps some of the ball-goers frequent the Center, though not many. Some use the resources of the Audre Lorde Project in Brooklyn (a community center for "lesbian, gay, bisexual, two-spirit and transgender people of color communities") or simply stay out of these organized forms of community. Sally's and Show World — clubs which are venues for transgender-identified sex workers and their clients — are both about fifteen blocks north of the Clubhouse. I have seen one or two of the ball-goers at Sally's, where the crowd is also mainly Latina and African American, though usually older. Karalyn's — the bar frequented mainly by white middle-class male cross-dressers — is a further ten blocks north and two avenue blocks west. Edelweiss — also a bar/club which caters to transgender-identified women and their admirers — is almost directly west from here on 11th Avenue. Positive Health Project (PHP) — a needle exchange program which has a Transgender Initiative — is less than ten blocks north on 37th Street.[3] Some of the ball-goers are clients or former clients of this agency. At this time of the night (it's one o'clock by now, and the ball shows no sign of starting anytime soon) all the agencies and community centers are closed but the clubs will no doubt be open. This being Wednesday, Karalyn's is likely empty (the cross-dressers from the suburbs who are its mainstay are a weekend and early evening crowd), and none of the Karalyn's girls would ever come to a ball like this.

On the streets of the Meat Market, and on the Christopher Street piers (just a five-minute walk from the darkened 13th Street Center), a few African American and Latina fem queens might be walking. They are likely being cruised by men in cars, maybe even some of the same ones who will be at Karalyn's on Friday night. But it's raining and the girls will probably come up to the Clubhouse by around two, when things usually start happening. There is a significant overlap between the Meat Market girls and those who walk the fem queen categories at the Clubhouse.

All across New York City, lines of connection, knowledge, friendship, and affiliation join these different places and the people in them together. I know these other places from having spent time in them, observing their rhythms, and noting their memberships, busiest times, comings and goings. It feels to me rather as if I, and the literature from GIP I carry, are the only real connection between all these places, and that somehow this thing called a "transgender community" is something of a misnomer. Pleased at the observation, I pull out my notebook to write it down, only to catch several people glancing in my direction. Taking field notes in venues like this marks me even further as "other" — at thirty, I am older than most of the participants, and I am one of the few white people in the club. While I try to fit in, wearing a trendy t-shirt and jeans, I stick out like a sore thumb.

At around two o'clock the ball is underway at last and the first category tonight, announced by Eric Bazaar — the MC for the evening — is "butch queen up in drags." At these balls the categories are predictable. There will always be a fem queen performance category, and a butch queen vogueing fem category, and generally one for butch queen up in drags, butch realness, butch queen realness, women's face, and butch queen body (see figures 2a and b for an example of the categories in a Clubhouse ball program). "Butch queen up in drags" is one of the most puzzling categories to me, but having said that, I need to step back and investigate what these categories signify.

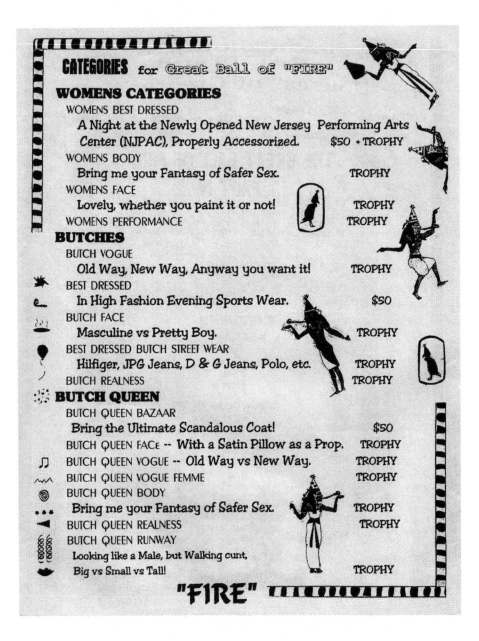

CATEGORIES for Great Ball of "FIRE"

WOMENS CATEGORIES

WOMENS BEST DRESSED
  A Night at the Newly Opened New Jersey Performing Arts
  Center (NJPAC), Properly Accessorized. $50 + TROPHY
WOMENS BODY
  Bring me your Fantasy of Safer Sex.   TROPHY
WOMENS FACE
  Lovely, whether you paint it or not!   TROPHY
WOMENS PERFORMANCE   TROPHY

BUTCHES

BUTCH VOGUE
  Old Way, New Way, Anyway you want it!   TROPHY
BEST DRESSED
  In High Fashion Evening Sports Wear. $50
BUTCH FACE
  Masculine vs Pretty Boy.   TROPHY
BEST DRESSED BUTCH STREET WEAR
  Hilfiger, JPG Jeans, D & G Jeans, Polo, etc.   TROPHY
BUTCH REALNESS   TROPHY

BUTCH QUEEN

BUTCH QUEEN BAZAAR
  Bring the Ultimate Scandalous Coat! $50
BUTCH QUEEN FACE -- With a Satin Pillow as a Prop.   TROPHY
BUTCH QUEEN VOGUE -- Old Way vs New Way.   TROPHY
BUTCH QUEEN VOGUE FEMME   TROPHY
BUTCH QUEEN BODY
  Bring me your Fantasy of Safer Sex.   TROPHY
BUTCH QUEEN REALNESS   TROPHY
BUTCH QUEEN RUNWAY
  Looking like a Male, but Walking cunt,
  Big vs Small vs Tall!   TROPHY

"FIRE"

FIGURE 2a and b: Ball Program for the *Great Ball of FIRE* (October 1997)

October 25, 1997

BUTCH QUEEN -- Foot & Eye Wear. $50

BUTCH QUEEN FAG OUT -- Revenge of the Nerds,
   Safer Sex is the Key, Keep It Clean Girls!   TROPHY

BUTCH QUEEN IN DRAG

FACE -- Cover Girl of the Year.   TROPHY

RUNWAY -- Serving from a Foreign Country!   TROPHY

REALNESS -- Presenting it Like a Lady!   TROPHY

BAZAAR $100

FEMME QUEEN

RUNWAY DIVA -- In All Black!   TROPHY

FACE -- With an Ovah Mask-Reveal the Carta! $50

BODY -- Bring Me Your Safer Sex Fantasy.   TROPHY

FOOT & EYE WEAR -- Fall '97 Pumps Please! $50

PERFORMANCE   TROPHY

GLAMOUR -- Done from Head to Toe!   TROPHY

OPEN TO ALL

EXTRAVANZA -- Sequins, Feathers and Beads! $100

PARENT/CHILD RUNWAY -- In Complimenting Outfits.   2 TROPHIES

TRIPLE THREAT AS A HOUSE -- 1 Face, 1 Vogue,
   1 Runway in Complimenting Outfits.   TROPHY

DESIGNER'S DELIGHT, HAUTE COUTURE
   Made out of Latex, Plastic, Vinyl or All Three. $100

GRAND PRIZE

FACE AS A HOUSE -- In All White with an AIDS Ribbon,
   Creativity is a Must! 4 or More. $250

SAFER SEX COMMERCIAL AS A HOUSE
   2 Minutes Limit, you will be timed! 4 or More. $500

RUNWAY AS A HOUSE -- In Safer Sex Costumes!
   4 or More. $500

----- **CATEGORIES CLOSED !!!** -----

A butch queen is, normatively (if such a category can be normative), a gay man who "passes" as a straight man in everyday life, or at least does not take on any culturally regarded feminine practices or behaviors in public. A fem queen, on the other hand, is a person born male who has taken various steps — hormonal, sartorial, and, in some cases, surgical — to feminize their appearances and identities.

A butch (as opposed to a butch queen) is best described as a female-bodied masculine person, that is, someone born female who takes on masculinized behaviors and/or identities. Butches may or may not identify as male and take on masculine names and pronouns. Some may also identify as lesbians, though a few of these same individuals could also be injecting "T" (testosterone). "Women" in the ball scene seem to be female-bodied feminine persons who may be heterosexual or may be fem lesbians. Fem queens who have had SRS (post-operative transexual women as they might be described elsewhere) represent a liminal category that, because of the recency of their appearance in the community, still creates confusion, concern, and disputes. The category "man" does not really make sense at the ball: if you are here, and male-bodied, you are assumed to be a queen of some variety, whatever your appearance, identity, or sexual practice.

Given this description, it is evident that two of these broad categories are available for interpretation as "transgender": fem queens and butches, whereas butch queens and women are more evidently describable as "gay" and "lesbian." Yet, as I soon discovered, everyone at the ball — fem queens, butch queens, butches, women, butch queens in drags — refer to themselves and each other as "gay." This, indeed, is the central puzzle at the Clubhouse, and one to which I will return.

Within these groupings, people compete in other broadly defined categories, which are themselves gendered in complicated ways. For example, "realness" categories require one to look as much like one's chosen gender as possible.[4] That is to say, butches (female-bodied masculine people) and butch queens (male-bodied masculine people) are scored by the judges according to how well they approximate the appearance and manner of a straight man. Such genderings are also shaped by class and racial meanings, as *Paris Is Burning* makes abundantly clear: the "realness" of masculinity can be expressed in terms of looking like a (white) business executive or a (black) banji boy. Similarly, fem queens who walk in realness categories are required to express their "realness" through a variety of genres: schoolgirl, runway model, and so on. There is no realness category for "women." Female-bodied people who present as women are not seen to have to prove their realness as they are considered "real" already—whatever their sexual identity.

In table 1, I have attempted to represent an idealized description of these identities and categories, but it can only be used as a heuristic, for things on the ground are more complicated. "Butch queen up in drags" is a case in point. This is a category for butch queens who dress and perform in fem drag. In ball programs, "butch queen" categories are listed separately from "butch queen in drags" categories (see figure 2), but they are also understood to be different from "fem queens." It seems that "butch queen in drags" acts in some ways as a liminal category between "fem queen" and "butch queen."

However, it is not always easy to tell who is or is not a fem queen, a butch queen in drags, or a butch queen. On one of my first visits to the Clubhouse when I was new to safer-sex outreach, I was hanging out with Jay, an outreach worker with another social service agency, who had promised to point out "the transgenders" (his term) to me. As we stood, trying to talk over the din, a person in a short skirt and heels walked past us and greeted Jay. He nudged me and nodded after her, but as I set off after her in the crowd, bearing condoms, Jay pulled me back.

"Sorry," he shouted above the music, "I just remembered, she's a butch queen in drags." In Jay's estimation, this person was therefore a "gay man" and thus outside the category of "transgender." We will see, when I discuss *Night of a Thousand Gowns,* that "gay men in drag" are sometimes also drawn into "transgender," as is evident from the examples in part 1. The point to note here is how "transgender" comes to be a way for external agents to try and sort out what appears to be a confusing conflation of gendered and sexual identities for the purposes of social service outreach and documentation.

I get further confused this evening. Prior to the ball, Eric Bazaar calls on well-known and popular individuals to walk, first calling them by their name, and then by the category in which they usually walk: "butch queen up in drags, walks like cunt, acts like cunt, cunty, cunty, cunty," he intones.[5] The butch queen in drags he has called on is, to my surprise, not in "drag" at all but rather in trousers, a shirt, and sunglasses, looking a lot butcher than some of the butch queens who "vogue fem," a category for ostensible butch queens who vogue in a manner associated with fem queens. Certainly, he looks nothing like the butch queen in drags I had

TABLE 1: The organization of performance categories, gender, and sexuality at a Clubhouse ball

Gender Presentation	Performance Categories	Gender Identity				Sexual Identity
		Male-Bodied People		Female-Bodied People		
			Transsexual Woman	Transsexual Woman	Woman	Gay
Feminine	"Realness"	Fem Queen			Woman	
↕	"Body"/"Face"	Butch Queen Up in Drags	↔	↔		
↕	"Performance"	Butch Queen Vogueing Fem	↔	↔		
↕	"Performance"	Butch Queen	[Transsexual Man]*			
↕	"Body"/"Face"					
Masculine	"Realness"	Butch Queen			Butch	

* I put "Transsexual Man" in square brackets because I have never met nor heard of a butch in the ball scene who transitioned or identified in this way. Even those who live full time in masculine gender are generally referred to as butches in my experience, though, as I have noted throughout, my data on butches and female-bodied people in general are relatively few.

tried to give condoms to earlier. He comes on to the runway, makes a few desultory turns, and goes back under the barrier to his seat. The calling goes on. Without the context of Eric's remarks, I would not have known that this person was known as a "butch queen up in drags."

But by far the most interesting event for me comes sometime around three o'clock from the two young butches—that is, female-bodied masculine persons—standing right next to me in the crush. They have a running joke about the butch queens vogueing fem on the runway. One of them starts, remarkably well, parodying the butch queens, but so convincingly I would have thought that s/he was a butch queen getting ready to get onto the runway if his/her friend was not falling about laughing, and if I hadn't already seen her/him walking in "butch realness: looking like a banji boy from the projects."[6] If there were to be a category for this layered performance, it might be something like "butch realness vogueing butch queen vogueing fem."

For all the layering of these performances, and the ambiguity to my observer's eye, though, there are very strict rules for participation in the performance categories and frequent disputes about who is permitted to walk in what category. At another ball I attended, Nadia, a transexual woman who used to walk in the fem queen categories but who had undergone SRS, attempted to walk in a category for women. The hall erupted in an uproar as one of the judges challenged her right to walk in this category. Despite the attempts of the MC to support her right to walk, the commotion and disputes drove her off the stage. Likewise, Bella, another ball-goer, told me that she had faced enormous opposition from judges and audience members when she first tried to walk in a fem queen category because, up until that ball, she had walked as a butch queen vogueing fem. Even within a category like "butch queen," different kinds of butch queens walk in the "vogue fem" category and the "realness" category, and it is uncommon for people to walk in both. Indeed, at another ball, the Father of the House of Omni, Kevin Omni, had made this point by noting that in the past, contrary to the usual way of things, he had first won a grand prize for walking as a butch queen in drags, then for walking butch queen vogueing fem, and finally for butch queen realness. "First I told you I was a woman, then I told you I was a man, and then I told you I was *real!*" he crowed to his audience.

Crossing over within categories (different kinds of butch queen categories, for example) rather than between categories (between fem queen and butch queen) may be easier to do, but the point is that the divisions are strictly enforced. Yet, at the same time, what is most interesting about the ball scene is that for all the policing of divisions, virtually all ball-goers see themselves as unified by the category "gay" (see table 1). That is, whatever the gendered presentation of the person, the category in which they walk, their embodiment, or any transitions they may have made across categories or within them, all ball-goers talk about themselves as "gay." Within the balls, "transgender" has little if any salience, and my concern about directing my safer-sex materials to the "transgender" participants was confounded not only by a difficulty in separating out fem queens and butches from the others but by a system of identification that is at odds with the social service and activist understanding of the distinction between gay and transgender identities with which I was working.

This is not to say that transgender is never used at the Clubhouse or at other balls. Those participants who access social services from organizations like the GIP, or who are members of the House of Latex (a house sponsored by the Gay Men's Health Crisis, an AIDS prevention organization), have knowledge of this category and will use it about themselves and others. But the same people will also refer to themselves as "gay," often in the same utterance. In short, the performance divisions, and the recognition of the differences between fem queens and butch queens, between butches and women, and between fem queens and women, are highly gendered and heavily policed. But this difference is not understood as one which precludes fem queens and butches from being "gay."

I will leave the Clubhouse for a while now and draw on these observations later. But the confusions that plagued me at the Clubhouse are those I want to draw on throughout this chapter. On the one hand, the division of fem queens and butch queens into "transgender" and "gay" is clearly an artifact of the analytic framework I (and people like Jay) bring to the balls as outreach workers. But on the other hand, what would it mean to talk about butch queens, butches, fem queens, women, transexual women, and butch queens up in drags as all, simply, "gay?" And what does it mean to talk about "drag" as a singular category when so many different levels of drag are apparent with a whole range of different meanings for the people involved?

But this is not the only way that "drag" is complicated, as we will see at our next ball.

The following evening, Thursday, at around six thirty, I am ten blocks north of the Clubhouse in a suite at a hotel in the West 40s. Tonight I am in a suit and tie, in honor of the formality of a Debutante Ball. This ball is not a ball in the sense of the one I described above: there will be no dancing, vogueing, or loud music. Nor is it a Debutante Ball in the sense of that tradition where young upper-class white women are presented to "society" as a mark of their eligibility to marry. Rather, it is an event where Cross-dressers International members step out into the "civilian world" (to use a phrase provided by Nancy Lamar, CDI's New York president) and social-ize over dinner while listening to show tunes performed by a Barry Mani-low lookalike on the piano. The venue — Judy's — is traditionally a gay bar, frequented by older gay white men, gay male drag queens, and occasion-ally cross-dressers. With its location in the theater district, the theme of the place is, perhaps inevitably, Broadway shows.

The hotel suite has been rented for the evening so that members can change into their fem personae. From here, it is only an elevator ride downstairs to the lobby, which has an adjoining door to Judy's. Already here are Nancy, Kristine, Irene, Gina, Electra, Alta, Incognita, Helena, and two Mary Kay ladies who do makeovers for the group. Apart from myself and the women from Mary Kay, everyone else is in various stages of dress or undress, removing male attire and putting on evening gowns, makeup, jewelry, and wigs. In the sitting room, Nancy is putting on her own make-up, though she does call over to the Mary Kay women to ask what kinds of beard cover they are using.

"Do you want an observation?" she says to me suddenly. I nod willingly and pull out my notebook. For cross-dressers, she says, "the two hours dressing up here is as important as the two hours downstairs in the restau-rant," implying that the act of dressing is itself an erotic activity.

Nancy is not only the president of the New York chapter of CDI but also keeper of the records. From these records, Nancy — who likes to map things out as much as I do — reports that the vast majority of CDI's membership lives in the suburbs of New Jersey and outer boroughs of New York City. The majority are married (the wives may or may not know about their husbands' cross-dressing), white, and while they range in employment from plumbers to executives, a significant proportion (40 percent, she estimates from her own rough tallies) are, like herself, freelance business or computer consultants.

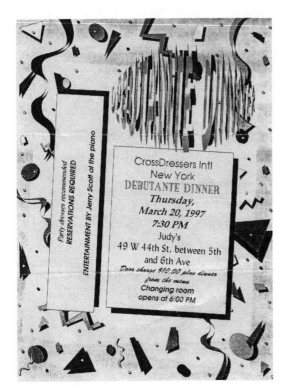

Inside the flyer image:

CrossDressers Intl
New York
DEBUTANTE DINNER
Thursday,
March 20, 1997
7:30 PM
Judy's
49 W 44th St. between 5th
and 6th Ave
Door charge $10.00 plus dinner
from the menu
Changing room
opens at 6:00 PM

Party dresses recommended
RESERVATIONS REQUIRED
ENTERTAINMENT by Jerry Scott at the piano

FIGURE 3:
Crossdressers
International
Debutante Ball Flyer
(March 1997)

Back at the hotel everyone but Helena is ready, and we set off in groups to the elevator. In the lobby and in Judy's bar we attract some mild attention, but the head waiter is happy to see us and sends us through to the restaurant, where there are eight or so people who had arrived earlier, already dressed. I sit with Jan, Incognita, Gina, Dana, and Merv. Merv and Dana are both retired firefighters who worked together, and Merv is, like me, in a suit and tie. I think perhaps he falls into the category of admirer, but etiquette prevents me from asking.

While the pianist plays show tunes we eat dinner. Later, there are prizes in a range of categories (made up on the spot so that pretty much everyone gets one), and many photographs are taken. Nancy, forever my champion, buys me dinner. "My treat," she tells me. When I leave at around ten thirty — a finishing time I appreciate, having gotten to bed at five this morning following last night's Clubhouse ball — people are beginning to head upstairs to change back into what Gina calls "boy drag."

The figure of "drag" looms large at the CDI ball and at CDI meetings. A common joke is that putting on makeup and spending two hours getting ready is "such a drag," and members often refer to one another and to themselves as being "in drag." At the same time, "drag" is complicated by the meanings it is often seen to index, especially male homosexual desire.

The official psychiatric profile for a cross-dresser (or someone suffering from "transvestic fetishism" to use the DSM term) is that of a heterosexual (often married) man who cross-dresses for erotic pleasure. This is certainly true of many CDI members, but cross-dressing is more complicated than this simple diagnostic category allows for. At Karalyn's, where I regularly hung out with Nancy and other CDI members, the crowd mainly comprised cross-dressers, all of whom are well aware of the DSM identification of themselves as "heterosexual men." This is another standing joke with cross-dressers, who, like postmodern theorists, speak the phrase while making scare quotes with their fingers to indicate an ironic stance toward the term. At Karalyn's, there are "heterosexual married" cross-dressers who are flirting and exchanging numbers with some of the male admirers or other cross-dressers. Some take feminizing hormones though their wives might not know it (if they even know about the cross-dressing). This practice is considered by psychiatrists to be a part of a *gender* transition — that is, of "gender identity disorder" or transexuality — and to be a radically different practice from the *sexual* "paraphilia" of transvestism. However, most of those who do take hormones have no plans to transition surgically. On the other hand, others who Nancy used to know as cross-dressers are now planning to transition and live full time as women. There are others, too, who are white *gay*-identified men who cross-dress for erotic pleasure, refusing the term "drag queen" which is usually applied to such individuals (see below). These members choose to socialize with the CDI crowd rather than at gay bars downtown where cross-dressing is limited to drag performance, and where there is little chance of finding sex partners who will share their erotic interests. For them, cross-dressing is an erotic practice, *not* a performative one, but there is no space for their desires in the predominantly white downtown gay male scene where masculinity in presentation and behavior is the accepted (and eroticized) mode.

Even more complexly, there are those who see cross-dressing not only in erotic terms but as an expression of a differently gendered self. Some, like Nancy and Connie, say that while they began to cross-dress as an erotic activity, cross-dressing has become as much about expressing a feminine self as it is about eroticism, though they do not consider themselves transsexuals. These dynamics further complicate the meanings of erotic practice and identification. When cross-dressed, some cross-dressers identify as women, and their sexual involvement with women or other cross-dressers is expressed in terms of lesbianism, even when both partners involved may have penises. Most of the cross-dressers refer to one another as cross-dressers or transvestites, sometimes as "trannies," but rarely as "transgender." Occasionally, in conversation, Nancy or someone else uses the phrase ("we're part of the transgender community" or "other transgender people," implying they are part of this broader category), but they rarely use it in conversation about themselves or their friends. And, unlike the queens, butches, and women at the Clubhouse balls, "gay" is not the unifying category. Rather, "gay" indexes the particular desires of some (few) cross-dressers who are exclusively attracted to men.

Indeed, most CDI members, even those who might have sex with men or other cross-dressers, strenuously refuse to identify as "gay" or even as "bisexual." This, indeed, is one of the difficulties of using "drag" for CDI members, since male "drag" is usually associated with male homosexuality. People like Nancy, who may be erotically drawn to other cross-dressers, do not experience that attraction as homosexuality and resist attempts to use that category to describe them. Moreover, the theatrical associations of drag also make it unattractive as a descriptive term for CDI members' activities. For them, cross-dressing is erotic and/or an expression of an inner self, not an opportunity to engage in explicit theatrical performance. Hence, while CDI members will joke about "drag," in discussion they far more often talk about "dressing," a term which distances them from homosexual desire and identity. While "drag" and "dressing" refer to, essentially, the same set of practices, the differences in meanings between them are highly salient for CDI members. Further, what makes the CDI group quite different from the Clubhouse ball-goers, apart from the obvious class and racial distinctions, is the strict separation of drag or cross-dressing from everyday life (represented in table 2 by the thick line). This contrasts with the ways that those lines are more blurred in the performative contexts of the Clubhouse balls, particularly with the category "butch queen up in drags."

A final point to make about CDI members is that they are virtually all male-bodied people who identify as men in their daily lives.[7] Unlike at the Clubhouse, there is no space here for female-bodied people who cross-

TABLE 2: The organization of drag, gender, and sexuality at the Crossdressers International Debutante ball

	Gender Presentation	Gender Identity	Sexual Identity
Male-Bodied People	Feminine (restricted to meetings/social events)	Man/Cross-dresser/ Transvestite/Woman	Straight Gay Bisexual Lesbian
	Masculine (the everyday)	Man	Straight/Gay/Bisexual

dress as men, a fact reflected in the absence of female-bodied people in table 2. In popular and medical understandings of cross-dressing, it is an activity restricted to male-bodied people. Female cross-dressing is seen as almost unintelligible, and conventional wisdom holds that women have more latitude to take on male items of clothing. Yet, as Califia points out (2003 [1997]: 199–200), this assumption ignores the fact that most items of clothing for women which are traditionally "male" (e.g., trousers, suit jackets) are clearly gendered as feminine. Judith Halberstam (1998a) further points to a long tradition of female cross-dressing in Western culture and argues for the importance of looking at what she calls female masculinities. However, CDI has no non-transexual cross-dressing women as members, and so "drag"—even as it is complicated by different understandings of that term—is, at CDI events, something that male-bodied people do.

Hence, even among the relatively homogenous group at the CDI ball and at Karalyn's, "drag" has a number of different meanings, indexing a variety of desires, identities, and practices that escape both popular and medical understandings, but different again from the young, gay-identified Clubhouse voguers. The absence of female-bodied cross-dressers at CDI also marks a significant difference in what "drag" can mean in these places. Finally, unlike at the Clubhouse, presence at the ball or participation in the activity of doing "drag"—or of "dressing"—does not imply that the participants are "gay." It is quite clear that doing "drag" is not a commensurate experience in these two contexts, and as we will see next, there are yet more ways to be in drag in New York City.

Two nights later and another ten blocks further north, I am in the same drag—that is, in the only suit I own—in the lavish ballroom of the New York Hilton. This is a far cry from the narrow darkness of the Clubhouse and the faded off-Broadwayness of Judy's, and for the first time, I really feel as though I am at a "ball" in the Cinderella sense of the word. Footmen and ladies-in-waiting abound, the hall is enormous, brightly lit, and full of people in fabulous gowns, military uniforms, and tuxedos. I feel positively underdressed and, far from being a guest or a safer-sex outreach worker, tonight I am a security volunteer, which means I don't have to pay $75 (the price of the cheapest ticket) to attend.

Night of a Thousand Gowns is an annual fund-raiser put on by the New York chapter of the Imperial Court,[8] and tonight's ball benefits AmFAR (the American Foundation for AIDS Research), the Lesbian and Gay Community Services Center, and its Community Health Project. The Imperial Court is an organization whose membership is made up of mainly white self-identified gay men who do performative drag. John Capazuca, who—as Maria Fabrizia—is a member of the Court, tells me that hardly any of the male-born members identify as women or as transgender.[9] Drag, in this environment, is considered to be in the realm of art and performance and to have no implications for members' gender identity or sexual practice/desire/identity. There are, moreover, an increasing number of gay men who are in the Court as "men," that is, male-bodied, gay-identified people who dress and present as men. "Drag" in this sense, therefore, does not only mean cross-gender dressing but also dressing as particular kinds of men, usually with historical military references. Like the Clubhouse balls, these balls draw on the long history of gay male drag performance (Chauncey 1994), but in sharp distinction to the Clubhouse ball, almost all those present are white and, to judge from the price of the tickets and the lavishness of the gowns and uniforms, literally and figuratively well-heeled.

In the ballroom, dozens of decorated tables are surrounded by hundreds of gorgeously dressed men and women of all genders, including a large number of non-transgender-identified men and women who are there as guests and donors. As I stand security at the door, the lights drop, voices are hushed, and a dramatic musical number unfolds on stage. This is to be the first of two or three big productions of the evening. *Night of a Thousand Gowns* is not only a fundraiser but also the annual showcase for the

Imperial Court, the event where "elevations" of Court members take place, culminating with the coronation of the new Emperor and Empress. The flavor of the coronation reflects the tastes of the Emperor and Empress being crowned, and this one is rather tsarist in mood with nary a Bolshevik in sight.

In between my security duties, I see friends and colleagues. Dr. Barbara Warren—as a director of the Center—is there, as well as Maria Fabrizia and Rosalyne, the director of the GIP. Rosalyne—who has coined the phrase "heterosexual woman of transgender experience" to describe herself—looks fantastic. She says that it had taken her three hours "to get dressed up like a drag queen." I wonder how she deals with the potential to be mistaken for a gay male drag queen since she is so insistent on her identity as a heterosexual woman. During the evening a lot of people apparently take her for a drag queen, which is not surprising in this crowd. But she seems to take it all in stride. None of the CDI members are here, though I heard some of them talking about coming. I see one person who is a well-known married cross-dresser activist from Pennsylvania, but most of the crowd seems to be—whatever they are wearing—non-transgender-identified gay men, like the membership of the Imperial Court itself.

Later, during dinner, Ruth Messinger, president of the Borough of Manhattan (and soon to be the Democratic candidate for New York City mayor), comes on stage to declare March 22 *Night of a Thousand Gowns* day in Manhattan. Her letter of support is also included in the glossy, bound program alongside letters from other state and national leaders, identifying the court's members implicitly as "gay." Later still, the different levels of the Court are presented one after the other: Lords and Ladies, Barons and Baronesses, and Princes and Princesses.

Once the new Court takes over, their style comes to define the events and mode of the Imperial Court for the coming year. They are elected by a committee drawn from the court, and once elected, John/Maria says, they have to be "virtually independently wealthy" to fulfill the offices of Emperor and Empress. As the Imperial Court is at least partly a philanthropic organization, the monarchs travel around the country and officiate at all sorts of events and balls, which requires them to have an abundance of appropriate outfits to fit the occasion.

Amid the drama of this extravagance, I am drawn again to think about what "drag" might mean in this context, and how it indexes—or, perhaps, maps onto—particular sexual and gendered identities. Despite the presence of people like Rosalyne, the married cross-dresser from Pennsylvania,

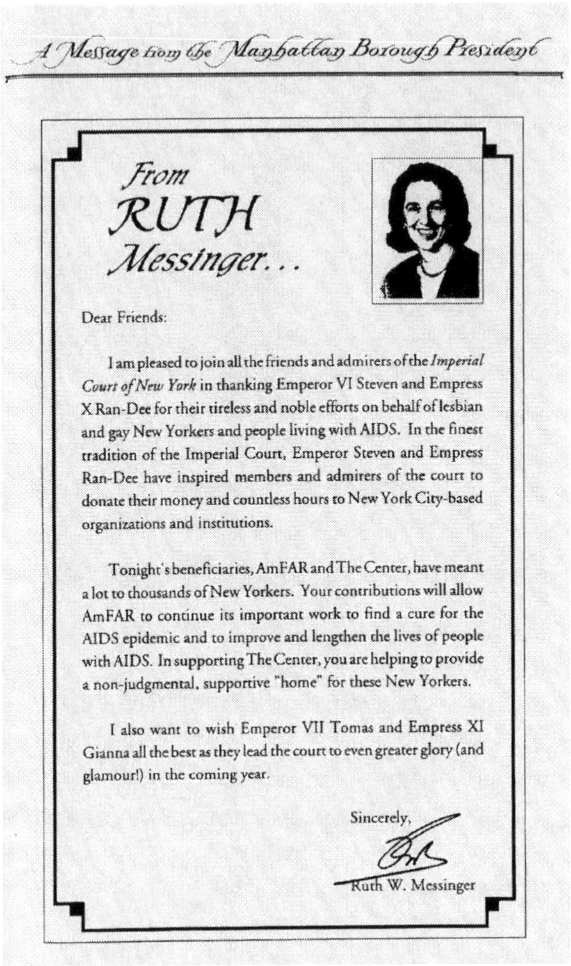

A Message from the Manhattan Borough President

From
RUTH
Messinger...

Dear Friends:

I am pleased to join all the friends and admirers of the *Imperial Court of New York* in thanking Emperor VI Steven and Empress X Ran-Dee for their tireless and noble efforts on behalf of lesbian and gay New Yorkers and people living with AIDS. In the finest tradition of the Imperial Court, Emperor Steven and Empress Ran-Dee have inspired members and admirers of the court to donate their money and countless hours to New York City-based organizations and institutions.

Tonight's beneficiaries, AmFAR and The Center, have meant a lot to thousands of New Yorkers. Your contributions will allow AmFAR to continue its important work to find a cure for the AIDS epidemic and to improve and lengthen the lives of people with AIDS. In supporting The Center, you are helping to provide a non-judgmental, supportive "home" for these New Yorkers.

I also want to wish Emperor VII Tomas and Empress XI Gianna all the best as they lead the court to even greater glory (and glamour!) in the coming year.

Sincerely,

Ruth W. Messinger

FIGURE 4: Ruth Messinger's letter of support for *Night of a Thousand Gowns* (March 1997)

Ruth Messinger, and Dr. Warren, the vast majority of the people at the ball are self-identified gay men in one form of performative drag or another. Here, drag is tied to performance and fun; that is, dressing in drag has few if any implications for the gender identities of the men who are in drag, nor is it understood as an erotic activity—or, at least, this is the claim Imperial Court members make. This stands in sharp contrast to the other two balls I have discussed in this chapter insofar as both the Clubhouse voguers and the CDI members understand their practice of drag/dressing not just in terms of performance or fun but also in terms of its implications for their gendered identities and/or their erotic desires. In table 3 I represent this

TABLE 3: The organization of drag, gender, and sexuality at the *Night of a Thousand Gowns* ball

Male-Bodied People	Gender Presentation	Gender Identity	Sexual Identity
	Feminine	Man	Gay
	Masculine	Man	

distinction at the *Night of a Thousand Gowns* by thick lines between the categories of gender presentation, gender identity, and sexual identity. This is to say, on the whole, members of the Imperial Court reject the idea that doing drag has implications for their core gender identity (to use a psychiatric term); correspondingly, that they remain gay *men* whatever their particular clothing choice or gender presentation; and moreover, that their "sexuality" as gay men is not expressed through drag.

This insistence on masculine gender is clear from an incident that took place prior to my fieldwork. In 1994 the Gender Identity Project was proposed as one of the beneficiaries of the *Night of a Thousand Gowns*. There was an enormous resistance to this from the membership of the Imperial Court, precisely because of an articulated fear that it would associate Court members with transgender people (and the category "transgender") and, it was believed by some members, imply that they themselves are, or desire to be, women. It took the work of Charles Chang (then-president of the Imperial Court) and an address to the membership by Dr. Barbara Warren before the membership relented (Philomena/Phil Stoehr, interview May 20, 1997).

In other words, most of the Imperial Court members reject the association of themselves with the category transgender. Yet *Night of a Thousand Gowns* is not without its own ambiguity. Rosalyne's statement that it had taken her three hours "to get dressed up like a drag queen" speaks in some ways to the instability of the Imperial Court members' positions in the gay/transgender identity divide. While it may be Rosalyne's identity — as a "heterosexual woman of transgender experience" — that becomes subsumed into the category "drag queen" in the context of this ball, her presence — "dressed up like a drag queen" — also destabilizes Imperial Court members' insistence on their identities as gay men, as does the presence of the heterosexual married cross-dresser. For if a transsexual woman can be mistaken for a drag queen, might not a drag queen be mistaken for a transexual woman, or a cross-dressing straight man? Similarly, the initial resistance to GIP as a recipient of Imperial Court philanthropic dollars speaks to a nervousness, a recognition by members that their gender identities as *men* need constant attention and work, particularly in a context where male homosexuality has been increasingly defined since the 1970s by hyper-masculine presentation (see Levine 1998).

The common insistence among Imperial Court members that "drag is for fun" or "my drag is a performance, nothing more" (both comments I heard on the floor of the Hilton ballroom that evening) is underpinned by an anxiety that their masculine gender is at risk. Still further ambiguity is added by the recognition of a few members, such as Maria Fabrizia, that there *is* an affiliation — and common political ground — between the Imperial Court and those grouped under the category "transgender." And finally, the insistence by some of my transgender-identified study participants that Imperial Court members are "really transgender" but are too "transphobic" to recognize the fact draws on this same dynamic.

I have no intention here of implying, like my just-quoted study participants, that gay male drag queens are "really" transgender or "really" feminine-identified. Rather, I am pointing to the ways that "drag" can index a variety of practices, identities, desires, and organizations of gender and sexuality. And as "drag" escapes a neat definition when you begin to look at the social contexts in which "drag" is drawn upon as a trope and enacted as a practice, so too the inclusion of cross-gender dressing as a feature of "transgender" in opposition to "gay" also begins to be complicated by cross-cutting demands, knowledges, and denials.

As should also be clear by now, however, these balls are not only differentiated by differing understandings of drag, or of gender and sexuality, but also by a variety of other markers of social difference we call by names such as class, race, or culture. And, as I will argue next, they are the very differences which animate the divergent understandings of "drag" that play out in these arenas.

DIFFERENCE BY THE BALLS

It is important to remember that my attendance at all these balls was prompted by two things: first, the guiding idea from my GIP colleagues that they all fell under the framing of "transgender"; and second, that it was "drag" (broadly conceived) which made their participants available for identification *as* transgender. But to simply say someone is "in drag" or part of a "transgender community" is to ignore a wide variety of other differences which shape both individuals' experience of being "in drag" and the ways that such practices gain meaning. Moreover, the idea that there is a similarity to the identities or practices at all three of these balls which overrides these differences — and which therefore constitutes the basis for a "community" — deserves attention.

However, the obvious differences between these three balls are not as clear as simply invoking "race," "class," or "culture" to explain them. Overlapping experiences and practices give these events a family resemblance along the axis of "drag." But as in any family, the differences are as striking as the similarities. So, in the interests of drawing out the similarities and differences in this particular family portrait of "drag," I want to look more closely at some of the factors that bring these three balls together and set them apart from one another.

Whereas the participants at the Clubhouse are mostly young, primarily people of color, and on the whole not too well off, the *Night of a Thousand Gowns* is awash with relatively wealthy (or unquestionably rich) white, and older, non-transgender-gay-identified men (and some few women, transexual and non-transexual). On the other hand, while the Imperial Court and CDI memberships might overlap in terms of broad racial and class identifiers, and are more likely to be over over thirty-five than under twenty-five, there are differences in terms of erotic interest and practices. Many of the CDI members are sexually attracted to men or to other cross-dressers, but many of them are also attracted to non-transgender-identified women, are married, and most refuse the identity label "gay." For the Imperial Court members, drag is about "performance" and "art," not erotic satisfaction or gender identification, and the membership is made up of insistently non-transgender-gay-identified men. Despite this, for both CDI and Imperial Court members, "drag" is a part-time affair. For the Clubhouse fem queens and butches, however, achieving "realness" in the ballroom is deeply significant beyond the walls of the Clubhouse. Many live and work in their gender of presentation at the ball, and this undercuts the notion of "drag" as purely performative in the theatrical sense.

The presence of Borough President Ruth Messinger at the Imperial Court ball and the lack of any such political support at the CDI ball, despite similar class and racial backgrounds, speaks to another difference. "Drag" as a (white) gay male performative genre has a certain validated space within an admittedly diverse New York City, and the Imperial Court's wealthy and relatively politically powerful membership can draw progressive politicians to their events, as many gay and lesbian events in the city do. However, the stigma attached to erotic cross-dressing — particularly among structurally heterosexual men — prevents such public validations (or the desire for them) by politicians for the CDI membership. Again, if CDI and the Clubhouse balls share a certain shadow-like existence in terms of the lack of participation of vote-hungry politicians, they are also strangers to one another in many other senses. White, middle- and upper-class cross-dressers are unlikely to consider that they have much in common with the young African American and Latina/o fem queens and butch queens up in drags at the Clubhouse, many of whom turn to sex work to support themselves.

Location, activity, and cost provide a further point of comparison. The Imperial Court meets at the Lesbian and Gay Community Services Center and has its annual ball at the Hilton, with tickets costing between $75 and $125. CDI members are reluctant to go to the Center as many of them fear being perceived as "gay," and attempts to start meetings there have not been successful. CDI has its own apartment in midtown (with a steep monthly rent) and holds its ball in an out-of-the-way middle-class bar attached to a hotel where they have rented a suite, spaces where they can dress and then return to their male personae without attracting attention. The cost of these spaces is distributed among its middle-class users, and supplemented through door fees of fifteen to twenty dollars. The Clubhouse on 28th Street is small, dark, and cramped, its runway marked out by roadwork barriers, and costs five to seven dollars to get in. Yet, as I have already pointed out, Clubhouse voguers also often avoid the Lesbian and Gay Community Services Center, if they even know about it. This avoidance is not a concern about being read as gay, though. The Center, with its location in Greenwich Village, is perceived as a "white" organization, and while many Center users are people of color, the perception still holds in the ball scene and other communities of color. Further, the Clubhouse ballgoers have their own forms of community — the Houses — which make the Center, with its focus on creating a space for community, somewhat redundant. The point of the activity, too, is a clear marker of difference among these balls: the philanthropic mission of the Imperial Court, which draws on American middle-class traditions of charity and volunteer work, is distinct from the competitive nature of the Clubhouse drag balls, where cash prizes of up to several hundred dollars in some events can be a real windfall for winners. (Of course, competition is clearly a part of the Imperial Court and CDI balls: it just isn't marked in the same way.)

To continue the comparisons, if the voguers at the Clubhouse can be seen to have a resemblance to the Imperial Court members as being all "gay," other differences can be found: to be "gay" in the Clubhouse can mean being a butch queen but it can also mean being a butch or a fem queen on hormones and with silicone breast, hip, or facial augmentations. Such gendering of the body beyond clothing itself is foreign to most of the Imperial Court members, who insist on their primary gender identity as men, and who would see such practices as feminizing — indeed, as "transgendered." Moreover, while neither Clubhouse voguers nor Imperial Court members use "transgender" to describe themselves, it is for different reasons. For Imperial Court members, transgender identification is actively disputed because it is seen to fundamentally contest their identities as gay men. For the range of people at the Clubhouse, while "transgender" is sometimes used (primarily by those who have close contact with social service agencies), its absence in that space has less to do with resistance to it than a lack of knowledge about the term itself. Further, among those who do use it, unlike the Imperial Court members, its use does not preclude them from continuing to talk about themselves as "gay."

Moreover, "transgender" and "drag" work complexly with and against one another in these spaces. Jay's interpretation of a butch queen in drags as "non-transgender" relies on the idea that the use of drag in that context is temporary, and that the person is really a "gay man," and so "transgender" contracts. But at the Hilton, it can (and threatens to) expand to incorporate structurally equivalent people into its purview.

Finally, the embodiment of the people involved in these different venues is also worth noting. At the Clubhouse, a respectable number of female-bodied people (both masculine- and feminine-identified or -presenting) were in attendance, though male-bodied people (again, both masculine- and feminine-identified or -presenting) predominated. At CDI, with few exceptions, the attendees were all male-bodied people who cross-dressed, while at *Night of a Thousand Gowns*, female-bodied people were present but primarily as guests, political figures, or allies. Few, if any, female-bodied people were dressed in "drag" as it is commonly understood.

The complexity of all the social distinctions at work here could take pages, but I hope I have made this observation clear: when the terms "drag" or "gay" or "transgender" are used in these contexts, they can mean quite different things, even within a twenty-block radius in New York City. These differences can be expressed in terms of other categories of social experience — such as class, race, age, embodiment — but not simplistically; they overlap, nudge each other aside, and reshape the contours of one another in the family portrait. Most significantly, these events also draw attention to the family portrait itself: while I attended all three balls as "transgender" events — or rather, they fell into the realm of my fieldwork as being part of a transgender community — this term was used by very few of the ball-goers. That is, it is difficult to imagine these different groups as being members in a community with equal access to or recognition of their membership. "Transgender," then, is *productive* of certain meanings — of creating the family portrait in the first place, of bringing the fem queens, drag queens, butches, cross-dressers (and, to cast my net wider, the transgender-identified women and men of the GIP support group) into the same portrait by elaborating certain differences while deemphasizing others. But most importantly, this portrait is enabled by not attending to those who resist, or lack knowledge of, the discursive power of "transgender" itself.

COMMUNITY AND DIFFERENCE

You may well ask after reading this: so what if there are different understandings of drag? Doesn't the family resemblance itself point toward a usefulness and reality of a category which could incorporate these ball-goers? Aren't the similarities as important as the differences? Indeed, this is the argument implicit in outreach efforts to different groups perceived as transgender by organizations like the GIP. Transgender, from this perspective, is a way of actively *creating* a community — a task that GIP and other agencies and organizations explicitly take on. The goal behind these activities is to create precisely the political and social entity that is needed in contemporary U.S. discourses of civil rights and identity politics in order to make claims for representation in a liberal democratic political system (Fraser 1997, Taylor 1992).

Central to this work is the assertion of a transgender community as a separate and definable group. Its underpinning source is seen to lie in variant *gender* expressions and identities, an origin which marks transgender identity and community as distinct from gay and lesbian identities. As we have seen, however, this distinction is not easily made in many contexts which are imagined by activists and social service providers to be a part of a transgender community. As a result, explanations must be sought by activists for why this might be. As noted above, Imperial Court members' resistance to being identified as transgender was dismissed by my social service provider colleagues as "transphobia." Likewise, fem queens' and butches' use of the term "gay" to describe themselves was dismissed by one social service provider who said to me, "They are working with the master's tools," invoking Audre Lorde.[10] That is, she saw the Clubhouse ball-goers (and others like them) as operating under a kind of false consciousness which disabled them from understanding the distinctions between gendered and sexual identities. In short, these different organizations of gendered/sexual selfhood which contest the institutionalized models of ontologized gender and sexuality (and a simple distinction between gay and transgender communities) are able to be dismissed as false consciousness or self-loathing, even as the people who profess them are drawn into the imaginary of a transgender community.

It should be noted that there is a crucial cultural space where the gender/sexuality distinction is complicated. Judith Halberstam, in her discussion of "transgender butch," writes that "transgender butch describes a form of gender transition that could be crucial to many gender-queer dykes' senses of embodiment, sexual subjectivity, and even gender legitimacy" (1998b: 287). Halberstam is pointing here to a subject position in which female-bodied butches, who do not see themselves as transexuals or FTMs, have access to the language and implications of transgender-identification in order to explore masculine identities and practices (see also Califia 2003 [1997]). This opens up the possibilities for the kinds of fluidity which characterize the Clubhouse balls.[11] There are two points to make here. First, Halberstam's argument is about female-bodied people; there is no analogous possibility for self-identified gay men to take on a "transgender fem" identity as a valorized or culturally salient role for themselves outside of the specific context of drag performance. Even in such performative contexts, as the Imperial Court members demonstrate, such a possibility is constantly foreclosed. As such, "transgender butch" elaborates a broader feminist interrogation of the lines between "sexuality" and "gender" as I discussed in chapter 1. Likewise, the drag king scene which developed in major U.S. and European urban centers in the 1990s is in many ways an elaboration of those kinds of explorations in lesbian and FTM transcommunities Halberstam describes (Halberstam 1997, Halberstam and Volcano 1999), just as drag has been repudiated in gay male communities as a form of identification outside of purely performative contexts (Levine 1998, Namaste 2000, McNeal 1999). Second, though, despite the experiential modes which might give "transgender fem" a lived reality, one goal of this book is to show how the institutionalization of "transgender," and the meanings of "gender" and "sexuality" which underpin it, work against these possibilities, for both male- and female-bodied people.

The point is that in academic, social service, and activist discourses and practices, these experiences *are* divided up as ontologically distinct. As such, then, in the space where a "gay and lesbian" community is contrasted to a "transgender community," "drag" — but most particularly "drag" engaged in by male-bodied people — becomes a node of category crisis not (just) for the categories "man" and "women," or "male" and "female," but for the categories of "gay" and "transgender" themselves, and consequently the categories of sexuality and gender which underpin them.

Moreover, "drag" can open up what kinds of distinctions are marked by "gender" and "sexuality" in discourses about and practices around male "drag." In my discussion above, I was at pains to point out the cross-cutting affiliations and differences between the three balls in terms of class, race, age, location, and so on. Like most contemporary anthropologists, I would argue that we must pay attention to the intersections of these social divisions and how they affect the practices and understandings of those who experience them or are understood through them. But the deeper point that I want to make here is that age, race, class, and so on don't merely inflect or intersect with those experiences we call gender and sexuality but rather *shift the very boundaries of what "gender" and "sexuality" can mean* in particular contexts. That is, in looking at the fuzzy edges of a "transgender community," the clarity of "gender" and "sexuality" also fades. If a fem queen sees herself as "gay" — defined by her desire for male-bodied people, and generated from her understanding of herself as male-bodied — then the category "sexuality" begins to leak into the space of "gender" in ways that cannot be accounted for by their separation as social differences. Simultaneously, if the figure of "transgender butch" enables a complication of what it means to be a lesbian or female-bodied masculine person, the complexities of this position are disabled in the *institutional* contexts where the differences between homosexual and transgender identification (and, of course, sexuality and gender) are stabilized.

I have used "drag," then, to demonstrate the complexities that arise in including those who do drag — be they fem queens, butches, cross-dressers, or drag queens — into an assumed transgender community. But I want to return finally to Cindy (who opened this chapter), who complicates the idea of a transgender community from other perspectives. Cindy, and others like her such as Melissa, often resist their inclusion in a transgender community because they see their identities as women or as men threatened by those who do not willingly take on a stable gender; who cross-dress for erotic pleasure; who argue against surgical transition; or who do performative drag. Cindy and Melissa resist the notion of a transgender community precisely because they are leery of its inclusivity, seeing the inclusion of drag queens, intersex people, or cross-dressers as diluting the specific political and social goals of transexuals, focused on surgical transition. And those who are on the "radical edge" of the category, those who refuse to adopt a gender identity or who see their gendered selves as fluid or androgynous, are equally leery of being included in a category which they see as too easily being captured by the firm categories of identity politics.

Yet, once more, a transgender community has come to have a certain institutionalized and experiential reality. In the last section of this chapter, I want to return to anthropological understandings of the community concept and draw out what they can contribute to this discussion.

MAKING COMMUNITY

In early 1998, a town hall meeting on violence directed at transgender-identified people was held at the Lesbian and Gay Community Services Center. The topic was a recent upsurge in violence against, and police harassment of, fem queen sex workers in the Meat Market. Apart from some gay- and lesbian-identified non-transgender activists and other community activists, most of the audience was MTF transgender-identified. On the table was not only the issue of violence but of class and race: sex workers and activists were blaming at least part of the upswing in police action on the mostly white local homeowners who had brought political pressure to bear on the police to step up action against the predominantly African American and Latina sex workers in the area. The topic was particularly controversial because the Center had recently moved its premises temporarily to the Meat Market to enable renovations to its 13th Street home, and this relocation was being blamed by some residents for the presence of the sex workers there.

Toward the end of the meeting, there was presentation by two young African American girls, Kerri and Nina, both of whom I also knew from the ball scene and the Meat Market (though neither engaged in sex work). Standing up in front of the packed room, they made a plea for tolerance from the police but also cast their claims as a broader call for acceptance of their practices and identities. "We're all transgender," said Kerri, appealing to the mostly white and transgender-identified people in the room. "We all have to stand together."

Kerri's use of "transgender" in this context further complicates the category, for, as I wrote above, "transgender" is not frequently used by Kerri and her peers in the Meat Market or at the balls. As I will argue in the next chapter, Kerri's use of "transgender" here (as opposed to something like "fem queen") is in part representative of her involvement in social service organizations which see her as transgender. Here, I am after something different, though: a recognition that, in this room on this evening, a transgender community was readily apparent. People had come together around this category, understanding it as having relevance to their experiences, and while most of the attendees were not Meat Market habitués (Kerri and Nina were the only two I recognized), the similarities in their experiences, rather than the differences between them, were foregrounded in this forum.

For, as Steven Gregory reminds us,

> Communities *do* exist. People move into them and are excluded from them. Public authorities chart their borders and "develop" them. Financial institutions invest and disinvest in them. Politicians represent and appeal to them. And those who inhabit these bewilderingly complex fields of political and socioeconomic relations struggle to define their needs, interests, and identities by constructing and mobilizing their own often oppositional version of "community." From my perspective, community describes not a static, place-based social collective but a power-laden field of social relations whose meanings, structures, and frontiers are continually produced, contested, and reworked in relation to a complex range of sociopolitical attachments and antagonisms. (1998: 11)

Miranda Joseph (2002a) further argues that the idea of "community" is deeply implicated in capitalist relations, and its imagining both depends on and produces communities even while, as a concept, it obscures the hierarchies that characterize them. Both Joseph and Gregory point to how communities are imaginary constructs, the result of certain political and institutional measures which are shot through with relationships of social power and inequalities, and both resist the smooth localization of "community" that characterize traditional social scientific frameworks. As with a transgender community, the neighborhood of Corona, Queens, that Gregory discusses is characterized by difference, and while its institutionalized boundaries may be traced onto a map of New York, the social realities of its makeup are far more complex. At the same time, like Corona, the town hall meeting I discuss above is one of the places where community exists because people say it does. By going to such a meeting — or attending a transgender support group, or engaging in transgender activism — participants affirm the existence of such a community over the differences and structural inequalities that exist within it.

Here, though, I ask another question: what about those spaces (physical or conceptual) where people do not necessarily understand themselves as doing the work of creating transgender community? Benedict Anderson's (1991 [1983]) notion of an imagined community is of use here. Anderson's work shows how nation-states cohered historically through appeal to common symbols and icons, creating an imagined national community where all its members could not possibly know one another. Anderson argues that despite the disparities of power between different citizens, it is precisely this feature of shared identity — the fact that citizens *do* imagine themselves as fellow citizens, despite other differences — which makes nation-states cohere. But in the case I describe here, the imagined community is an imagining of one group, where other putative members might *not* imagine themselves as belonging to such a community, or might not even know that such a community exists. Further, others (such as the Imperial Court members) may actively resist the idea of a "transgender community" as including the variety of people some claim it contains. The question is thus: what issues of power are revealed by asking who imagines a community and its membership, and what relationship do they bear to larger structures of inequality and stratification (Joseph 2002a)?

In contemporary identity politics, community is predicated on an assumption of shared identity. As many critics have noted, the notion of "identity" in contemporary politics does much the same that an imagined national community does: it irons out difference and elides power relations.

Eckert and McConnell-Ginet offer another model for thinking about community which escapes the problems of identity, that of a "community of practice" (1992). In many ways, this provides a better way of thinking about a "transgender community," conceptualizing it not in terms of shared identity but in terms of shared practices. Yet here too we face a problem, for practices such as "drag" do not stand simply as practices but are imbued with different meanings in different contexts. Moreover, the practices I am interested in here are not only the (different) practices of "drag" but the practices of ethnography (and social service provision) which are as much responsible for this family portrait as "drag" itself. That is, the "community of practice" which might gather together these balls as part of a "transgender community" — comprising ethnographers, social service providers, activists — is as significant to the process of building a transgender community as the people who were present at the Clubhouse, at Judy's, or at the Hilton.

The idea of a "transgender community," then, is complicated along different axes — of identity, of group experience, of practice — even as it is posited as (and increasingly experienced as) a social reality that gives meaning and structure to people's lives, much like the idea of the nation-state. I am arguing, therefore, that the concept of a "transgender community," while a powerful category, mobilized around salutary motives, also works against other less powerful understandings of gender and sexuality and fixes into place particular meanings to the exclusion of others. That is, if we understand "community" as a series of practices, then the notion of a "transgender community" is produced through certain kinds of work which incorporate members who are not necessarily engaged in doing the same kind of work. In turn, this incorporation obscures the racial and class structures which characterize the transgender community.

Now that I have done some mapping in a patchy, incomplete fashion, I want to move back into some of these places and spaces and forward into new territory, to draw out some of the themes I have begun to work out above in order to look at some of the consequences of imagining a transgender community. In the next chapter, I focus primarily on the social spaces of the Meat Market and the Clubhouse balls, and the ways in which participants' professions of self further complicate the category transgender.

3

"I Know What I Am"

Gender, Sexuality, and Identity

"I am a woman of trans . . ." Tara pauses: "trans*African* experience!" she laughs. Later, while Nora is interviewing her on video, Tara says with more confidence: "I am a woman of transAfrican, transgender experience." I am again in the conference room at New York Hospital for the semi-monthly support group for HIV-positive transgender-identified people. My way into this group has been through Nora, an HIV-positive Latina heterosexual transgender woman (her own definition) who also works at the Gender Identity Project as a peer counselor and safer-sex outreach worker. However, while Nora has a similar history to those in the room — she is a person of color, a former sex worker, and HIV-positive — they do not say the same kinds of things about themselves.

Today Nora is interviewing Tara and the other group members about their experience with "transgender sex work" for a conference presentation she will be making. Tara's declaration of self gets my attention precisely because I have never heard her or any of the other group members use such a formulation before. As with the Clubhouse ball participants and the Meat Market sex workers, it is more common to hear participants refer to themselves as gay, fem queens, girls, and sometimes (though often jokingly) as women. I do not know how long Tara has used this formula to describe herself, but I'm pretty sure I know the origin of the "of transgender experience" construction. Rosalyne Blumenstein, GIP's director, formulated "woman of transgender experience" to describe her own identity and experience about a year before I started doing fieldwork.[1] Rosalyne's position at GIP has resulted in the distribution of this term in many contexts in New York and nationally, so that it has become widely used not only in GIP materials but in outreach work, in print, and increasingly in people's self-identifications. So Tara's statement is not just a statement of self but also indicates her location in a web of relations in which identity labels become distributed and simultaneously intelligible.

It seemed to me that Tara's statement that morning was elicited by the formal situation of a videotaped interview in the context of a hospital-sponsored support group, for at no other time did I hear her or any of the other group members use such an identity label about themselves or others. How is it, then, that Nora or Tara can access—strategically, and in different ways—the language of "transgender" while others who are assumed by social service agencies to *be* transgender often have never heard of the category at all? Moreover, what does it mean that Tara can employ —and creatively extend— "woman of transgender experience" in this context while using different terms in others, some of which resonate with "transgender" and some of which do not? Finally, how does her creative assertion of "transAfrican" modify what "transgender experience" can mean?

In much of the literature about transgender, transexual, or gender-variant people, the concept of "identity" (or its kin in a family of concepts —subjectivity, personhood, selfhood) is generally an organizing principle, a chapter heading, or a theme that runs through the text. Indeed, "transgender" is culturally unintelligible without a concept of "identity." In these accounts, transgender identity tends to be invoked in standard ways. First, psychological and psychiatric approaches seek to explain how and why the process of gendered development works differently (or, in many accounts, *fails*) in transgender-identified people. Sociological and ethno-methodological investigations tend to focus on gendered practices, careers, and strategies, looking at how transgender-identification both subverts and upholds binary gender. And different arms of feminism take up this latter point, seeing on the one hand the embodied performativity of transgender identity as a site of radical gendered possibilities, or, on the other, the manifestation of false consciousness and the assertion of patriarchal gendered norms in

Lesbian and Gay Community Services Center
208 West 13th Street , New York City
(212) 620-7310

GENDER IDENTITY PROJECT
Winter & Spring, 1997

Are you living with HIV /AIDS ???

Do you identify as a person on the transgender spectrum ???

Fem queen, male to female transexual, female to male transexual, drag queen, drag king, male of transexual experience, female of transexual experience, gender non-conformist, crossdresser, etc. etc.

We need you to share your experience, strength and hope with others while healing yourself.

LIVING WELL WITH HIV
FOR TRANSGENDER PEOPLE AND FOR PEOPLE OF
TRANSGENDER EXPERIENCE

Fridays, 3:00 PM - 4:30 PM
Starts late February

This will be a 12 week program offering a variety of healing techniques including meditation, acupuncture, tarot readings, feeling sessions, REIKI, guest speakers, and positive affirmations.

Get involved, get it going, get down.
You deserve this time to take care of yourself.

All participants need to pre-register with the Gender Identity Project.
To register call the GIP at 212-620-7310.

FIGURE 5: Gender Identity Project Flyer (1997)

the individual body. For transgender-identified people themselves, identity, whether understand as internal and eternal or as socially produced and contingent, is deeply felt indeed. However, I am not particularly interested in exploring any of these approaches, questions, or debates. Rather, I want to examine the idea that there is a transgender identity that can be located in a distinct domain called "gender."

The title of this chapter is drawn from a common assertion—"I know what I am"—professed by many study participants. When these participants described what they knew about themselves, however, their explanations moved out of the realm of what is usually understood by "transgender" in contemporary mainstream LGBT politics. In this chapter I want to look more closely at those who are included on the "transgender spectrum" by activists, scholars, and others but who do not usually use "transgender" to talk about themselves and their peers or who may not even know that it is a term which applies to them. In particular, I focus mostly on the talk of African American and Latina fem queens of the balls and Meat Market whom I discussed in the previous chapter. Some of the people I discuss below claim to "know what I am," and others claim not to know who or what they are. But, I will argue, none of these people's understandings of themselves or their desires are intelligible in political categories of collective agency, because of the gap between their understandings of personhood and the political categories of identity which claim to represent them. However, I do not want to simply conflate this process with racial and class differences. As with my comparison of the three drag balls in chapter 2, I complicate the picture by looking at the organization of gendered/sexual identity across lines of class, race, age, and embodiment.[2] And, as with the previous chapter, I want to look at the margins of the collective "transgender" rather than at its center. Thus, I will not discuss at any length the experiences of self-identified transexual women or men, about whom much has been written.

Moreover, in analyzing this talk, I foreground not only what people said about their gendered/sexual practices and identities—their knowledge of "what I am"—but also what I made of this talk. I ask the reader to pay close attention to the questions I felt compelled to ask. That is, I want to consider how I myself was reproducing a theoretical understanding of transgender identity—and of gender and sexuality—which itself threatened to produce these accounts as incoherent and unintelligible.

My concern in this chapter is thus to document the instabilities of the category transgender when it is applied to individual lives, and how individuals' use or non-use of the category complicates the terms in which it has become institutionalized. In turn, it shows how the institutionalization of transgender produces these selves as unintelligible. The broader goal of this chapter is not to call for a more accurate representation of these lives or the elaboration of new categories to account for them. Rather, I will argue that the goals and logics of identity politics themselves produce this apparent unintelligibility and erase an analysis of the entrenched inequalities that underpin them.

THE MEAT MARKET

The Meat Market is only one of several "strolls" in New York City to which fem queen — or transgender-identified — sex workers come to meet their clients.[3] Whatever the language I, the GIP, or the sex workers themselves use, in the sexual marketplace of New York this niche is usually referred to as "chicks with dicks." Almost all the girls (as they call themselves most often) who walk these streets are African American or Latina; some are immigrants to the United States from Latin America or the Caribbean; and many of them have an affiliation with a ball House.

The Meat Market is particularly popular with clients who come from New Jersey and the outer boroughs. Even today, on a Friday and Saturday night, cars can be seen crawling past the curb as their occupants (mostly white men) observe the girls on the sidewalk. A pickup is made by a man coming to a stop and hailing a girl. Most sexual encounters take place in parked cars, though with increased policing and the presence of many bar-goers, finding a quiet venue is hard. Sometimes a motel room may be hired, which the girls like because they can charge more. The girls do not live in or around the Meat Market; rather, they come from different parts of the city to congregate here. Some live in low-income public housing, others have their own apartments in lower-rent areas in the city. The Meat Market, then, is a space in which they work, exchange information, gossip, socialize, and come to understand themselves as constituting a group.

Talking about the Meat Market regulars as "sex workers," though, is complicated by the different experiences that people have of doing sex work. Some, like Sugar, have been out here for years — nineteen in Sugar's case. But there are also those like Mona, out for the first time, and others like Tamara, who sometimes works, sometimes doesn't. There are also several core groups of younger girls who work the cars intermittently, hanging out at Dizzy Izzy's bagel store or on the Ninth Avenue loading docks. India, Charity, Rita, Yolanda, Sybil, and others will chat and ki ki (or laugh) together for hours, often spending more time talking, it seems to me, than working.

Groupings in the Meat Market draw on social networks developed at the balls or in the Meat Market itself. Some girls, like Julip or Anita, who are in their twenties, are rarely if ever in a group, tending to walk alone in the quieter streets further west. They are not here to socialize but to make money. Anita does not like hanging out in groups because she hates to be gossiped about, and gossip is a major activity here. In the even darker corners, I meet girls like Giana. Giana has a serious drug habit about which she is very frank. Sometimes she is willing to be drawn into conversation, but more often not. Other girls stray into the areas north and south of the Meat Market proper, working alone on quieter, more residential streets. They do not have much contact with other workers, tend to be older, non-English speaking immigrants, and are outside the social networks of the younger girls on Ninth Avenue. But if the cops are actively rounding up, then the younger ones will also scatter north of 14th Street (the boundary of the sixth precinct) or along 14th Street to Eighth Avenue where they can blend into the larger crowds of pedestrians and subway users. It is here that I usually lock up my bicycle and begin my evening's participant-observation and outreach.

Among those people who hang out with the core group of fem queen sex workers on the stroll are a range of others: their butch queen friends, boyfriends, and other gay- and lesbian-identified youth of color. As well as the fem queens and butch queens, there are also some butches, most of them African American, who hang out on the loading dock or at the corner of Ninth Avenue. Some of them are boyfriends to the fem queens or to female-bodied femmes, but they are rarely willing to talk to me. Often, they hang out with the male-bodied masculine people — those people who, outside this study, might be understood unproblematically as "men" — who are also boyfriends to the fem queens.

The fem queens' experiences on the street are not always distinguishable from those of their peers and friends. Here, as in many U.S. urban centers, young people of color are frequently targets for police action, whatever their identities or appearance. The public space of the street can be dangerous simply because one is African American or Latina/o, since nonwhite racial identification in the United States is heavily coded by assumptions about criminality, drug use, and excessive sexuality. And as the realm of the public has contracted under neoliberal economic policies, evident in the gentrification and redevelopment of much of New York's public space in the 1990s, the pressure on poor youth of color from police and other authorities has become increasingly severe (Chesluk 2004; see Davis 1992 [1990]). The fem queens out in the Meat Market, though, have the added stigma of being male-bodied feminine persons, a fact well known to police, their clients, sightseers, and potential assailants (see Manalansan 2003: 80–81).

Among the array of people who engage in different forms of sex work here, virtually all were born as male-bodied people but present as feminine on the stroll. For some of them, their feminine presentation may be a part of their daily lives; for others, it is guided by the requirements of the work. One summer evening, I was handing out GIP safer-sex kits in the Meat Market when I came across a group of three young African American male teenagers hanging out by a car. To my surprise (since they had not seen me giving kits to anyone else), one of them asked for a kit. Sorry, I said, they're only for the girls, invoking my instructions that the kits only be distributed to those I could read as "transgender."

"I'm Tamara!" said the boy who'd asked for the kit. "Don't you recognize me?" He and his friends laughed as recognition dawned on my face. He said that he wasn't working tonight, just hanging out.[4] Some weeks later, I saw Tamara again, still dressed as a boy. He told me he had stopped working the stroll, though he still hung out there as a "butch queen." And though he was a butch queen in appearance, he told me she had started taking feminizing hormones. A few weeks later still, I saw her dressed as Tamara again, but a week after that Tamara was dressed as a boy once more. When I asked him why, he showed me a mark on his face: she was robbed, he said, and she's scared of being robbed again.

Other fem queens in the Meat Market may shift back and forth between butch queen and fem queen style (or identification) on the streets, but as at the balls, this distinction is often unclear and style in and of itself does not necessarily indicate an internal "gender identity." Sybil—twenty-something and Puerto Rican—for example sees herself as a "butch queen," even though she also sees herself as "real" and lives full time in her feminine presentation. When I asked her why she called herself a butch queen, she said it was because she was not on hormones. For Sybil, even living full time as a feminine person made her neither a fem queen nor a woman.

Sybil's claims about herself, Tamara's shifting presentations, and his/her reasons for such shifts and use of hormones indicate that for at least some of the girls in the Meat Market, being a "fem queen" is more complex than the ball categories would imply.

This presented me with some practical, ethical, and epistemological problems. From the beginning of my fieldwork, I adopted the claim of activists and social service providers such as Melissa and Rosalyne that people should be addressed with the pronouns and descriptive gender categories appropriate to their gendered presentation. Indeed, sensitized as I was to these claims, when I first started fieldwork in the Meat Market I referred to the girls as women in conversation. However, this was frequently contested by the girls themselves. On another evening in the Meat Market, while hanging out with Monica and Sugar, I referred to Monica as a woman. Sugar said: "You call her what you want, but I'll call her a man." This did not seem to faze Monica, who laughed and retorted with a comment about Sugar's penis. "Yeah, well, yours is bigger than mine," she shouted, causing more laughter yet. This encounter left me feeling very uncomfortable. It seemed, again, to reduce Monica's gender identification to genitals, precisely the kind of claim that social service providers like Rosalyne would hotly contest. Yet I would also note that the description of themselves as "men" offended neither Monica nor Sugar.

But even here, I am unwilling to make broad claims about fem queen identity and their understandings of self through conventionally gendered terms. On another warm summer's evening on Little West 12th Street, I bumped into Julip, to whom I had given a safer-sex kit earlier. She was walking past me, ignoring me (as the girls often did when we had had an interaction and they were now working), when she suddenly turned to me and asked: "Do you think I look like a man?" "No," I said, caught off guard, "you don't. Why do you ask?" I added, thinking of a group of men whom I had earlier seen taunting her out of a car window. She told me that she had just taken a photograph of herself and some friends with a Polaroid camera, and in the photo something in her face had told her she looked like a man. She said she was hollow-cheeked and looked "hard." "Do I have a round face?" she asked. "No," I admitted, "but you have a nice face." I added: "The light is bad, and Polaroids aren't the best kinds of photos." She nodded, turned away, and marched off down the quiet street, wounded.

Julip's concern over "looking like a man" complicates Sugar's and Monica's jokes about each other's penises. While there is not the same articulated differentiation that I heard among white, middle-class transexual women between being a man and being a woman, there are also clear investments on the part of many of the girls out here in being "soft." The distinction between "hard" and "soft" is one of the most important in the Meat Market (and at the Clubhouse balls too, where "softness" is a major criterion for winning a fem queen face category). Hardness and softness — with their clearly gendered implications — have no easy correlate to any physical or sartorial appearance, though suppleness of skin, smoothness of features, and perceived femininity in facial and bodily contours count for a lot. The softer you are, the more "real" you are. "Softness" also applies to perceived femininity in style, body movement, and language use. And while the use of feminizing hormones is seen as essential for developing softness, girls often deny that they are using them, claiming that their softness is "natural." In moments of gossip and tattling, someone may be described disparagingly as "hard" or admired for being "soft." Pussy, out in the Meat Market one night, told me that the "hard" girls are the ones who will fuck, that is, the ones who will be the penetrative partner in anal sex, something many clients desire but girls may not want — or may not be able — to do. For many of the girls who are taking hormones, the capacity to sustain an erection is often impaired. This is a complex condensation: "hardness" is a general term for the visible signs of masculinity but also the capacity for sustaining an erection for the purposes of anal sex, and the desire or willingness to be the penetrative partner.[5]

The cross-cutting forms of identification, presentation, desire, and style in the Meat Market make it hard for me to justify the characterization of "fem queen sex workers" any more than I could that of "transgender sex workers." My use of the former term is, then, as much a selection of certain meanings to the exclusion of others as the latter one is. Next, I will draw on taped interviews to show how fem queens' (and butches') understandings of self resist any easy form of identification in the terms of the organizations which do outreach to them.

I KNOW WHAT I AM

The Meat Market is also a space (represented by my own presence there) where the fem queen sex workers will meet outreach workers from a variety of social service organizations who offer condoms, safer-sex literature, and information about services to which they are entitled as trans-

gender-identified people. The same outreach workers (again, myself included) are also likely to be found at the Clubhouse on a Wednesday, at the
Christopher Street Piers on a weekend, or at some of the bars, like Sally's,
where older fem queens tend to congregate. As such, Meat Market regulars like Tamara, Julip, or Sugar are likely to know that they are considered
transgender but, as with Tara at the New York Hospital group, it is rare to
hear them use it in conversation about themselves.

If I and other outreach workers were giving safer-sex materials to transgender sex workers, our work was made more difficult by people like
Tamara who shifted back and forth between masculine and feminine presentation, or by Sybil, who loudly proclaimed that she was a butch queen
and not "a transgender." In interviews with some of the Meat Market girls,
this attempt to define fem queens as "transgender" became even more
difficult as they situated themselves in terms of this category and others.

In my interview with Anita (Puerto Rican, age twenty-four), for example, she told me she had been on feminizing hormones since her teenage
years. This practice marked her as "transgender" in my understanding,
one which was borne out in the first part of our interview:

3.1
ANITA: I identify myself as a drag queen, you know, and [laughs] and you
know this is my lifestyle. I live my lifestyle like this twenty-four hours a day.
DV: You live as a woman.
ANITA: I live as a woman everyday, you know. (Interview, June 26, 1997)

It is notable that I read Anita's statement that she "identif[ies herself] as a
drag queen" as "you live as a woman." Later in the interview, though,
Anita complicated my assumptions. I asked her:

3.2
DV: Do you know what this term "transgender" means?
ANITA: No.
DV: You never heard it before?
ANITA: No.
DV: Um, but, OK do you know what transsexual means?
ANITA: Transsexual means a sex change right?
DV: Uh, yeah. You don't consider yourself to be transsexual?
ANITA: No.
DV: No, OK. But, and do you consider yourself to be a woman?

ANITA: I consider . . . yes, yes, but *I know what I — I know what I am,* but I . . . I . . . you know, I treat myself like a woman, you know I do everything like a woman. I act like a woman, I move like a woman, you know. I do everything like — everything like a woman. [My emphasis]

Later still, shortly after I explained the collective meaning of transgender to Anita, she talked about herself as "gay." In return, I asked:

3.3
DV: You do you consider yourself to be gay then?
ANITA: Yes!
DV: Yeah.
ANITA: Yes.
DV: Yeah. Um.
ANITA: Yes.
DV: Even though you live as a woman.
ANITA: Yes.
DV: Right, OK.
ANITA: I know I'm gay and I know I'm a man.

Like Rita (who I quoted in the introduction), Anita claims a number of different identities: gay, drag queen, man. While she did not claim to be a transexual or a woman, she did not dispute my characterization of her as "living as a woman" (3.1) and noted that she does "everything like a woman" (3.2). In other words, being on hormones and living as a woman did not make her either transexual or a woman. But later in the interview, she said: "I don't wanna go back to a man, you know," implying that even if she is not a woman, she is no longer a man, despite her earlier assertion that "I know I'm a man" (3.3).

Anita's long experience on the stroll might account for some of these claims, but others such as Mona who have not been out here as long say similar things. Mona was new to the Meat Market when I met her and had not spent much time socializing (or being socialized) by the other girls. She had heard about the Meat Market from some friends and had gotten dressed up — rather androgynously compared to the more extravagantly fem style of Sugar or Julip — to see if she could make some money, but she had not been too successful. The visual economy of sex work in this context requires a certain constellation of clothing, embodiment, and style to be successful.[6] Despite this, her statements resonate with Anita's. In our interview, she began by saying:

3.4

MONA: My name is Mona, I'm a butch queen up in drags, I live my life as a
woman, I'm twenty-two years old, African American, born and raised in
Brooklyn. (Interview July 18, 1997)

Mona's simultaneous identification of herself as a "butch queen up in
drags" and her claim to "live my life as a woman" raises questions about
what these categories might mean. When we started discussing "transgender," Mona said that she wasn't sure what it meant but that she had
"heard the girls you know, talk about transgender, you know, like talk
about like fem queens, you know, female impersonators." Clearly, "transgender" is not entirely absent from the vocabulary of the Meat Market
girls but it is compounded with others like "fem queen," "female imper-
sonator," and "girl." Moreover, when I asked her about her experiences
with social service agencies, Mona said: "I would like to participate in a lot
of gay activities," indicating that this was also a category she understood
herself to be part of. During the interview, as with Anita, I explained to
Mona the meaning of "transgender" in its collective sense as used by the
GIP, and then asked her to position herself in relationship to it:

3.5

DV: Given that description that I've just told you, would you consider
yourself to be included under that category?

MONA: Exactly.

DV: Yeah? Um, so do you consider yourself to be gay?

MONA: Exactly.

DV: You are? OK. So what—what does that mean to you to be gay?

MONA: What does it mean to me to be gay?

DV: Uh huh.

MONA: It's not just only having feelings for someone of the same gender but
also being turned on by the same gender.

DV: But you say that you're a woman as well?

MONA: Exactly.

Note that Mona's initial lack of certainty—about what "transgender"
means—is the only thing she is not sure of in these extracts: she is certain
that she's a woman ("exactly"), that she's transgender ("exactly"), and that
she's gay ("exactly").

Similarly, Anita's exasperated "yes!" to the same question—"You do you consider yourself to be gay then?" (3.3)—as well as the confusion apparent in the questions I ask, indicates a more complex system of identification than I was bringing to the interview. The significant point is that for both Anita and Mona, "liv[ing] as a woman" does not preclude being "gay" where "gay" indexes erotic desire for someone who is male-bodied. My attempts to get Anita and Mona to define themselves in terms of one category or another speak to how powerfully this distinction had structured my research questions. Just as significantly, on a nightly basis, outreach workers from social service agencies across the city must decide whether the clients they meet are "transgender" or "gay" (like Jay at the Clubhouse ball in chapter 2), a product of the institutional and funding requirements of their agencies. Like me, they often find it difficult to enumerate on their outreach reports how may of their clients are "gay male" and how many are "transgender, MTF."

These modes of identification are not the only ones in the Meat Market, however. Other young people of color in this context are very clear about the differences between themselves and gay men and were much easier to count in outreach reports. Cherry (African American, age twenty), who often hangs out in the Meat Market and at the Piers, is adamant that she is a woman, that she has never been "gay," and she embraces transgender as a category to describe herself. Unlike Anita or Mona, though, Cherry is a regular attendee of GIP support groups, as well as other social services around the city which are organized around the category transgender. Cherry responded to my "how do you identify" question in our interview as follows:

3.6
CHERRY: I identify as female. I mean just because I have this penis doesn't mean that I consider myself a man. I don't even consider myself being born male, like I mean, I was just born with a penis, that's the way I look at it. And I consider the penis a clitoris. (Interview April 12, 1997)

Unlike Anita or Mona, Cherry also was able to give me a definition of "transgender" which excludes homosexual identification:

3.7
CHERRY: I know transgender can mean a person who may or may not go through the sexual process, the sexual reassignment surgery. A transexual can mean that a person who's already had it done but may or may not be totally happy with it.

Cherry explicitly rejects "fem queen," "gay," "drag queen," or "butch queen in drags" as terms that could apply to her. She spends a lot of time informing her peers that they are "transgender" and not "gay," and had she heard Monica or Sugar referring to one another as "men," she would no doubt have told them they were wrong. Indeed, she argued "as I have gone through my process," she has been able to resist these labels by insisting on her femaleness and by using the term "transgender" (or "transexual") to describe herself. Cherry's narrative and her employment of identity categories is very similar to many (usually white, middle-class) transexual women's stories of transition that I heard: an explicit rejection of homosexual identity, a repudiation of their maleness, and an identification as a heterosexual woman.

The significant difference between, on the one hand, Cherry and Tara, and those like Anita and Mona is not so much their class, racial identification, or age but their contact with those formalized contexts of community — support groups, social service agencies, clinics, and so on — which employ the understandings of "gay" and "transgender" that I am analyzing here. Both Tara and Cherry, for example, access services through GIP and have had individual counseling with Rosalyne. Both make use of a variety of services throughout the city which are part of a network of agencies and events — GIP, Positive Health Project, Harlem United, the annual Transgender Health Conference, and others — that provide services under the framework of transgender. That is, these contexts have provided for Tara and Cherry a language through which to interpret their experiences outside the more commonly distributed categories in the communities through which they move — fem queen, butch queen, drag queen, transvestite, and so on — much as the New York Hospital group provided Tara with the language of "woman of transAfrican, transgender experience."

For Cherry, this has given her a way of conceptualizing herself that few of her peers do. Cherry frames her own life experiences in terms of "my process," a common metaphor for transition employed in transgender discourses. This framework draws on a broader processual model in mental health, twelve-step programs, and support group settings and one deeply rooted in middle-class American understandings of self-transformation and remaking. For Cherry, her process involves a repudiation of those terms which imply homosexual identification and a movement toward eventual surgical transition and identification as a heterosexual woman. As such, she is able to see her penis as a clitoris (3.6) and to elaborate upon the differences between transexual and transgender (3.7). This is in sharp contrast to those like Anita or Mona — neither of whom access such services — who see themselves, simultaneously, as gay, as drag queens, as transgender, as men, as "liv[ing] as a woman," and so on.

Even so, this is not to say that involvement in such formalized contexts of social service provision necessarily results in a radical split between these two conceptual organizations of identity. Certainly, as I pointed out at the beginning of this chapter, Tara much more frequently refers to herself as gay, as do other members of her group. Likewise, peer outreach workers in the employ of social service organizations, like Renee or Jade (whom I discuss below), are quite aware of the use of transgender, yet they will often use a different model to describe themselves and even the people to whom they do outreach. Renee, who was a peer outreach worker for Harlem United, spoke of doing outreach to "transgenders in the Meat Market" but later in our interview she said, of herself and these same "transgenders":

3.8

RENEE: I really think we're all in the gay community [. . . .] But I don't really think that we're all united, the transexuals are kinda off on their own. And that's why, you know, the transexuals have to come together and start their own shit up because of the — I mean a lot of the gay organizations, they don't give us any support. (Interview June 11, 1997)

For those like Renee, Cherry, or Tara who involve themselves in such organizations, "transgender" is a discourse through which they can mount demands of the "gay" community that in their view should respond to their needs and concerns. And it is through recourse to "transgender" — and the assumptions which underpin it — that these demands are made, a process which, almost inevitably, requires the participants to position themselves in relation to "gay." But this positioning, in turn, complicates what "gay" and "transgender" can mean, blurring the lines that seem so solid on outreach reports.

All the people I have discussed so far have been male-bodied feminine people. As I wrote above, butches — female-bodied masculine people — also hang out in the Meat Market, and they too become incorporated into the institutional terms of transgender. One example of this was Harlem United's hiring of Jade as a peer outreach worker to the butches in the summer of 1997. A Harlem United staffer, Jay (the same person who was pointing out "the transgenders" to me in chapter 2), told me that Jade was an African American "transgender man" and suggested that I interview him. But some weeks later, at the Clubhouse, Jay informed me — rather sheepishly — that Jade was not transgender-identified; rather, she was a "butch lesbian." Like the butch queen in drags he had pointed out to me at the Clubhouse ball as "a transgender," his initial identification had been wrong. However, even the latter appellation turned out not to be entirely accurate.

Jade's story is one which is indicative of the complex land between "gay/lesbian" and "transgender," and how institutionalized categories come up against personal experience. Jade's experiences and narratives are both different from and similar to the claims of people like Mona or Anita. Jade explicitly does not identify as transgender, but not because her experience does not match those of the set understood as transgender.[7] Now approaching fifty, Jade had worked for twenty years as a man in the postal service, dating women and socializing with her co-workers as a man. Though she has never taken testosterone shots, she passed as a man and was accepted as such by her co-workers and friends.

In our interview, Jade initially defined herself as both "gay" and as "a butch," but these claims were also complicated by other things she said about herself. In ways structurally equivalent to Anita and using the same terms, she saw herself as a woman (that is, an identification framed by her embodiment) but simultaneously understood herself in some ways as a "guy":

3.9

JADE: *I know what I am.* I know that I'm an aggressor, a very aggressive-thinking woman. I think just like a guy thinks. (Interview, November 6, 1997, my emphasis)

Jade's use of "transgender," like Cherry's and Renee's, has been framed in terms of her contact with social service agencies, in particular her employer, Harlem United. When I asked Jade what her understanding of "transgender" incorporated, she replied:

3.10

JADE: Well I heard the word when I came to Harlem United. I had never heard it before. I was like transgender? Transgender, the word "trans" was only used in "transexual," meaning that you were flipping over, changing

your organs. That's the only time that I was familiar with the word "trans."
Then when I came to Harlem United and I started coming down here on the
West Side, I started hearing gay guys talk about being transgenders. I'm
like, what the hell's a transgender? And that if you go to a ball, it's live like a
woman, walk like a woman, eat like a woman, you know. And I guess —
their description of a transgender is what I am or what I was.

Here, Jade seems to see herself as describable through "transgender,"
but a short time later she also said: "Do I consider myself a transgender?
No." To complicate matters further, though, Jade returned to the question
of transgender at the end of our interview, saying:

3.11

JADE: I think it's [the use of "transgender" at Harlem United] great, I think
it's great, it opens up Harlem's eyes that there are gay men here, we're right
here, and we ain't going nowhere.

In the latter quote, Jade makes the most complex statement of all, seeing
"transgender" as making people aware that "there are gay men here, we're
right here." This is a dense claim in which she seems to include herself in
the category "gay men," but even more interestingly she equates "transgender" to "gay" as she also did earlier in the interview (3.10). Moreover,
Jade's understanding of transgender — and her relationship to it — is complicated (at least for me) by her experience as a mother to her fifteen-year-
old daughter. To her daughter, she is Mommy, "the best mommy she could
ever get," and at one point she noted that her daughter was the only reason
that she would not transition to living as a man. Indeed, she noted that
prior to motherhood, she would have considered it:

3.12

JADE: I did then! I would have, yeah, back in the days if I would have had
the money or the knowledge. I don't know if the knowledge was that good
then. I would have did it, I would have did it.
DV: Right, so but what's um — what's different now. Why not now?
JADE: I've gotten older. Um — your ideas change. Society is more accept —
they accept the gay life. It *is* a gay life.

Here again, Jade confounded my attempts to understand her as either a
transgender man (someone who would have transitioned if they'd "had
the money or the knowledge") or as a butch lesbian ("It *is* the gay life"). In

the end, in my attempt to get Jade to position herself in my terms, I asked, somewhat desperately:

3.13
DV: Tell me about your gender in ten words.
JADE: My gender.
DV: You—I mean—I know you've been very eloquent about it but I just want you to give like some—like if you could just do it in ten.
JADE: I'm a hard daddy. I'm a hard daddy. At times, more times I think I'm a man than not. Um . . . my demeanor is very aggressive.

There are other apparent incoherencies in Jade's account that make me strive to get a statement of "ten words" about her gender: she is a mommy to her daughter and a hard daddy to her lovers; she is a woman, but "more times I think I'm a man than not"; the reason she *used* to want surgery was that the "gay life" was difficult and it would have been easier to be a man; yet even though she claims it is acceptable and easier to be gay now, she says she would still like the surgery if it weren't for her daughter. She recognizes that others may see her as transgender, but she says she's "gay." Overall, she is just a hard daddy.

Jade's statements clearly draw on a vocabulary of masculinity available to butch lesbians, as well as a long history and vocabulary of masculine-identified passing women, and invoke the "border wars" between FTMs and butches which I will discuss in the next chapter (see Halberstam 1998b; Hale 1998; Kennedy and Davis 1993; G. Rubin 1992; H. Rubin 2003). At the same time, Jade's understanding of herself is not equivalent to the self-conscious appropriation of "transgender butch" that Halberstam (1998b) describes. Rather than drawing on the possibilities of "transgender" to elaborate her identification, she positions herself simultaneously against and through its terms. Again, "transgender butch" certainly captures some of those qualities and experiences that Jade describes, but Jade's identification is more complex still, since she explicitly states that she does not see "transgender" as a category that describes her even as she recognizes that others may see her as such.

My difficulty in pinning down Jade's relationship to identity categories is not in the different ways she identifies as butch, as a hard daddy, or as a masculine female-bodied person. Rather, it lies in the fact that we are operating from different perspectives about two broader categories: "gay" and "transgender." Jade sees herself defined by a variety of characteristics:

her attraction to women, as a "hard daddy" or "an aggressor," as a mommy to her daughter, as a guy, and as a woman. I am attempting to get Jade to talk about her gender apart from her sexual desire, about some kind of internal desire to be a man: that is, I am trying to get her to pin herself as *either* a butch-lesbian-hard-daddy ("gay/homosexual") *or* as a (straight) man ("transgender"). Consequently, my confusion is less about those descriptors of "female masculinity" (Halberstam 1998a) than about how to account for this masculinity in terms of the primary categories through which it can be understood in *institutional* terms.

While Jade's experience is clearly different from Anita's or Mona's — they are younger, male-bodied, have experienced sex work — their experiences come together insofar as their ways of understanding themselves escape easy classification through broader, more powerful discourses about possible identifications. There is no room at Harlem United for simply a "hard daddy." Jade was hired to do outreach to "the transgenders." This is the category through which her salary is funded via HIV/AIDS funds, the newly developing epidemiological category which captures the girls and guys she gives condoms to, and which organizes the support groups, social services, and funding (minimal as they might be) which support the nascent attention to this group.

Jade's account is marked by apparent incoherencies and contradictions that obviously, from my line of questioning, were making no sense at the time of my interview. To others, Jade's claims could be gathered into one of several opposing stories: that she is really a butch, who used to want SRS because of the homophobia she experienced; or that he is really a transman who, in other circumstances and with more education, would have made that choice and lived happily as a man. Yet it is also clear that Jade, in her own words "know[s] what I am." When I pay attention to the context of those answers, to their place on the map that I am drawing her into, it becomes apparent that it is my questioning that is producing the incoherence. Like Anita, Jade's claim to "know what I am" is the key to my mapping here.

These different accounts — drawn from interviews and social interactions — are intended to make the broader point that despite the differences between Jade and those like Anita or Julip or Tamara in terms of embodiment, age, gender identification, and sexual practices, all these individuals can be incorporated into the explanatory force of the collective mode of transgender, even as they contest some of its basic assumptions. Julip's concern that she "looks like a man," Sugar's and Monica's joking about being "men," Tamara's masculine dress (though having just started feminizing hormones), Mona's androgynous style, Sybil's description of herself as a butch queen, Jade's seemingly contradictory relationship to transgender, and Cherry's rejection of "gay" and adoption of "transgender"— all complicate any assertion of a stable identity for those on the Meat Market or at the Clubhouse. By this I do not mean that these individual fem queens, butches, or transexual women do not have "stable identities." Rather I am making two other points: first, even using locally derived terms for people does not capture the range of (sometimes contested) meanings that animate people's understandings of themselves in particular contexts. More importantly, though, the complexity of these identifications *does* lead to some social service providers (like the one quoted in chapter 2) seeing them as having "false consciousness," of shifting between apparently stable categories of identification because of a lack of education or an adherence to outmoded systems of meaning.

So what happens to those like Anita or Mona or Jade who have not taken on the understanding of "transgender" as something different from "gay" or even for those like Renee or Tara who employ it in strategic moments to make particular demands? One could argue that Anita or Mona are using "the master's tools," and that they should be "educated" into the new language and meanings of transgender as a liberatory and "true" description of their identities and experiences. But this implies that the new tools—those subsumed into "transgender"—are free of the social power relations that my colleague sees condensed in these people's statements about themselves as, simultaneously, woman, man, drag queen, gay, and transexual; or as woman, guy, butch, hard daddy, and mommy. Moreover, such an "education" also implies that what Mona or Anita or Jade know—about themselves and the world—is inherently false.

I heard many of these claims to and statements about knowledge of the self on the streets of the Meat Market and at the balls phrased in just these terms: "I know what I am." I am arguing that these are politically significant claims. At the same time, if at least some of the Meat Market girls (like Cherry) can understand themselves through transgender, it might seem that my concerns are cautionary at best. But what happens when people try to mount these claims about the self in particular social contexts? Next, I want to look at how, in conversation, competing claims over what counts as identity — what counts in knowing about oneself — become adjudicated.

THE ALTERNATIVE LIFESTYLES GROUP: "SOMEONE LIKE ME"

The Communities Together Services Center (CTSC) is about a ten-minute bike ride from the Meat Market, on the Lower East Side.[8] This center offers services for residents of the low-income housing in the area and in 1996 included an "Alternative Lifestyles" group. The participants were a group of friends from the projects — mostly young African American or Latina/o people who could be described as gay, lesbian, bisexual, and transgender — who came to the group weekly to talk about their experiences. Like the mix on the loading dock of the Meat Market, they included female- and male-bodied people with differing identifications. Though I never met any of the group's participants at the Meat Market, some of them told me that they attended the balls, and, like the fem queens there, some had engaged in sex work.

My way into this group, as with the New York Hospital group, was through Nora. Though Nora shares common life experiences with group members (as she did with the New York Hospital group), the way she and group members talked about themselves was quite different, underpinned by Nora's experience in social service settings both as a client and as a counselor. In the analysis that follows, based on exchanges during an Alternative Lifestyles group meeting in October 1996, I focus on this difference in the escalation of Nora's attempts to get one of the group members to identify as *either* transgender *or* gay.

While this was not a transgender-specific group, Nora was called upon to define the term at the beginning of the meeting, to which she gave the standard response of contemporary New York City social service providers. Transgender, she said, is an "umbrella term which includes [. . .] transexuals, pre-op, post-op, uh, transvestites, drag queens, female impersonators." We had not been talking long when Miss Angel entered the room, late as usual. Miss Angel — African American and in her mid-twenties, a former drug user and sex worker — was one of the central participants in the group, the acknowledged linchpin of the core group of friends in the group. Like Mona in her interview with me, Miss Angel felt the need to give a brief narrative for my tape recorder:

3.14

MISS ANGEL: My name is Angel, I'm a pre-op transexual. I dunno *what* I am, I'm a woman, simply . . . OK? I'm HIV-positive.

As such, Miss Angel seems to be reiterating the central tenet of transgender identity: that she is a woman, despite her male embodiment. However, later Miss Angel talked about her experience at high school in ways that complicated this assertion:

3.15

MISS ANGEL: I had to get to know new friends when I turned gay and it's not easy being gay.

NORA: How was your experience when you became a woman, a transexual woman?

MISS ANGEL: I was thirteen years old when I did everything.

NORA: Was it even harder?

MISS ANGEL: Was it harder? No.

NORA: Did it go from bad to worse?

MISS ANGEL: No [. . .] Um, when I was thirteen. It was hard, I went to school —

BEN: With breasts.

MISS ANGEL: The breasts.

Nora's questions to Miss Angel (3.15) are significant because she is proposing to Miss Angel two different states of coming out: as "gay" when she was thirteen, and as a "transexual woman" at a later date. Miss Angel, however, dismisses this: she was thirteen, she said, when she did "everything." This becomes clearer still in a later exchange between them, when they were discussing Miss Angel's sexual history:

3.16

MISS ANGEL: I went to bed with my own kind. I tried it once.

BEN: How was it?

MISS ANGEL: How was it?

BEN: Uh huh.

NORA: Now what is your own kind mean by definition, because you're always telling us —

MISS ANGEL: I'm a woman, well you know.

NORA: You're a woman, transexual, you're gay, you're homosexual.

BEN: A man.

MISS ANGEL: Look, me, like me, someone like me. Someone like me . . .
Someone like me.

NORA: [Who] changes sexuality, uh huh.[9]

BEN: With breasts.

MISS ANGEL: With breasts.

NORA: OK.

MISS ANGEL: I went out with someone like me. Her name was Billie Jean, she lives in Coney Island.

In both 3.15 and 3.16 Ben offers "breasts" by way of explanation of Miss Angel's being, which Miss Angel affirms. This reference to Miss Angel's breasts — the result of hormone therapy — is the final word in both cases. The reference to her body is particularly instructive, for Miss Angel's changing body shifts her — in contemporary understandings — into the category of "transgender" or, more specifically, "transexual," the latter category which she indeed uses to describe herself. Yet, as is clear from the preceding conversation, Miss Angel does not always stick to this definition of self. Indeed, Nora implicitly recognizes this in her attempts to get Miss Angel to define what her "own kind" is. She lists the identity categories that Miss Angel has used about herself in this group and in others (woman, transexual, gay, homosexual) (3.16), implying that she cannot be all these things. To this, Miss Angel insists: " Look, me, like me, someone like me. Someone like me . . . Someone like me." In the end, Nora leaves it there: "OK."

Toward the end of the meeting, Nora told us of her days of sex work when non-transgender men who were her clients would ask her what their desire for her meant for their own sexual identity:

3.17

NORA: And they're attracted to that [a feminine person with a penis] So they would tell me, "Well, what am I? I said, Well, I can't tell you what you are unless you know and I can't not tell you this is what you are and this is what you're gonna be, you know, because it's not my life." My life, *I know what I am.*

MISS ANGEL: ⌈ *I'm a woman with a large clit.*

NORA: ⌊ *I know what I am.* [My emphasis]

Nora's and Miss Angel's talk overlaps in the last two lines of 3.17: they speak at the same moment. Both profess, simultaneously, a knowledge of the self, but what they know is rooted in different ideas about *how* to know oneself. Nora's attempts to get Miss Angel to pick one of the definitions of self that she has used in the group fail precisely because they do not share the same understandings of how gendered and sexual identity works. Miss Angel claims to be gay, but also a transexual, and a "woman with a large clit." Like Cherry, she has reread parts of her anatomy to claim an identification as a woman, but like Anita or Mona, she also claims other kinds of identities, including "gay." Nora, as I have noted, shares much of Miss Angel's history and experience but she has an understanding of gendered and sexual identity gained through social service agencies, defined by a distinct split between gay identities on the one hand and transgender identities on the other. Miss Angel has no such model of personhood. All she can respond when Nora puts her on the spot is: "someone like me" (3.16). In the final quoted passage, Nora states, "I know what I am" (3.17). Like Anita, Mona, and many others, Nora asserts a knowledge of the self that is mounted against conventional understandings of bodily sex and gender identity. But, unlike those people, her statement of self never varies: she is a heterosexual transexual woman.

Miss Angel, at one point claims "I dunno *what* I am" (3.14), but it becomes clear that, in fact, she has a strong idea of "what I am": simultaneously gay, homosexual, transexual, and "a woman with a large clit." Even in the friendly atmosphere of a peer-led support group, certain statements of identity and experience can become interpreted—by Nora, by myself, and by others—as inconsistencies, but only because we are interpreting them within a theoretical framework which cannot make sense of them unless they are dismissed as false consciousness or a lack of education.

However, as I wrote above, I do not want to turn this into a simple story of how young, poor people of color are excluded from dominant discourses and practices around "transgender." Indeed, it is not that easy to make such a case, as Tara, Nora, and Cherry make clear. Moreover, the kinds of complexities I have discussed above are not restricted to the young kids hanging in the Meat Market or the Clubhouse. In other places around the city, I also met people whose understandings of self, practices, and identifications similarly confused an easy distinction between gay and transgender.

From the Lower East Side and the Meat Market, let's go back to Karalyn's, the bar on 10th Avenue and 55th Street frequented mostly by white male cross-dressers, though it has its share of transexual women, admirers, and some people of color too. It doesn't take me long to get up there from the Village — it's about a twenty-minute bike ride. Here, one of the regulars is Sherry. Sherry is white, in her mid-thirties, and lives in Pennsylvania, traveling into the city on the weekends in her Porsche to come to Karalyn's or Tranny Chaser.[10] She used to own and run an insurance company but has retired, partly because she is HIV-positive. Despite these markers of upper-middle-classness, Sherry has lived frugally since her retirement. She cross-dresses on weekends and has been on hormones for a year or so but does not believe she is transexual; and indeed, while she was quite aware of the concept "transgender" and all it implies, she most often referred to herself as "gay" in our conversations. One evening she told me "I'm going up to P-town with two other guys," indicating through this structure that she also understood herself at times as a "guy."

After talking over this issue — being gay, being transgender — over drinks at Karalyn's in the summer of 1997, I received this e-mail from Sherry:

> You asked about the differences between someone like myself and the [. . .] queens [a category to which she had opposed herself in our conversations]. Well, for one, none of them take hormones. They like using their penises, while myself i prefer impotence. So in that regard, our identity and gender are somewhat different. They consider themselves gay drag queens, and to a degree i suppose i consider myself gay as well, although a post op-TS friend of mine thinks i should go thru the change, and that i'd be more happy living as a straight woman. That's HER opinion. I really don't know. I do know that i love men, and that i could be quite happy living fulltime as a woman, but i also accept the fact that physically i don't think i can pull it off. Therefore i feel like i'm trying things like hormones, and i'm planning on having some cosmetic surgery done to see just how far i can take this. (E-mail, May 9, 1997)

A few months later, this time at Tranny Chaser, I saw Sherry again. We caught up on news, and she told me a bit more about the visit of a non-transgender woman friend from Germany, whom I had met the last time I had bumped into Sherry here. She divulged the fact that they had had sex the evening I had seen them together at the bar. I was rather startled at this: how did it feel to have sex with a woman? I asked. She shrugged: it was fine. It wasn't the first time for Sherry, whose fourteen-year-old son lives with her.

A month after this, I cycled up to Karalyn's for the last time, as it was about to close down. Karalyn had lost the battle to keep open a bar that only really had a weekend crowd, a business not sustainable with New York rents. At the bar, I leaned over to say hello to Tina the barmaid and caught sight of a half-familiar face to my right. Half-familiar because it was Sherry, but she was in masculine clothes — jeans, a loose shirt, and a vest — and was sporting a goatee. I was startled again, and she was amused at my surprise. There was some reason for the goatee that I couldn't quite make out, something to do with a cut on her chin, which had led to her coming to Karalyn's in her male persona.

We settled down to a long talk, occasionally greeting other people we knew as they came in. She told me she was still having electrolysis on her cheeks and repeated that she was on hormones, but her beard still sprouted powerfully. I asked her how it felt being on hormones, and she startled me once more by taking my hand and placing it on her chest, visible under the loose cotton shirt she was wearing. Her breasts were soft. She used to have a lot of muscle mass there, she said, but it has all gone due to the hormones. I asked her how she would like me to refer to her as a man, and she said simply "Shay" would do, as it would work for both Sherry and Shane, her male name. Despite the hormones and electrolysis, Sherry still had no plans for surgery and shuddered when I mentioned it.

Unlike Anita or Miss Angel, Sherry does not claim to "know what I am." In fact, her e-mail claimed that she "really do[esn't] know" whether she is a gay man or a transexual woman. The indeterminacy of Sherry's identity and presentation seems to make sense in the collective mode of transgender, yet Sherry was clear that "transgender" could not describe her experiences, especially since she was attracted to gay men as a man. And at other times, Sherry told me that she was content not to know. Indeed, Sherry's lack of certainty could be understood not as a function of an innate uncertainty about who she is but because of the way she feels compelled to describe her desires through a set of discourses that do not make sense of them. While Sherry is white, upper middle class, and in most ways shares very few of the social experiences of Jade, Anita, or Miss Angel, like them she is hard-pressed to align her self-understandings with discrete categories of identity.

Sherry is just one of a heaving crowd of regulars who come and go at Karalyn's. There are plenty of others who easily fit into "transgender" here, and who understand its boundaries and see themselves as incorporated within it in different ways. But far more often, the boundaries of categories — transgender, gay, transexual, transvestite, and others — blend and blur around the bar. Often, the regulars simply refer to one another as "trannies," a useful catchall, like "transgender," but one which can incorporate the gay male cross-dressers who sometimes come and hang out. There is Chris, who says she likes men and used to think she was gay, but now she's not sure what she is. Her psychoanalyst believes she is just too homophobic to come out, but Chris rejects this analysis. "I have one self, but two lives," she says. And Gwen likes being a gay man most of the time, but sometimes she gets the urge to dress and hang out at Karalyn's. "I can't do this downtown," she told me, referring to gay male bars in the Village and Chelsea. "What gay man would want to fuck someone in a dress?" Here, she might score with a heterosexual cross-dresser.

What I describe here may seem to be a reiteration of the power of transgender — to incorporate many different kinds of gendered expression and desire under its umbrella. But the point is that for many of the people at Karalyn's, "transgender" (in its implicit opposition to "homosexuality") cannot make sense of the way they experience their desires and selves precisely because they see their desires fueled by their "sexuality." Whether these people are secure in their knowledge of "what" they are (like, in very different ways, Cherry or Miss Angel) or not (like Sherry), none of their experiences are easily accounted for through the categories of either homosexuality or transgender.

FRACTIOUS FRACTURES

The critique of identity politics is certainly not new and has been developed in feminism, queer/LGBT studies, critical race theory, and other bodies of critical theory (e.g., Moraga and Anzaldúa 1981, Epstein 1987, Warner 1993, Scott 1993). The stories that I have told above demonstrate the usefulness of those critiques which point out that "identity" can erase the intersections of different kinds of social experiences, more often than not asserting the experience of white, middle-class U.S. American social actors as the implicit exemplary center. The basic argument that animates these critiques is that in privileging one "identity" ("woman," "gay," "American"), the intersections of these social differences are erased, disabling those who are multiply engaged by racial, ethnic, sexual, gendered, and other kinds of differences. Identity politics also, as Scott (1993) points out, simply affirms the differences between groups and extends those differences back into history.

However, these stories are useful not simply to show how identity categories such as "gay" or "transgender" cannot account for the complexity of people's desires, understandings of self, and experience (though they do this too). Rather, they are most useful in showing that the complexity of experience can disrupt the very analytic categories by which social theorists and others attempt to describe the intersections of different forms of lived experience. That is, Anita or Jade do not simply demonstrate the ways that gendered and sexual experiences escape the boundaries of identity categories: rather, they show how that which counts as "gender" or "sexuality" is itself the contested ground.

The point of these ethnographic anecdotes and theoretical discussions of "identity," then, is not to reveal "transgender" or "person of transexual/ transgender experience" as empty categories. Rather, they show that the *category* of transgender is (as much as the category of "homosexuality") an *effect* of the distinction between what "gender" and "sexuality" have come to mean in much contemporary politics, theory, and social service provision. What I am after here is the increasing institutional power of "transgender" to order certain experiences, even as it erases their complexity. If someone like Nora or someone like Jade argues that "I know what I am," that knowledge becomes differently understood — and judged — in terms of a categorical system where Nora's knowledge is intelligible in institutional contexts but Jade's is not. For Jade, being gay, a woman, a hard daddy, and a guy are equally and simultaneously possible. And for Mona, there is no necessary conflict between being gay ("exactly") or a woman ("exactly") or transgender ("exactly"). That is, for Mona, knowing you are a gay man does not exclude the possibility of knowing that you live as a woman, in the same way that for Jade, being a hard daddy and "thinking like a guy" does not mean you can't be a mommy to your daughter and a woman. This, I would argue, is *not* the same understanding which underpins dominant ideas about gender and sexuality in the United States, the "master's tools" version of gendered and sexual personhood in which cross-gender identification is a restricted possibility for people who are "really" homosexual. Nor is it evidence that homosexual identification among those perceived as "transgender" is the result of not being "educated" into the possibilities of transgender identification. If the emergent idea of gender and sexuality as separable and separate entities has been opposed to the conflation of these experiences in mainstream U.S. society, then Mona or Jade's or Tara's understandings are different again. That is, in their view of the world, *any difference sets you apart from heteronormativity, a difference which can be named in a variety of ways:* for Mona, as gay, a butch queen up in drags, or as transgender; for Jade as a woman, a guy, a hard daddy, a butch, or as gay; and for Tara as both a gay girl and a "woman of transAfrican, transgender experience."

The significant difference between Mona's or Jade's or Tara's understanding of "gender" and "sexuality" and that employed in mainstream LGBT organizations is that in mainstream gay and lesbian politics, difference from heteronormativity is that which is to be elided. That is, contemporary mainstream gay and lesbian politics works to minimize the difference between homosexuality and heterosexuality, precisely by removing the visibility of (class-inflected and racialized) gender difference from the category "gay," part of the dynamic that Lisa Duggan neatly captures with the term "homonormativity" (2003: 50). This is possible only through a conceptual shift which produces gender and sexuality — and the identities that are seen to flow from them — as radically different domains and experiences. And it is for this reason, I have argued, that "transgender" has been able to emerge as a distinct category of being, predicated on an autonomous sphere of "gender." However, because Mona, Jade, Tara, and a host of others do not share in this binarized conception of their experiences or identities, their statements of self become unrepresentable — and incoherent — to those who claim to represent them. To "know what I am," in other words, is not enough to be accounted for in mainstream identity politics.

Moreover, this is not simply a story that can easily be made along lines of race, age, or class. While Anita, Mona, and Jade are people of color, poor, working class, and in many ways disenfranchised, Sherry is white and middle class. Cherry — Mona and Anita's peer — hangs out on the Meat Market but explicitly rejects the idea that she was ever "gay" and employs "transgender" as a category which makes sense of her experience. The white, middle-class gay male drag queens of the Imperial Court discussed in chapter 2 are very clear about the differences between themselves and transgender-identified people, even though they are described as transgender in many contexts. Jade is approaching fifty and has a long experience in the butch/femme communities of color in New York City, while Mona — male-bodied and identifying simultaneously as gay, transgender, and a woman — is just twenty-two. And Tara condenses racial, gendered, and sexual identity by claiming to be both "gay" and "a woman of trans-African, transgender experience."

By noting these divergences and convergences, I want to resist any attempt to reduce my analyses here to one simply about class, race, or age. Rather, if there is a commonality, it is one of involvement in formalized institutions which employ transgender as a category for the purposes of community building and social service provision. Cherry is distinguished from her peers by her heavy involvement in GIP and other organizational support groups. Sherry, Julip, Anita, and Mona do not participate in these contexts. But even this does not fully explain all these differences, for Jade and Renee, who work for a social service agency as "transgender peer outreach workers," shift between seeing themselves and their clients as "transgender" and "gay."

After reading this chapter, one might justifiably ask: so what if Jade or Mona or Miss Angel or Sherry come to understand themselves as — or are understood through — transgender? If, as it seems, at least some of them are comfortable with using the category about themselves at least part of the time or can make sense of the category as incorporating them (for example, Jade, Mona, Renee, or Anita), then doesn't it make sense to educate them into a distinction that enables them to organize their selves in this way? In the end, I would say that this is not necessarily a negative outcome. For some, like Cherry, this has proved a powerful tool of self-understanding.

Yet, at the same time, I have some cautions. First, from a purely utilitarian perspective, one of the central tenets of the kinds of public health–oriented social service outreach I have been invoking here — a central site for the production of transgender as a category — is to pay attention to the experiences and identifications of those to whom such outreach is done. That is, in order to reach people you wish to help, you need to understand and use the categories by which they understand themselves. As such, instrumentally, it makes sense to think about the implications of these stories for the kinds of public health models being developed under the rubric of "transgender."

But second, from a more abstract but still political perspective, the "education" of Jade or Anita or even Sherry in the meanings of transgender ignores the fact that for someone like Sherry the category simply does not make sense of who she feels she is. And, for Jade or Anita, it implies that the way they understand themselves now is inherently false, and that to "know what I am" is, in fact, not really to know at all. Sherry, motoring down to New York in her Porsche, may not in the end have to choose between being gay or being transgender. Jade or Anita, on the other hand, may not have this luxury, dependent as they are on social services and (dwindling) institutionalized social safety nets, institutions which operate through discrete categories of identity. So, while I have argued above that I do not want to reduce this analysis to race, age, or class, my concern here finally is that the young, the poor, the people of color who are understood as being transgender are increasingly having to un-know what they know about themselves and learn a new vocabulary of identity.

And even here, there is nothing inherently — ethically, morally — wrong with this. Culture is produced in the constant, shifting emergence of meaning as people engage with one another as social actors in particular contexts. That is, I am not invested in romanticizing Jade or Anita as "natives" whose "culture" should be left alone or "preserved." But simultaneously, I am cautious about the other possibility, where for them to become "transgender" requires a recognition of another organization of their identities as being, inherently, false and outmoded.

In writing about her experience of being subject to surgeries at an early age because of an intersex condition, Cheryl Chase (1998) writes that her genitalia — understood in popular and medical discourses and practices as "ambiguous" — were not, prior to surgical intervention, ambiguous at all. They were exactly what they were. Rather, a powerful system of binary gender and sexed bodies produced them *as* ambiguous. Chase's point is similar to one of the earliest observations in American anthropology. In his classic article "On Alternating Sounds" (1889), Franz Boas contests the claims of Euro-American observers that Native American languages were "primitive" because there was no consistency in the pronunciation of words in those languages. Boas's counterargument was revolutionary. He proposed that it was the investigators' inability to understand the phonemic distinctions of those languages, rather than the speakers' imprecision, which resulted in the interpretation of primitivity.

With the stories I've told above, what struck me most while they were being told to me was how ambiguous and shifting they were, an impression not dissimilar to those held by Chase's doctors and the nineteenth-century linguists Boas took on. And, like those linguists, the call to "educate" fem queens into the language of transgender and the repudiation of their homosexual identification as outmoded smacks of an implicit claim about their primitivity. Yet one can make the same discursive move here that Chase or Boas makes: in their own terms, these stories are entirely coherent. They are ambiguous only in a binary system where primary "gender" or "sexual" identity must be conceived as two distinct arenas of one's experience. As Mark Johnson writes: "there is nothing ambiguous about ambiguity, sexual or otherwise. Rather, ambiguity is the specific product or effect of different historical relations of power and resistance through which various cultural subjects are created and re-create themselves" (1997: 13–14).

If, as I argue, these professions of self exceed identity categories, another way of reading these interview excerpts and ethnographic anecdotes is to celebrate them as queer, indeed to see them as breaking down or resisting the solidity of identity categories. Jacob Hale, writing of what he calls genderqueer positions which contest a strict division between FTM and butch identities, argues that "our dislocatedness provides us with subject positions. This might sound paradoxical but it is not, for dislocatedness is not the absolute absence of location. Because borders between gender categories are zones of overlap, not lines, our dislocatedness is constituted by our locations in the overlapping margins of multiple gender categories: we bear Wittgensteinian family resemblances to people who occupy multiple gender categories" (1998: 336). However, while Hale's argument is convincing for the subject positions he is discussing, it does not necessarily account for the experiences of the people I have discussed here. A perspective which celebrates dislocatedness in the Meat Market would ignore the fact that in this context, fem queens, butches, and others are highly active in maintaining categorical boundaries such as at the Clubhouse balls or in the Meat Market where being called "hard" is itself a form of categorical policing. That is, I do not believe that these stories demonstrate a system outside representation itself. Rather, it is still a system of categorical orderings, but one that is differently organized from, and cannot be accounted for in, the relatively more powerful terms of mainsteam identity politics.

It is true that even though they may not identify as "transgender" as such, people like Jade, Miss Angel, or Anita nonetheless benefit from the outreach done in its terms. Yet, from both a theoretical and utilitarian perspective, "transgender" cannot account for the complexity of their understandings of self. It is important to note that I am not calling for "better representation" of those I discuss above, or the simple elaboration of new categories, but rather a reexamination of a system which, in both practical and theoretical terms, marks Miss Angel, Anita, or Jade as "other." This is the case whether they are understood as suffering "false consciousness" or as representative of a queer, subversive selfhood beyond categories. I am suggesting, in short, that their claims about themselves should be taken seriously, in their own terms. Indeed, as I will argue in more depth in Part III and especially in the conclusion, this suggestion is only the beginning of a broader analysis of a system of identity politics where "representation" as a trope itself erases more complex analyses of political and economic injustices.

Having laid out some of the institutionalized politics of identity and community that are shaped by — and shape — the category transgender and its differences from homosexuality, I want to move, in Part III of this book, to consider three realms in which this category has become institutionalized: academic and popular literature, the contexts of political activism and social service provision to which I have alluded throughout the previous chapters, and the recourse to narratives of violence in making claims for the state's attention to transgender lives. Here, I want to consider how the development of a body of knowledge around the category transgender, shaped by an ontological distinction between gender and sexuality, is doing similar work in contexts as diverse as literature reviews, social justice activism, and telling stories of violence suffered. And again, my analysis — and my political concerns — revolve around what these orderings achieve, for whom, and what the implications are for the increasing use of transgender in these contexts, even as they produce remarkable social achievements.

Part III

Emerging Fields

Introduction to Part III

The Transexual, the Anthropologist, and the Rabbi

"So, a transexual, an anthropologist, and a rabbi walk into a bar," says Linda, handing me my drink and motioning over my shoulder. I turn around to see an Orthodox Jewish man walking through the door of Tranny Chaser, the Thursday night party for transpeople and their admirers at a downtown Manhattan bar.[1] The humor of Linda's remark depends on the idea of the radical differences between the three figures she draws together, each of which can represent a thematic strand in the literature on transgender and transexuality: deviance represented by the transexual body; moral opprobrium represented by religious, legislative, judicial, and medical authority; and the values of objective science, for which the anthropologist, in this case, will stand.

In contrast, the concept of transgender has enabled a new set of counterclaims: first, an understanding of gender variance as socially valid, publicly claimable, and free of the stigma of pathologization. Second, as transgender gains hold in academic and popular discourses, it has enabled the coalescence of an emerging field of transgender studies which, like other fields of critical inquiry, challenges the claims of scientific, objective knowledge. Finally, transgender has reframed the moral and ethical questions in terms of the negative impact of medical, religious, scientific, and legal practices and theories on transgender lives. The following three chapters examine these counterclaims. In chapter 4, I examine how transgender is becoming a trope through which scholars from many fields are understanding the phenomena of gender variance in order to map out how — and with what effects — transgender is making it into the academy. In chapter 5, I consider how transgender-identified activists are demanding "inclusions" in lesbian and gay organizations and in agencies of the state, and in chapter 6 I specifically take on the issue of violence against transgender-identified people. However, I am concerned not simply with the efficacy of these counterclaims but with how the institutionalization of transgender as a category of knowledge production, social action, and moral argumentation also, and unintentionally, reproduces some of the very inequalities it aims to overturn. The concerns I have raised earlier follow me into this section of the book: when and how might the knowledge production, activism, and moral claims enabled by transgender actually produce the kinds of elisions I have discussed in part II? Whose voices are heard in these accounts, and why? Does the promise of transgender activism and scholarship extend equally to all those imagined to occupy its boundaries? And what are the broader implications for progressive politics in the contemporary United States?

4

The Making of a Field

Anthropology and Transgender Studies

On a hot summer's afternoon in August 1997, a group of us chatted around a conference table before the regular GIP staff meeting at the Center. With the exception of myself and Dr. Barbara Warren, everyone present was a transgender-identified woman, and with the exception of Arlene, who is African American, everyone was white. As I was talking to Rosalyne I heard Chloe mention to Melissa that she was reading Leon Pettiway's *Honey, Honey, Miss Thang* (1997), a collection of extended narratives of five Philadelphia sex workers whom the author identifies variously as "gay," "transvestite," and "transgender."

"You didn't get here on the gay track, did you?" Chloe asked Melissa, to which Melissa responded in the negative.

I asked Chloe what she meant by this. She explained that while many transexual women had lived at least part of their lives as gay men, she found Pettiway's book annoying because he seemed to conflate gay male sexuality with transexual or transgender identification. When I mentioned that many of the Meat Market girls we both knew identified in ways similar to those described by Pettiway, Chloe nodded. Yes, she said, she knew this. But they aren't really gay, they're transgender, she argued, and it was only a lack of knowledge which prevented them from abandoning gay identification.

In this brief anecdote, the themes of the previous two chapters are immediately apparent. However, my interest in this chapter is in how Pettiway's book found its way into Chloe's hands, or rather, the reasons that Chloe might have picked it up. Its subtitle — "Being Black, Gay, and on the Streets" — makes it, implicitly, a part of the ever-growing literature in "lesbian and gay studies." But its contents — about people who are identified by the GIP and its staff members as being "transgender" — shifts it into a different (if related) category, the emerging and fast-growing field of "transgender studies."

In this chapter, I investigate this new field of knowledge, transgender studies, and the complexities, contradictions, and confluences that have enabled its emergence. I look at how many different kinds of texts (from autobiographies and ethnographies, to journal articles and political manifestos) in a range of different fields (from anthropology, literary criticism, history, and philosophy, to psychology, public health, and criminology) get grouped, or come to be understood, as being about a set of people who are defined as transgender. In particular, I want to focus on anthropological texts and their co-option into this field because anthropological knowledge is frequently cited (or contested) by transgender-identified people as a source of knowledge about themselves.

These processes are intimately connected, for the appropriation and contestation of scholarly work (and the subjects of that work) is part of a broader cultural process whereby a field of knowledge is being produced about people — historical and contemporary, Western and non-Western, male-bodied and female-bodied — who are seen to be understandable through the category of transgender. Like the practices of community building, social service provision, or activism organized by this category, these intellectual and hermeneutic practices are part of a broader reorganization of what "gender" and "sexuality" are coming to mean in the United States.

There are three primary themes in this chapter. The first is precisely this diverse set of social practices around creating something that can be understood as a field of transgender studies. The decision about whether a book or article can be understood to be part of this field is not only a decision on the part of an author, bookseller, or library cataloguer. It is also a social practice of figuring out the "transness" of a particular text by teachers, scholars, and readers, both transgender- and non-transgender-identified (by, for example, including it in a bibliography or syllabus or appropriating it in a critical reading, such as this one). As such, while this chapter is in some ways a traditional literature review, it is simultaneously a critical investigation of a set of social practices on the part of scholars, readers, and cataloguers which enables me to discuss this literature as a body in the first place. (This is also not a conventional literature review as I cannot do a comprehensive review of the many texts that could be drawn into such a chapter.)

The second theme is the way the indeterminacy of "transgender" simultaneously enables and complicates the stabilization of this field. "Transgender studies" is not an isolated field — it intersects with and is incorporated into "queer studies," "LGBT studies," "women's studies," and "gender studies" in different institutional contexts. Given the operative distinction between transgender and homosexuality, though, I am particularly interested in those texts about "homosexuality" which tend to get drawn into a discussion of "transgender" — and vice versa. This is not to say that these texts should not contribute to interconnected intellectual trajectories (and indeed, they do). But, as I will argue, at crucial moments the absorption of certain texts into transgender studies engages the same distinction that results in the dilemmas noted in part II. My concern here is: what does transgender achieve in organizing knowledge about people?

The third theme of this chapter is the differing places of male-bodied and female-bodied people in this literature, a difference which is marked by geographies of physical space, historical location, and contemporary politics. I will argue that these differences contribute to and are shaped by the power of the collective mode of transgender. More importantly, these different placings speak to another difference — the way that gender and sexuality are differently understood in feminism and LGBT/queer studies (Butler 1994).

In short, I examine the production of this emerging field to further develop my arguments about the power of transgender to generate and maintain a particular theorization of gender and sexuality as distinct categories of human experience. To do so, first we must look at the emergence of transgender studies itself.

In her introduction to the 1998 *Transgender Issue* of the journal GLQ, Susan Stryker writes that "as a field, transgender studies promises to offer important new insights into such fundamental questions as how bodies mean or what constitutes human personhood. And as individuals, transgender scholars who can speak intelligibly from their positions of embodied difference have something valuable to offer their colleagues and students" (1998: 155). Judith Halberstam, in her review of three books frequently understood as being part of transgender studies — Holly Devor's FTM (1997), Leslie Feinberg's *Trans Liberation* (1998), and Jay Prosser's *Second Skins* (1998) — notes another feature of this emerging field in her observation that "these new texts fail, fortunately, to form a coherent and noncontradictory body of work; in fact, there is as much difference among them as there is within a transgender community" (2000: 313). These statements point to three central features that characterize the emerging field of transgender studies: first, the capacity for new insights into embodied experience; second, the heterogeneity of theoretical positions, identification, embodiment, and disciplinary backgrounds that characterize the contributors to this emerging field; and third, the importance of transgender-identified scholars in producing these insights (see also Stryker 2006).

In its outlines, transgender studies shares a genealogy and its broad concerns with other areas of cross-disciplinary critical inquiry that developed in the latter part of the twentieth century — feminist scholarship, lesbian and gay studies, queer theory, critical race theory, subaltern and postcolonial studies, and disability studies — all of which emerged in the context of wider postmodernist and poststructuralist critiques. Broad shifts in the intellectual, social, and political climates of U.S. and European academies have enabled a questioning of both knowledge production about subordinated groups but also epistemological questions about the status of knowledge itself.

If transgender studies is genealogically linked to other areas of critical inquiry, its closest relative is the equally diffuse fields of queer/LGBT studies (the latter, indeed, including the "T" of "transgender" in its name), but one with which it has a complex relationship. Stryker (1998) points to Sandy Stone's "The Empire Strikes Back: A Posttranssexual Manifesto" (1991) as an early and central text in the emergence of this field, for not only its content but the way its call for transexuals to actively speak from their subject positions foreshadows the tensions in the relationship between "queer" and "transgender." As Stryker notes, Stone's essay makes no reference to "transgender," but in 1991, just as it was published, transgender was emerging simultaneously as an alternative to transexuality and as a collective organizing term. At the same historical moment, "queer" was gaining steam as a repudiation of gay and lesbian accommodationist politics, fueled by the anger of self-proclaimed queers over the inattention of the U.S. government to the AIDS pandemic. The propinquity of these movements produced a complex dynamic around what transgender could mean, both as a personal identification and as a way of knowing about the world: "*transgender* became associated with a 'queer' utopianism, the erasure of specificity, and a moralizing teleology that condemned certain practices of embodiment that it characterized as transsexual. From other positions, 'queer' became something that excluded the consideration of gender altogether. Depending on one's subject position and political commitments, these trends could be embraced or bemoaned" (Stryker 1998: 153, emphasis in original). As such, Stryker argues, "transgender," "transsexual," and "queer" have "become hopelessly tangled in subsequent attempts to carry out the critical project I understand Stone to have envisioned with her neologism 'posttranssexual' " (148; see also Prosser 1998 and Namaste 2000 for a critique of queer theory and its relationship to trans scholarship, politics, and activism).

In other words, "transgender" in activism, identification, and scholarship is enmeshed in a complicated set of contradictory meanings. It can be read as a mode of revolutionary and utopian action but also one which recognizes the specific trajectories of certain identifications. Further, its coming to prominence at the same time as "queer" raises questions about the differences between or similarities among "transgender" and "queer" identities. Transgender studies, then, is inevitably implicated in questions about history and social change on the one hand, and its relationship to queerness and/or homosexuality on the other. As such, transgender studies is complicated not only by the heterogeneity of voices and the question of embodiment and experience but also by how certain voices, experiences, and embodiments come to be understood *as* transgender in the first place.

So, what does — or can — transgender studies incorporate? The "can" is important because this field is characterized precisely by disagreements about what transgender itself incorporates. However, it contains most evidently, at its center, texts by contemporary self-identified transgender and transexual people and people who prior to the 1990s identified as transexual or as transvestite. One of the few venues in which transgender-identified people have historically been able to express their voices is in the realm of autobiography, and the list of such books is long indeed. Such texts are frequently discussed in other books as precursors of knowledge production about transgender-identified people by transgender-identified people (see Prosser 1998 and discussions in Califia 2003 [1997] and Meyerowitz 2002). Since the emergence of transgender activism in the 1990s, autobiographies have been joined by popular texts like Feinberg's *Transgender Warriors* (1996), which makes a case for everyone who transgresses gender norms ("from Joan of Arc to Dennis Rodman," as its subtitle states) as transgender warriors. Other books authored in the 1990s by nonacademic writers offer different perspectives, such as those by Wilchins (1997) and Bornstein (1994, 1998), who argue for the deconstruction of gender itself rather than the simple reclamation of historical figures under the banner of transgender.

This raises the question of the relationship of trans-identified authors to the category which incorporates them and their work. Books, collections, and journal articles by transgender-identified scholars (e.g., Cromwell 1999, More and Whittle 1999, Namaste 2000, H. Rubin 2003, Towle and Morgan 2002, Prosser 1998, Stryker 1998, and others) exhibit a complex relationship to the category. The tension at the center of most of these texts is the desire to bring a critical perspective on broader cultural and historical dynamics while, simultaneously, not wanting to erase the specific subjectivities of transgender identification. Jason Cromwell (1999) and Henry Rubin (2003), for example, insist on the specificity of FTM and transmen's experience, but their books are simultaneously available for consolidation as part of a broader transgender studies with those by Wilchins, Feinberg, and Bornstein by virtue of their authors' identities and their subject matter. Despite this, the issue of trans identity and the authority it conveys are key tropes in this diverse corpus, made most explicit in Hale's *Suggested Rules for Non-transsexuals Writing about Transsexuals, Transsexuality, Transsexualism, or Trans*_____ (n.d.).

Perhaps the next area of investigation which can be placed in this field is contemporary social research authored by non-transgender-identified people. This book is one example, as are books by Meyerowitz (2000), Pettiway (1997), Ekins (1997), and King (1993), and edited collections like that by Ekins and King (1996), which incorporates both transgender- and non-transgender-identified authors and subjects identified as transexual, transvestite, or transgender. Others, like Califia (2003 [1997]), Devor (1997), and Halberstam (1998a) could also be slotted in here, though all three authors express varying affinities with transgender identification (both Califia and Devor have subsequently transitioned to different gendered identities since their books were first published).

Most of these texts are authored from the position that transgender identification is neither morally nor politically objectionable, often arguing that transgender practices or identification are potentially socially transformative. However, there are also a range of texts which take the opposite view, primarily from certain lesbian feminist perspectives. Raymond's *Transsexual Empire* (1994 [1979]), which argues that transexuality reasserts patriarchal standards of femininity and masculinity, is perhaps the best known — and, among transgender-identified people, the most reviled — of these. Many other authors decry transexuality and transvestism as politically retrograde (e.g., Jeffreys 1996, Mantilla 2000, McNeill 1982, Millot 1990, Yudkin 1978; see also Billings and Urban 1982), and more recently have applied the same analysis to transgender-identification specifically (e.g., de Motier 1998, Mantilla 2000, Raymond 1996). Others see transgender identification itself as politically progressive but have a similar analysis of SRS specifically (e.g., MacKenzie 1994). As I will discuss below, however, these texts too can be pulled into transgender studies even as their authors reject the terms of transgender identification.[1] On the other hand, other feminist texts which celebrate what could be understood as transgender practices as transformative of binary gender — notably Judith Butler's *Gender Trouble* (1990) — are often considered central to the theoretical developments that characterize transgender studies.

It is also not possible to consider transgender studies without invoking a range of historical medical and sexological texts which are also available for appropriation as part of the field. These would include the works of sexologists like Magnus Hirschfeld (1991 [1910)] and Havelock Ellis (1927) who elaborated distinctions between gender and sexuality early in the twentieth century. Later twentieth-century works which engage transexuality in particular (e.g., Benjamin 1966, Lothstein 1983, Stoller 1968, 1975) are also important to consider in the critical and reflective project of transgender studies, as is related work on intersexuality. Some contemporary texts — especially the controversial book by J. Michael Bailey (2003)

— are descendants of this tradition. This medical and psychiatric literature is critically engaged in virtually all texts written in the post–*Empire Strikes Back* literature under the rubric of transgender.

On the margins of this field (and again, it is with margins that I am most interested) lie anthropological studies of non-Western and Western subjects. Here, I am referring to not only contemporary ethnographic texts like those by Besnier (2002), Blackwood (1995), Boellstorff (2005), Elliston (2002), Kulick (1998), Johnson (1997), Manalansan (2003), Robertson (1998), and Sinnott (2004) but also early-twentieth-century works like Devereux's (1937) work on the "institutionalized homosexuality of the Mohave Indians," mid-century ethnographies like Esther Newton's (1979 [1972]) groundbreaking study of gay male drag performers in urban U.S. centers in the 1960s, and Anne Bolin's (1988) ethnography of Midwestern transsexual women in the 1980s.

Anthropological accounts are particularly of interest because of the ways that ethnographic subjects have been incorporated into the field of transgender studies, and vice versa. On the one hand, some transgender-identified authors have drawn on anthropological texts to argue for a commonality with historical and non-Western subjects (e.g., Feinberg 1996; see below). Moreover, anthropological and ethnohistorical accounts of Native American "*berdache*" or two-spirit people (Jacobs et al. 1997b, Lang 1998, Roscoe 1991, Williams 1986), Indian *hijra* (Nanda 1990), or Omani *xanith* (Wikan 1977, 1991) were often invoked by study participants in conversation to argue that "traditional societies accept transgender people" or as models for how people could identify. In these accounts — both published and anecdotal — "traditional" models of apparent transgender identification in non-Western contexts stand opposed to the cold modernity of the Western gender binary.

On the other hand, "transgender" has itself entered into the anthropological, medical, sociological, and other literatures with relatively little attention to how it carries certain assumptions and meanings with it. Within anthropology, "transgender" is rapidly becoming a term which is drawn on to describe and categorize *gender* non-normativity cross-culturally while, simultaneously, enabling anthropologists to engage in the (important) work of separating out the identities they are investigating from contemporary, modern homosexual identities. As we will see, the debate over whether certain people are best described through the frameworks of "transgender" or "homosexuality" is at its heart a debate over whether such subjects are understood best as either (and primarily) gendered or sexual subjects. I will argue that these debates obscure a more central issue: how it is that certain practices, identities, and ways of knowing come to stand in an unmediated fashion as simply "sexual" or "gendered."

As before, I am not so much interested in the center of this field but its boundaries, the places where there are disputes over what the collectivity of transgender contains. These debates often predate the emergence of transgender studies, but they have been transformed through the possibilities of transgender studies as an emerging field. Moreover, these debates also show — through the historical and geographical location of the authors and their subjects — how and where transgender comes to order particular kinds of bodies and desires, but in other cases, not. The first of these is the so-called border wars between butch lesbians and FTMs — and the lack of any analogous debate between gay men and transexual women.

BORDER WARS

Images of borders figure large in published debates over the distinctions — or rather, what the distinctions might be — between butch lesbians, transexual men, and other "female masculinities" (Halberstam 1998a). As many scholars point out, though, it is an unclear distinction at best (Halberstam 1998b, Hale 1998, G. Rubin 1992, H. Rubin 2003). These debates have arisen out of the politics of lesbian-feminism, the differentiation of butch/ femme roles in the United States in the twentieth century, and the ambivalence of (at least some) butches toward their female bodies (Kennedy and Davis 1993). Henry Rubin's chapter on the topic (entitled "Border Wars") locates the very possibilities for the solidification of FTM/ transman identification in the attempts to distinguish between "women-identified women" and "male-identified" female-bodied people in early 1970s feminism (2003: 64). Rubin writes that "this category confusion resolved itself by the consolidation of two distinct identities, male-identified transsexual men and women-identified lesbian women" (89). In these discrete territories, Rubin argues that transsexual men reject the idea that they were ever lesbians, and butches contest the idea that they are men. Yet, as Hale and Halberstam both point out, the territory around these borders is not always so clearly defined. Halberstam (1998b) wants to claim a territory for the possibility of "transgender butch" while Hale (1998) stakes out a claim for a "gender-queer" position in this borderland itself.

These border wars/borderlands/frontier fears (all titles taken from these texts) also play out on the historical stage. Hale, for example, notes how the late musician Billy Tipton has become a flashpoint in these debates, claimed by both butches and FTMs as an ancestor. The radiologist Alan/Lucille Hart, who died in 1962, is another case in point. Lillian Faderman, in her history of lesbian life in the twentieth-century United States, sees both Tipton and Hart as "passing women" who took on male personae in order to achieve career goals (1991: 41–45, 316 n. 9). On the other hand, an entry on transhistory.org identifies Hart as a man and gives a link to a web page hosted by Penn State University which identifies Hart as a woman. The transhistory authors encourage readers to "let them know that His Name Was Alan Hart!!!" (Morris and Brown, n.d.; see also O'Hartigan 2002, Hale 1998: 325). Another contested lesbian/butch/FTM/transgender figure is the fictional (and semi-autobiographical) character of Stephen Gordon in Radclyffe Hall's *The Well of Loneliness*. While this book is usually represented as a classic of lesbian literature and history, Gordon's masculine identification also make him/her available as a transgender avatar (see, e.g., Devor and Matte 2004, Prosser 1998, Taylor 1998). Perhaps the most contested person in these debates, though, is Brandon Teena (or, in some accounts, Teena Brandon), whom I will discuss in chapter 6 (see Hale 1998, Halberstam 2003).

I am particularly interested here in the way that these debates are characterized as "border wars" and "frontiers," not only for what it says about the broader argument of this book but also because, by contrast, there is a silence in the structurally equivalent terrain between feminine gay men and transexual women. While the idea that homosexual men are characterized by femininity has a long history in Western thought, there is no structurally equivalent contestation over iconic historical figures of gay male femininity. Indeed, it seems that contemporary gender-normative gay men are quite content to have the drag queens and fairies of yore be absorbed into a transgender history. All these points, as I will argue below, are central in the work being done to establish a field of transgender studies.

The furor over the publication of J. Michael Bailey's *The Man Who Would Be Queen* (2003) is worth some discussion here, because it is closest to this kind of frontier guarding, though the players are differently aligned. One of the most controversial aspects of Bailey's book is his claim that transexual women are either sexually aroused by the idea of themselves as women ("autogynephilia") or else very feminine gay men who have dealt with their femininity by transitioning (see Conway n.d.). This is a controversial claim because it locates transexual identity in *sexual* desire rather than, as is conventionally understood, in core gender identity. However, what is so striking about the outcry over the book is the almost total silence from gay male writers. Attempts to discredit Bailey's work have resulted in a very public debate, which has even found its way into the *Chronicle of Higher Education* (Wilson 2003a, 2003b). But the participants in this debate have virtually all been transexual women, and not gay men, and unlike the butch/FTM debates, it has no broad dissemination in gay male media.[2]

In summary, unlike Halberstam's valorization of "transgender butch," there is no analogous *culturally valorized space* for male-bodied "transgender fems," gay men who adopt, play with, or assert femininity as a central aspect of their senses of self, beyond the figure of the performing drag queen. Likewise, the absence of equivalent "border wars" and the relative silence of gay men in response to Bailey's book indicate, at the very least, an unwillingness to engage with the question of femininity in gay men.[3] As such, historical drag queens and other male-bodied feminine people appear to be available for absorption into the category of transgender (and into transgender studies) without the attendant critical attention that such a reordering has received for contested figures like Tipton or Hart. Part of this dynamic lies in the different meanings of gender and sexuality in feminist and mainstream gay and lesbian activism/scholarship as I discussed in chapter 1, a theme I will return to later.

These examples have been drawn from debates about contemporary and historical U.S. subjects. Next, I turn to anthropological subjects and recent debates over how to define and describe them. They are all the more interesting since, contrary to the cases above, most of these debates have focused on femininity in male-bodied people.

THE "BERDACHE" AND THIRD GENDER DEBATES

In anthropology, the place and definition of the "berdache"[4] (or "institutionalized homosexuality") in Native American societies, has been long debated (see Lang 1998: 17ff.), and in those debates, the problem of explaining this phenomenon has revolved, at least in part, around whether "berdache" are best described through the framework of sexuality or that of gender. For Western observers, from the earliest colonial accounts to twentieth-century writers (such as Devereux [1937]), "berdache" were evidence of Native American degeneracy and, from the late nineteenth century on, of institutionalized (male) homosexuality within Native American tribes (see Lang 1998: 26ff.). While there have been many interpretations of the meanings of "berdache" (e.g. Whitehead 1981, Blackwood 1984, Callender and Kochems 1983), most of the contemporary debate revolves around this reduction of the broad range of such roles to homosexuality (e.g., Jacobs et al. 1997a, Lang 1998, Cromwell 1999).

Califia's (2003 [1997]) analysis of anthropological and historical texts which focus on "berdache" by white gay male scholars such as Will Roscoe, Walter Williams, and Jonathan Ned Katz is particularly critical in this regard. Califia argues that while these scholars implicitly or explicitly frame "berdache" as a form of homosexual identification, Native Americans themselves perceived "berdache" as being in a different *gender* category rather than as "homosexual." He argues that this point should be accounted for "rather than distort[ing] these phenomenon [*sic*] by insisting on seeing them through the paradigm of modern Western male homosexuality" (125). For example, Califia takes issue with Roscoe's use of "he" to refer to the Zuni "man woman" WeWha when, Califia argues, all her contemporaries refer to her as "she"; and Califia cites many examples in Williams's book where he refuses to accept a gendered analysis of "berdache" identity.[5] Indeed, Califia argues "that we cannot understand third-gender roles without making use of the paradigm of transsexuality" (149) and not, he implies, homosexuality. Thus, for Califia, explaining "berdache" through a framing of sexuality and analogy to homosexuality is a stubborn refusal to recognize that they are best understood through a framing of gender and analogy to contemporary transsexual/transgender people.

Cromwell, himself an anthropologist and a transsexual man, is more subtle on this point. Cromwell's focus is on transmen and FTMS, and while he uses the term "transpeople" to refer to both historical and contemporary subjects, he is careful about not interpreting those subjects through contemporary categories of identity. At the same time, Cromwell also decries the reduction of such behaviors and identities to homosexuality, making the conventional claim that "sexuality and gender (as well as sex) are separate entities" (1999: 46). Like Califia, he insists on the primacy of gender variance as the analytic framing for discussion of "berdache" and other non-Western or historical subjects rather than that of (homo)sexuality. Cromwell makes the important distinction between transgender *identity*, which is a very recent possibility, and transgender *behavior* "that has occurred widely both historically and cross-culturally" (17). However, for all his care, elsewhere in his book he slips from "behavior" to "identity" in order to assert a gendered over a sexual explanation. For example, in the case of a Kaska female-bodied person who was understood as a man and took a woman as a wife, he writes: "it seems reasonable to assume that this person was a female-bodied man" (56). My interest here is not so much the reasonableness of this argument but rather Cromwell's implicit assertion of a "gendered" explanation for this individual over a "sexual" one.

Making the field more complex still is the identification of contemporary Native American Two Spirit people. Lang (1998) points out that contemporary Native Americans (who might have been what she calls "women-men" or "men-women" had they lived in precolonial times) often identify as gay or lesbian or alternate between women-men/men-women status among tribe members and gay/lesbian identity in urban environments. Jacobs et al.'s (1997a) use of the recently coined "Two Spirit" further complicates the easy assertion of gender over sexuality as a source of identity, for as they note, Two Spirit incorporates contemporary self-identified gay and lesbian Native Americans, Native American transgender, transvestite, transgender people; other non–Native American gender-variant people, drag queens, and butches; as well as those subsumed under "berdache" (2).

I do not intend to make an argument either for or against these different framing rubrics (homosexuality or gender variance/transgender) for discussing Native American "berdache." Rather, what I am interested in is the way this debate has been enabled by the assertion that, to quote Cromwell again, "sexuality and gender (as well as sex) are separate entities" (1999: 46). The problem with both of these arguments is that they are based on an assumption that "sexuality" is *experienced* as separate from "gender." In other words, for Califia to say that the "berdache" are best analogized by contemporary transgender/transexual/gender-variant people invokes, as its shadow, a modern model of gender-normative "homosexuality," one untouched by gender variance. This assumption results in anachronistic claims. For example, Califia writes: "While third-gender identities may serve as roles that can be adopted by people we might label as transsexuals, hermaphrodites, and effeminate homosexuals, I believe that if hormones and surgery were made available to third-gender people in traditional societies, the great majority of them would opt for sex change. And I doubt that even Williams, Roscoe, and Katz could disagree, in all good faith, with that hypothesis" (149). While I would not necessarily disagree with Califia — we simply cannot know — the more significant point is that like hormones and surgery, the distinction between gender-normative homosexuality and transgender identity is *also* a modern technology.

At the center of much of the debate over "berdache" is the contention that "berdache" should be understood as an institutionalized *third sex* or *third gender*. Other non-Western groups — such as the *hijra* of India (Nanda 1990; see Cohen 1995) and the Omani *xanith* (Wikan 1977, 1991) — have also been read through this category (see Herdt 1994) even as the category has been critiqued (Boellstorff 2004, Cohen 1995, Towle and Morgan 2002, Weston 1993: 354, Wieringa and Blackwood 1999: 25).[6] As with the debate over "berdache," figuring out the place of "third gender" subject positions in contemporary social research also engages the operative distinction between gender and sexuality.

At their heart, these claims and counterclaims revolve around three central issues. First is the problem of historical or cultural accuracy of using terms like "homosexuality," "transgender," or "third gender" to describe non-Western people. From a Foucauldian, social constructionist perspective, categories such as "homosexuality" or "transgender" can never escape the implications of modern homosexual or transgender identity. Second, the debates center on a kind of typological battle where some people will see "berdache" or (*xanith* or *hijra*) as evidence of the universality of homosexual desire, while others claim them for the category of gender variance, arguing that sexual desire is a result or elaboration, not a cause, of non-normative expressions of gender.

Finally, these debates revolve around the adequacy of "third gender" to account for the experiences of female-bodied people and the relative absence of female-bodied people from these accounts. Wieringa and Blackwood (1999) are also critical of the "third gender" framework precisely because it does not distinguish male- and female-bodied experience. They ask, "Why is it that male-bodied individuals transgress gender boundaries more freely than female-bodied individuals?" (25). To this question I would add some more: if it is the case that many of these debates revolve around the differences between homosexuality and transgender (or, at least, forms of selfhood that can be analogized as homosexual or transgender), then why is the discussion of female-bodied people relatively absent from cross-cultural accounts when it is so heatedly debated in the United States in the butch/FTM border wars? Concomitantly, if there is an overwhelming focus on male-bodied people in the anthropological literature on "third gender," then why are there no debates in the United States analogous to the butch/FTM border wars for male-bodied people?

I should note that I have glossed over the complexities of the debate I've laid out above (including longer-standing debates over whether "berdache" were occupational or gender/sex categories; see note 5). There is no absence of discussion of the relationships among sexuality, gender, and bodily sex in these texts. But I have focused on the way these debates are predicated, at their center, on a particular understanding of "gender" and "sexuality" as ontologically distinct across time and space. This debate, then, is less about the experience of Native American "berdache" or other "third gender" people themselves than one which has been enabled by an analytic distinction between gender and sexuality within Western academic discourses and identity politics. As a result, these issues raise a central question: how does this distinction produce certain subjects as being part of transgender studies, and other subjects as not?

This assumption is, moreover, complicated by Towle's and Morgan's (2002) concerns with the third gender model: its inability to account for transnational processes; the appropriation of Western identities and categories of knowledge by non-Western subjects; and the centrality of contemporary neoliberal forms of international capitalism to social and cultural changes globally. In the next section, I consider how these latter concerns fall out both theoretically and institutionally in relation to some other, mostly recent, ethnography which engages transnational appropriations of modern Western identities.

IS TRADITION TO MODERNITY AS TRANSGENDER IS TO HOMOSEXUALITY?[7]

In a 1993 *Annual Review of Anthropology* article, Weston notes that the emergence of the cross-cultural study of homosexualities in the 1970s and 1980s, especially by gay male anthropologists, was at least in part informed by a desire to argue for the universality of homosexual desire, if not of homosexual identity itself (1993: 342–43). She argues that the cataloguing of homosexuality so defined had resulted (by the early 1990s) in an implicit typological framing of non-Western gender/sexual variation across the globe, embodying an assumption that even if it was organized differently in "traditional" societies, it was the same innate sexual desire that animates "modern" homosexual identities (see Vance 1991). Manalansan (1997), in his analysis of similar representations by gay and lesbian activists and scholars (e.g., Adam 1995, Likosky 1992), finds a more explicitly teleological schema, with Western gender-normative, egalitarian (and implicitly, evolved) homosexuality contrasted to "traditional" forms. The latter, based on age-graded socialization into adulthood (as in parts of New Guinea) or institutionalized "third gender" roles, implicitly or explicitly stand as atavistic forerunners of modern Western homosexual identity. In turn, transnational appropriations of Western identities such as "gay" or "lesbian" are seen as evidence of contemporary "traditional" people adopting "modern" homosexuality in a way analogous to how Chloe imagines the Meat Market queens will adopt transgender identities. That is, in these accounts, if tradition is the antecedent to modernity, then gender-variant and age-graded homosexuality appears to be the antecedent to modern, egalitarian, and gender-normative homosexuality.

In the decade after Weston's article was published, there were two important developments. First, the rise of transgender activism and scholarship challenged this appropriation—not for its teleologies but rather in order to claim some of these same historical and non-Western subjects for the category of transgender and to repudiate the notion that these individuals are precursors of modern homosexuals. For example, Califia's confidence in assuming that "berdache" would have chosen hormones and genital surgeries is precisely the same move made by gay and lesbian authors who assume that they are observing premodern forms of homosexual identity. Both perspectives presuppose the delinking of gender and sexuality not only from each other but also from a range of other social experiences that we name through categories like culture, kinship, gender, household, status, community, caste, class, ethnicity, race, and so on and assume the capacity of individuals to adopt such identities outside the bounds of (premodern) social organization and personhood.

The second development since Weston's article, though, is a complication of 1980s gay and lesbian anthropology by anthropologists whose work is informed by feminist and queer theory, postcolonial and subaltern studies, and a critique of the simplistic distinction between modernity and tradition. I want to examine some of these ethnographies next, showing how they complicate both the understanding of a universality of homosexual and/or transgender identification but also the easy separation of gendered or sexual experience. Despite this, as I will show in the concluding section, these accounts are still available for appropriation into, alternately, gay/lesbian and/or transgender studies.

Problematizing "Gender" and "Sexuality"   Don Donham (1998) draws on the story of a male-bodied resident of Soweto, Linda (a conventional Zulu male name), to look at how "gay" identity became available to urban black South Africans in post-apartheid South Africa (see also McLean and Ngcobo 1994). Donham describes Linda's funeral in 1993, where he was valorized by local gay and lesbian activists as a gay man. However, Linda had not always been "gay." Writing of Linda's upbringing in the apartheid townships of Johannesburg, Donham argues that "instead of sexuality in the Western sense, it was local notions of sexed bodies and gendered identities — what I shall call sex/gender in the black South African sense — that divided and categorized" (7). As a young person, Linda thought of herself as a girl, was raised as a girl by parents, and was seen by others in the township as having biologically mixed sex or as a *skesana*. Donham writes that "in sum, black townships during the apartheid era found it easier to understand gender-deviant boys as girls or as a biologically mixed third sex" (9), and consequently their sexual partners were not considered *skesanas*, but (normative) men (10; see also Epprecht 1998 for a comparison to Zimbabwe). However, with the breakdown of the apartheid system, closer contact with white gay and lesbian communities, and the new availability of media about homosexuality, "the notion of sexuality was created for some black men, or more precisely, an identity based on sexuality was created. The classificatory grid in the making was different from the old one. Now, *both* partners in a same-sex relationship were potentially classified as the same (male) gender — and as 'gay'" (11, emphasis in original). For Linda "gay identity meant literally a new gender and a new way of relating to his body" (11).[8]

Despite the complexities Donham discusses, however, he ends with an assertion that deserves some attention: "A certain communicative density is probably a prerequisite for people to identify as gay at all, and it is not improbable that as media density increases, so will the number of gay people" (15). Here, Donham sounds very much like Califia in his contention that "if hormones and surgery were made available to third-gender people in traditional societies, the great majority of them would opt for sex change" ([2003] 1997:149). Yet these two authors imagine very different outcomes in the availability of modern Western technologies — both physical (mass media, surgery) and epistemological (identity categories). For Califia, it is self evident that "third gender" people would have opted to be transgender or transexual; for Donham, the development of an essentially gender-normative "gay" identity is the outcome of the availability of such technologies.

Linda's adoption of "gay" identity, however, does not simply mean that Donham got it right and Califia got it wrong. As Donham himself notes, as a gay man Linda still engaged in some practices which would make him/her part of the classificatory schema of "third gender" or "transgender," including occasional cross-dressing and chores in the home which were coded as feminine. Given Califia's rereading of the "berdache" data, or Chloe's contestation of the "gayness" of Pettiway's informants, it could also be possible for Linda to be read as a transgender person who, "if hormones and surgery were made available . . . would opt for sex change." But the point is that neither "third gender," "transgender," "gay," nor "homosexual" adequately describes the complexity of Linda's identification or experience.

Mark Johnson's (1997) study of the *gay/bantut* population of Jolo in the Southern Philippines provides a subtle reading of these kinds of distinctions. While "bantut" is a "traditional" term for boys and men who adopt feminine practices, dress, and occupation, and who are also erotically drawn to and seek out male partners, they themselves prefer to call themselves "gay," a term adopted from the United States. But like Linda, it is clear that they are not doing "gay" in the same way as contemporary Western gay men. Working in beauty salons, organizing pageants, weddings, and school events, the gay/bantut residents of Jolo see themselves simultaneously as feminine persons and as defined by their desire for a normative male partner.

The gays/bantut look to the United States for models both for themselves and their lovers. They imagine the United States as a place where they would find a gender-normative, supportive, and loving boyfriend or husband. As in other parts of the world (see, e.g., Donham 1998, Lancaster 1992, Kulick 1998), the male lover of a gay/bantut is not understood as gay/bantut himself but retains his status as a normative man. The reciprocation of sexual attention is neither offered nor desired in these encounters, Johnson argues. Those men who might best be understood as homosexual in the modern sense — that is, gender-normative men who desire gays/bantut but also desire their gay/bantut partner to be active in penetrating them — are derided by gays/bantut and non-gays/bantut alike as *silahis* or "double blades" (91).

As such, it seems that gays/bantut might be better understood through the category of "transgender" than that of "gay" or "homosexuality." The subtitle of Johnson's book — "Transgendering and Cultural Transformation in the Southern Philippines" — makes this implication. However, Johnson's focus on the "transgendered projects" of the gays/bantut is intended precisely to complicate what homosexuality and gender-variant behavior might mean in this context. Johnson argues that the adoption of "gay" by his study participants is neither a wholesale adoption of Western homosexuality nor an imposition of Western sexological models. Rather, he argues for "the possibility that there may be other histories of sexuality/gender in the Philippines which, while growing out of the . . . entangled skein of colonial and post-colonialism, may have as much to do with the discourses of state and nation, cultural and religious identity and identifications, and variously gendered ethnic bodies as it does with the proliferation and circulation of social scientific discourses of sexuality" (36).

Manalansan's (2003) study of Filipino self-identified gay male immigrants to the United States likewise contests gay male Filipino writers who decry the *bakla* (another subject position of male-bodied feminine people in the Philippines) as a feudal, false imposition which is giving way, naturally, to modern gay identity (35 ff.). Manalansan sees the cross-dressing of his U.S.-resident study participants not as a vestige of pre-Stonewall, pre-modern gender-inflected homosexuality but rather as an "alternative modernity." He writes: "I argue that cross-dressing practices and rituals are vehicles and spaces through which Filipino gay men in New York city create and promulgate their sense of belonging and citizenship amid competing images and practices of the 'gay community' and the nation" (127). In a similar fashion, Boellstorff (2004, 2005) notes that the *waria* of Indonesia must be seen neither as a simple "traditional third gender" role for male-bodied feminine people nor as a precursor to "modern" homosexuality. Rather, he argues that the waria subject position is a specific mediation between local and transnational understandings of gender and sexual identity and behavior but, just as significantly, is equally shaped by understandings of home, marriage, kinship, modernity, and state bureaucratic categories.

In short, all these authors point out not only the dangers of describing their subjects through contemporary Western conceptions of gendered and sexual selfhood but that the analysis of their experiences far exceeds the boundaries of "gender" and "sexuality." Local conceptions of home, "the West," kinship, occupation, travel, beauty, style, as well as the facts of missionization, state violence, immigration, bureaucratic categories of identification, local and global political economies, and so on are all as significant to the formation of gay/bantut/bakla/waria identity as the restricted domains referred to by "gender" and "sexuality."

As such, they also demonstrate the dangers of presupposing any of these subject positions as natural precursors of *either* modern homosexual *or* transgender identity. Despite these careful analyses, however, the implication for some Western readers might be the assumption, like Califia's, that given the opportunity, the gays/bantut or waria would opt for hormones and surgery and a transgender identity. Kulick's *Travesti* (1998) complicates this assumption. Among the *travesti* population of Salvador, Brazil, Kulick observed many of the same practices associated with MTF transgender-identification in the United States — early childhood cross-gender identification and behavior, cross-dressing, feminizing body modification, and the adoption of feminine names by male-bodied people. Poor, and subject to horrifying levels of violence, the travestis eke out a living primarily as sex workers. But, he argues, a central feature of travesti narratives about themselves and each other is their explicit assertion that they are homosexual men, not women. Indeed, the idea that one is or can be a woman is seen as nonsensical by travestis themselves, and calling another travesti a woman is an insult, Kulick claims. Likewise, his travesti informants, fully aware of the possibilities of transexuality, were horrified by the notion of genital surgery, though they engage in extensive (informal) feminizing body modification of the buttocks and breasts through the injection of industrial silicone.

For the travestis, Kulick argues, gender is not linked simply to genitalia or a notion of internal identity but rather to the act of penetration in sexual encounters. Kulick shows how when a normatively gendered male client of a travesti desires to be penetrated by the travesti, he becomes "she" in his informants' accounts. Likewise, boyfriends of travestis are desired for their masculinity and capacity to anally penetrate them. Should a boyfriend desire to be penetrated by his travesti girlfriend, however, the relationship is terminated since he — she — ceases to be a man. Kulick, a gay man, was himself understood by the travestis as sharing this gendered position; and he notes how they deride Brazilian middle-class gender-normative gay men for believing themselves to be men. In short, Kulick argues that the travesti are neither a third gender nor, to extend his argument, are they uncomplicatedly either "transgender" or "gay" — rather, he argues, they share a gender category with women, and all people who are penetrated: "not men." As such, though the travestis may appear to be transgender to many Western readers, and though they claim to be homosexual, neither of these categories in the contemporary Western sense can account for their understandings of self.

It should be apparent by now that, beyond the complications evident in these ethnographic examples, there is also one similarity: the focus on male-bodied people. As Wieringa and Blackwood (1999) have noted, as with the historical absence of women and female-bodied people in the anthropological record, the ethnography of non-normative genders/sexualities is marked by a dearth of discussion of the experience of female-bodied people. They argue that the gendered inequalities that result in the absence of female-bodied people in the record also structure the (in)ability of female-bodied people to enact non-normative gender/sexual desire and practices. Indeed, while there have been several recent ethnographies of gender/sexual non-normative female-bodied people (e.g., Robertson 1998, Sinnott 2004), the relatively greater possibilities cross-culturally for male-bodied people to enter the public sphere is an important reason for the disequilibrium of representation in the anthropological record.[9]

However, the discussion of non-normative female-bodied people enables a further complication of the representation of non-Western gender/sexual variant subjects. Blackwood's (1995) contribution to this field is particularly productive, for not only does she discuss the case of Dayan, an Indonesian female-bodied masculine person who was also her lover, but she discusses how her own desires, framings, and ambivalences shape her understandings and representations of Dayan. As in the Southern Philippines, Indonesians have adopted and transformed Western categories of identity, including "lesbi" and "gay" (see also Boellstorff 2005, Oetomo 2000). Blackwood notes that "due to the close connection of alternative gender with homosexuality in West Sumatra and Indonesia" (62), the categories of lesbi and gay are used synonymously with categories of alternative gender which in West Sumatra are *bujang-gadis/becong* (for male-bodied feminine people), and *tupik-fantan/tomboi* (for female-bodied masculine people). This close connection plays out in complex ways for Blackwood and her lover. While Blackwood sees Dayan as a strong and brave woman who resists Indonesian gendered conventions, Dayan expresses the desire to be a man and for Blackwood to adopt the role and demeanor of a wife. Blackwood writes:

> Our sexual practices were informed by these differences in gender identity and gave me further insights into the gender distinctions that Dayan drew for herself. She preferred to take the "male" role in sex, as she understood it from men she had talked to, and was little interested in being touched. Acts that emphasized her female body made her uncomfortable; she perceived them as corporal negations of her maleness. My own practices reflected an American lesbian feminist's rejection of male-defined and hierarchical sexuality; however, my attempts to negotiate greater latitude in lovemaking, in effect, to insert "equality" into sex, were generally unsuccessful. (68)

The candor with which Blackwood writes exposes, as she notes, the ways in which this relationship challenged and reshaped both her and Dayan's understandings of what it means to be a female-bodied person who desires other female-bodied people. Blackwood does not refer to Dayan as "transgender," though through her description it is clear that all those salient markers of "transgender-ness" — desire to transition to another gender, reshaping of the body, adoption of non-ascribed gender roles and behaviors — are present. Blackwood, indeed, refers to Dayan throughout as "she" and as a lesbian. Once more, I do not want to imply that Blackwood is "wrong" nor to make the claim that Dayan is "really transgender" (though this claim would certainly be made by some of my study participants). Rather, the point is to show again how "gender" and "sexuality" become deeply entangled with one another (and again, with occupation, kinship, locale . . .), indeed, inseparable for those subjects whose senses of self are not mediated through an understanding of gender and sexuality as experiences separate from one another or from other aspects of daily life. This entanglement between "gender" and "sexuality" is not specific to West Sumatra; rather, it is (as she recognizes) Blackwood's own assumptions about their separateness that produce the complexity of their relationship, and its representation in print.

These latter cases thus complicate both Donham's and Califia's assertions about the possibilities raised by the availability of categories and technologies. Admittedly, the people discussed by Johnson, Manalansan, Boellstorff, Kulick, and Blackwood are poor and on the lowest stratum of local and global systems of socioeconomic status. Perhaps, as Donham's argument implies, urban residence and access to information would enable the kind of "sorting out" of identities Meyerowitz identifies in the mid-twentieth-century urban United States (as I outlined in chapter 1); the kinds of "education" some social service providers believe will enable Anita, Jade, or Sherry (whom I discussed in chapter 3) to identify explicitly as transgender; or the accessing of medical technologies as Califia suggests. Yet this misses the point that Johnson so cogently makes: that "there may be other histories of sexuality/gender" (1997: 36), inflected by cultural frameworks of knowledge, colonialism, global connections, and border crossings, which make a simple reading of discrete gay and transgender identity untenable in these contexts. That is, those-experiences-we-call "sexuality" and "gender" *themselves* may be organized in very different ways and be understood through other kinds of orderings (see also Besnier 2002).

My argument is, then, that "gender" and "sexuality" are not simply universal experiences or categories that are shaped in different ways by different "cultures" but, rather, *that they are themselves transformed as categories* in different contexts. Jolly and Manderson (1997) make a similar point in their introduction to a collection of essays on sexuality in Asia and the Pacific. Noting the theoretical separation of "sexuality" from "gendered" topics such as reproduction in gay/lesbian and feminist scholarship, they argue succinctly that "the issue extends beyond the separation of sexuality and reproduction to the broader supposition that sexuality has ontological status in all times and places, that it is a thing that can be named and to which a set of behaviors, feelings, and desires can be attached" (24; see also Butler 1994).[10]

This extended discussion of the analytic place of homosexuality and transgenderism (or their assumed place) in these accounts serves to make two points: first, that a clear distinction between "gender" and "sexuality" is confounded by the observation that these categories do not contain the same experiences, understandings, ideologies, or frames of reference for all subjects. Like "homosexuality" and "transgender," they also have a history. These contemporary anthropological accounts do not simply point to the differences between different "forms" of homosexuality or of transgenderism but show how gendered and sexual experience exceeds the boundaries of those categories themselves. Indeed, it is crucial to note that all the authors cited above explicitly complicate the relationship between gender and sexuality (and other categories of analysis) in their work and raise questions about the utility of these discrete categories to account for their informants' identities and experiences. Their ethnographic data indicate that the status of "gender" and "sexuality" are complicated and transformed in locales where they are unable to be disaggregated from phenomena that are referred to as occupation, kinship, religion, state formation, marriage, travel, separatist warfare, modernity, capitalism, and so on. Second, though, once written, these texts enter a field where they are themselves subject to another set of social and meaning-making practices. Because they are read, taught, and put on syllabi and bibliographies, Western readers are able to see in these accounts — and argue over — analogies to Western gay, lesbian, and transgender identities. More significantly, as they come to be organized through the syllabi and bibliographies of a cohering transgender studies (as each of these texts is), their presence there reproduces the distinction between gender and sexuality upon which discrete homosexual and transgender identity depends, obviating the subtlety of these ethnographic analyses which aim to complicate that very distinction. I turn to this set of social practices next.

CONSOLIDATING A FIELD

So what is "transgender studies"? I have argued that it can gather unto itself a wide range of different texts, but what is the "it-ness" that produces this unity? As Halberstam notes, transgender studies is characterized by heterogeneity and a profusion of theoretical positions — similar to the profusion of identities that inhabit the imagined collectivity of transgender as a category of identification. So in this regard, there is no unity in the sense of theoretical, methodological, or political framings. Moreover, as I noted above, like any field of critical studies, transgender studies draws in a range of texts across disciplines and from different historical periods, all of which engage variously situated social actors as their subjects, further complicating the idea of a unified field.

However, despite this heterogeneity and diversity, there is a unifying center, the very reason for the constitution of the field in the first place: the idea that there is a group of people who can be understood through the category transgender. Or perhaps it would be better to say that there is a recursive relationship between transgender studies and a transgender community, one that engages an uncomfortable doubleness common to many fields of interdisciplinary inquiry. That is, even as transgender studies critically engages "transgender," its very institutionalization and naming presupposes a referent. Simultaneously, for all its critical impulse, transgender studies comes to stand as evidence *of* such a community for those concerned with its representation in the academy and beyond. This is, indeed, the central tension between a field of study which takes the category as a critical starting point, and the movement which enabled its emergence, which depends on the notion of fixed and distinct transgender identity. Finally, and again despite its critical impulse, its institutionalization privileges a particular understanding of "gender" as the primary experience around which transgender understandings of self are organized, and in turn is predicated on the assertion of difference from other fields of knowledge and states of being, in particular, that of homosexuality.

In exploring this claim, there are two broad — and interrelated — themes in scholarly and intellectual practices in which I am interested. The first is authorial and editorial. In this set, I include all those dynamics I have discussed above: the citation of historical texts in books or journal issues about transgender; the reinterpretation of anthropological and historical data as evidence of transgender behaviors and/or identities; but also the reiteration of the modern distinction between gender and sexuality as the truth against which local, non-Western ontologies are to be understood. The second is institutional: the way in which certain texts come to be understood as part of a field of transgender studies, however it is that they characterize their subject(s).

It is useful at this point to return to the *Transgender Issue* of GLQ in 1998. This issue embodies many of the dynamics I discuss above: even as Stryker's introduction thematizes the fissures and fractures of the field, the issue itself frames the collection of essays as texts about transgender. The articles in this issue include Cheryl Chase's (1998) discussion of intersexuality and the intersex movement; Joanne Meyerowitz's (1998) historical reconstruction of the formation of transexual identities in the early-twentieth-century United States; two articles which take on the issue of transgender/transsexual embodiment and subjectivity (Elliot and Roen 1998, H. Rubin 1998); an article on bioethics (Nelson 1998); a paired set of articles by Halberstam (1998b) and Hale (1998) on the aforementioned butch/FTM "border wars"; and an interview with a former San Francisco police officer, Elliot Blackstone, through which members of the Gay and Lesbian Historical Society of Northern California (GLHSNC) (Members 1998) explore the history of radical "MTF transgender activism" in San Francisco.

This issue is a dense enactment of both of the themes I laid out above. On the one hand, it consciously exploits the trope of transgender to incorporate a range of different texts, positions, disciplinary locations, topics, historical contexts, and critical perspectives. Hale, Halberstam, Meyerowitz, Stryker, and the GLHSNC members are all cautious about the framing of transgender, noting the ways that it intersects and overlaps with other kinds of experiences, and how "transgender" subtly, if significantly, reshapes the experiences of historical subjects (see, for example, Members 1998: 351). On the other hand, by their inclusion in a *Transgender Issue*, these texts (and their subjects) can be read as constituting a field. That is, "transgender" as a framing trope for this issue allows for a critical reading of this diversity — intersex infants, Tenderloin queens, butches, and FTMs — but also for producing the diversity itself as characteristic *of* transgender. For, like the anthropological accounts discussed above, the institutional framing of transgender as a discrete entity *also* enables the effect of erasing the complexities so central to these authors' analyses.

I must also note that my own scholarship and teaching is implicated in this process. This book itself (with "transgender" in the title) is available for appropriation into transgender studies, one of my essays (Valentine 2006) has been reprinted in a transgender studies reader (Stryker and Whittle 2006), and I have also twice taught a class called "Transgender Histories, Identities, and Politics" (Valentine 2004) which includes many readings that have been discussed above. I ask two central questions in the course description: "How is it that all these texts have been grouped together in a class about 'transgender'? What does this syllabus itself tell us about the category, and about emerging notions of gender and sexuality in the United States in the early twenty-first century?" Yet despite these critical questions, like the articles in the *Transgender Issue* of GLQ, this syllabus contributes to the ordering of these texts together as forming a body of work.

I certainly do not intend to argue that these processes are complete or without complication. As much as the *Transgender Issue* or my syllabus might order texts and their subjects (provisionally) through transgender as a collective term, other institutional uses are apparent. For example, the Library of Congress (LOC) had several subject headings for variations on the root term "transgender," but (at least in 2006), each of these was empty of references and referred users to "transsexualism" or "transsexuals." Reading emergent intellectual practices from library cataloging practices is tentative at best: in early 2006 the LOC category of "gender identity" had over three hundred entries, including books on gender and schooling, gay male masculinity, butch/femme, and homosexuality in general, while others like Meyerowitz's or Wilchins's, which arguably lie at the center of transgender studies, are listed under "transsexuals" or "transsexualism" but are not cross-listed under "gender identity." Another important point to bear in mind is, as Stryker reminds us, the relationship between "transgender" and "queer" studies, and how homosexuality and transgenderism can be read against and with one another in ways that subvert the easy division between them, historically, cross-culturally, or in the contemporary United States.

Yet my concern is still that the increasing use of "transgender" as a term to order knowledge produces the possibilities whereby certain subjects become appropriated into a reading of transgender that obscures the complexities of their identification and experience. Chloe's reading of Pettiway's *Honey, Honey, Miss Thang* at the beginning of this chapter reminds us that the practices of ordering and reading are not simply the product of scholarly work, syllabi, bibliographies, literature reviews, journal issues, library cataloguing practices, and so on, but of the way individuals make sense of such texts. From Chloe's perspective, Pettiway's book (listed under, among other headings, "transvestites" and "male prostitution" in LOC) is clearly about "transgender" sex workers. Their own, and Pettiway's, use of "gay" as a description of their selves is seen by Chloe as nonsensical or, at least, a reiteration of a "false" framework. Califia's rereading of Roscoe's and Williams's characterizations of the "berdache" is a similar kind of move. In both these cases, it is self-evident to these readers that the subjects of these very different books are best described as or analogized by transgender, and, moreover, that the reading of those subjects through a schema of "sexuality" rather than one of "gender" is, simply, wrong.

In the end, then, it is the distinction between gender and sexuality which produces, and is manifest in, these debates. Yet, as I have argued throughout this book, that distinction is, like contemporary categories such as transgender or homosexuality, a modern and recent innovation. It is this ordering of experience more than identity or institutionalized categories that results in the ways that texts — and their subjects — are increasingly coming to be framed. Hence, anthropological texts — those that explicitly draw on "transgender" as a category to describe their subjects (e.g., Besnier 2002) and those that use the term to qualify their informants' practices (Boellstorff 2004, Kulick 1998, Johnson 1997), as much as those that don't (e.g., Blackwood 1995, Manalansan 2003) — can be absorbed into a field of transgender studies in readers' selection of those aspects of personhood and experience which are evidently "(trans)gendered." At the same time, the operative distinction between gender and sexuality allows readers simultaneously to contest that such subjects are (or ever were) "homosexual."

In these readings, the anthropological and historical framing of (self-evidently) transgender behavior and/or identity as a precursor to "modern" homosexuality can be contested and reclaimed *as* transgender. This reclamation depends on the conviction that the modern reading of gender and sexuality as separate and separable has ontological status, to paraphrase Jolly and Manderson (1997), for all time and all places. And "modern" here indexes not simply the assertion of a contemporary intellectual framing but also a modernist and progressivist claim: that the separation of gender and sexuality is a universal truth which has been finally revealed, and through which anthropological, historical, and contemporary Western and non-Western subjects can now be reinterpreted and given their correct place in the order of things.

This reading of gender is, as I have argued, significantly different from feminist understandings of gender as a site of relationships of power, linked in complex (though not causal) ways to sexuality and reproduction. And it is here that we can find one reason for why, in the field of transgender studies, the majority of the debates over non-Western anthropological subjects engage those ascribed male at birth; and why there is an elaborate debate over the butch/FTM border but none over the analogous border between male homosexuality and MTF transexuality in the United States. The success of the separation of gender and sexuality in queer/LGBT studies has rendered discussions of femininity in homosexual men dismissable as "stereotyping," a rejection of sexological and psychiatric models of homosexuality as gendered deviance. For female-bodied masculine people or FTMs, however, while the legacy of sexology and psychiatry is also significant, "female masculinity" is refracted through the history of second-wave feminism and a framing of gender which departs significantly from sexological and psychiatric models. Most contemporary feminists reject gender as simply "difference" and see it as a primary site of social power relations, necessarily inflected by sexuality because of the historical and cultural linkages between female sexuality and the politics of gender, even as they recognize that sexual identity is not linked to gender identification in causal ways. Hence, the butch/FTM border wars are a product not simply of a new conceptualization of gender and sexuality but of the working out of the status of masculinity in female-bodied people in the context of much broader gendered inequalities.

Likewise, the debates over anthropological and historical non-normative genders/sexualities are framed by the different, if intersecting, histories and politics of feminist and queer/gay concerns. As Wieringa and Blackwood (1999) point out, the more general absence of female-bodied people in the anthropological record is the legacy of the historical dominance of men in the field as well as the broader gendered patterns of inequality which make it harder for female-bodied people to engage in gender/sexual non-normative practices. Similarly, the concern of gay male anthropologists to describe and valorize non-Western (male) homosexualities has produced a context in which "traditional," "gendered" homosexualities can be interpreted (if not by anthropologists themselves, at least by others) as forerunners of modern ("sexual") homosexuals.

Transgender studies, then, is an emergent field of knowledge that, while impacted by feminism (and opposed to those varieties of lesbian-feminism which see transgender identity as retrograde), is being institutionalized through an understanding of "gender" that sees it primarily as a social difference, a conceptualization that flows more from the history of sex research, gay/lesbian scholarship and activism, and the concerns of MTF people than from feminism and the concerns of FTMs. Clearly, the debates over the butch/FTM borders engage these different understandings of gender. But that there is a "border war" at all (and the lack of its analogue for fem gay men/MTFs) is evidence of that very distinction.

So, what is the reason for engaging in this long discussion of transgender studies, and the place of gender and sexuality in its formation? As I wrote above, this is the first of three chapters in which I look at how "transgender" (and particular theories of gender and sexuality) are being institutionalized in certain contexts. The problem is, once more, not that this framing is false or wrong but rather that it cannot account for the complexities of lived experiences; that it reproduces the distinction between gender and sexuality as ontologically secure and universally relevant; and that, as a result, the subjects of academic investigations — and of a range of other institutionalizing venues — are increasingly ordered by this distinction. Such institutionalization is indeed a feature of knowledge production itself, especially in an academic system where the establishment of fields of knowledge is vital for such scholarship (and the scholars who do its work) to be validated, as Chauncey argues for gay and lesbian studies (2000: 305). However, Chauncey also cautions against the narrowing potential of institutionalization and how it may close down analytic possibilities, a concern echoed by Butler (1994). Thus, while individual scholars who work within the framework of transgender studies may complicate these meanings of gender and sexuality, the broader push toward institutionalization produces conditions which obscure key critical questions at its heart. This is, indeed, the central problematic of institutionalization, and so I would argue that the very constitution of the field of transgender studies *as* a field must remain a central question *in* the field.

If, as I have argued, these debates are rooted in a modernist narrative of progress whereby the truth of the separation of gender and sexuality has come to be accepted, other conditions of modernity apply too. As Giddens (1990: 40–44) points out, one of the features of late modernity (or, in other readings, postmodernity) is that academic knowledge and social practices are related in recursive ways, so that academic models of society and its subjects come to be the ground against which social action is produced. In turn, such action becomes the source of anthropological and sociological data, framed as local knowledge. In the next chapter, I will look at how transgender — and the theories of gender and sexuality evident in anthropological, historical, sociological, and other framings — orders people in a different institutional context, that of social service provision and political grassroots activism. Indeed, to extend Giddens's argument, I believe it is in the intersection of transgender studies and transgender activism that the critical questions of transgender scholars become evened out. For even if the scholars cited above recognize the inability of discrete analytic categories to fully describe their subjects, activists and social service providers fully depend on the notion that transgender experience, even in all its diversity, is located discretely in the realm of gender.

5

The Logic of Inclusion

Transgender Activism

One busy morning at the Lesbian and Gay Community Services Center I was on my way out to get some coffee, down the narrow steps from the Gender Identity Project on the third floor and through the busy lobby. I stopped to look at the notice boards where there were announcements, posters, and signs — a support group, a party, a fundraiser, a housemate sought — the stuff of community centers everywhere. But my eye was caught by one which read:

DO YOU FEEL EXCLUDED FROM THE CENTER?

There followed a list of acts that the Center staff were supposedly guilty of: the ejection of transgender people from the Center; disallowing transgender groups from meeting there; discrimination against transgender people in hiring practices; and a demand that the Center own up to — and end — this perceived discrimination by "including" transgender people in its operations and its name. I went back upstairs to find Rosalyne, who had already seen the poster. She was understandably grumpy because, as the director of the GIP, she felt that the poster's author had ignored her efforts to have transgender issues addressed at the Center. But the poster — and Rosalyne's frustrations — speak more broadly to the idea of *inclusion* of the "T" of transgender (and the "B" of bisexual) in the names, mission statements, and politics of formerly gay and lesbian organizations in the United States.

INCLUSION AS A TROPE

The anonymous author of this poster was apparently a disgruntled Center user who was claiming that certain practices on the part of the Center administration resulted in the exclusion of transgender-identified people from the physical space of the Center, but also from a broader discursive space. By invoking exclusions — the ejection of transgender-identified people from the Center and the absence of "transgender" in the Center's name — the author was drawing on contemporary demands for the explicit inclusion of transgender people in gay and lesbian organizations.

This demand for inclusion, however, is complicated by the fact that, as I have described in previous chapters, transgender-identified activists and scholars simultaneously assert their difference from gay and lesbian identity, history, and activism. This contradiction is dealt with in one of two ways. First, the relationship between the gay and lesbian and transgender communities is often presented as one where transgender issues were *incorrectly subsumed* into gay and lesbian concerns throughout history, and in which their contribution to gay and lesbian history has been ignored (e.g., Feinberg 1996). As I discussed in chapter 1, a crucial argument made by activists and others is that transgender-identified people — and especially, transgender-identified people of color — were at the heart of the Stonewall riots, the moment to which the gay and lesbian liberation movement is conventionally traced. A second and related argument is the claim that the transgender and gay/lesbian communities are *analogous* to one another, but that distinct histories can be traced and compared across time and space (e.g., Devor and Matte 2004, Lombardi 1995). These accounts also depend on an assertion of clear historical differences between transgender and gay/lesbian histories but further solidify that difference through the figure of analogy itself.[1] However, in both arguments, calls for inclusion also produce the effects of ontological difference between gay/lesbian and transgender communities, identities, and histories, even as they complicate that distinction.

In this chapter, I examine claims about "inclusion" to think about the historical and contemporary meanings that have enabled transgender-identified and gay and lesbian activists to simultaneously come to an agreement on a recognition of shared histories while insisting on their differences. The analysis of inclusion I undertake here is focused on the processes whereby certain categories are produced as having certain kinds of boundaries in the first place, so that some people may see themselves as being included or excluded from them. Thus, "inclusion" for me is not simply a positive political act but an object of analysis itself, for it already assumes a coherence to the working categories of these politics. As with the debates over the identification and categorization of anthropological and historical subjects, the trope of "inclusion" points to the ambiguities in the working out of distinct histories and contemporary identities. And, as with the reordering of those anthropological and historical subjects, this ambiguity is worked out in the margins between homosexuality and transgender, margins that are shaped by race and class.

Whatever the complications, however, these claims have certainly had effects: in the 1990s gay and lesbian organizations — from national activist groups like the National Gay and Lesbian Task Force (NGLTF) to professional organizations like the Society of Lesbian and Gay Anthropologists (SOLGA) to university and community social groups — have increasingly included "transgender" (and "bisexual") in their mission statements, programming, and even their names. Indeed, "LGBT" (lesbian, gay, bisexual, and transgender) has become a common acronym in press releases, conference titles, mission statements, and so on, replacing simply "gay" or "gay and lesbian." While there has been — and continues to be — resistance from both lesbians and gay men to such inclusion, the mood has shifted significantly since the early 1990s toward a consensus that transgender-identified people should be included in lesbian and gay organizations.

This consensus has been achieved mainly around two related arguments which also attempt to resolve the contradictions noted above. First, there is a broad agreement that gay/lesbian political and social issues — such as hate crimes and employment discrimination — are similar to transgender political and social issues. Second, though, there is a simultaneous insistence by gay, lesbian, and transgender-identified people that gay/lesbian issues are qualitatively different from transgender-related issues and therefore require different goals and strategies (e.g., Devor and Matte 2004, Frye 2000, Lombardi 1995). Drawing on a model of democratic representation that sees political interests best addressed through representation of interest groups, "transgender" is incorporated in contemporary LGBT politics as a distinct entity, even as the acronym implies a similarity of concerns (see Phelan 2001: 115–38).

Transgender activism around "inclusion" is part of a much broader field of activism and advocacy which developed through the category transgender in the 1990s. Such activism has been directed at the medical establishment, media outlets, the judiciary, legislative bodies, and corporations by organizations such as Transexual Menace, GenderPAC, Transgender Nation, the International Conference on Transgender Law and Employment Policy (ICTLEP), the National Center for Transgender Equality (NCTE), the New York Association for Gender Rights Advocacy (NYAGRA), It's Time, America! (ITA), and many others (see Califia 2003 [1997], Wilchins 1997, Feinberg 1996, Meyerowitz 2002). While I will also discuss judicial and legislative advocacy in this chapter and the next, I have several reasons for focusing on the activism around "inclusion" in gay and lesbian organizations. First, during my fieldwork this was a central site for the production of meanings around transgender. Second, while the distinction between sexual and gendered identities is central in most of the activist and advocacy contexts mentioned above, the activism directed at gay and lesbian organizations is particularly interesting because of the tensions between the similarities and differences posited as important by both transgender and gay and lesbian activists.

The practices and discourses of inclusion are also impacted by those categories of social experience we call race and class. From the claims of contemporary transgender activists that it was poor transgender people of color who led the charge at Stonewall, to current demands that LGBT organizations address issues of poverty and racism, "race" and "class" are broadly salient as categories of analysis and action in this activism. Yet, as we will see, "gender," "sexuality," "race," and "class" come to take on distinct lives in this activism. I will show how, even as race and class are drawn into activist contexts, they are, like "gender" or "sexuality," relegated to a social difference represented by certain groups. Drawing on my analysis in chapters 2 and 3, I will argue that the bracketing of gender, sexuality, race, and class as attaching to particular groups undermines the potential of this activism but also produces some subjects, who are seen to be constituents of this activism, as incoherent.

I conduct this analysis — of explicit inclusions, implicit exclusions, and their histories — through three quite different but equally politically and emotionally charged contexts. I start with a local community center, then move to a meeting of national LGBT activists, and finally to the U.S. Congress. Claims over inclusion and exclusion are fraught with high emotion precisely because these are places where categories of personal identity *and* national politics are being negotiated. As Mary Douglas writes, "all margins are dangerous" because "any structure of ideas is vulnerable at its margins" (1992 [1966]: 121). I will look at how both gay/lesbian and transgender activists negotiate the margins between these categories, but also how the discourse of "inclusion" actually helps produce another kind of exclusion: that of gender variance as an experience underpinning gay and lesbian identities. In short, I will argue that the "inclusion" of transgender-identified people in gay and lesbian organizations actively stabilizes the vulnerable margins of "gay" and "lesbian." And because those margins are also shaped by race and class, I want to show how such inclusion is itself undercut by the "difference" model of democracy that underpins it. Before looking at these events, however, we need to consider the context within which such activism has become possible in the first place.

COLLECTIVE ACTION AND NEW SOCIAL MOVEMENTS

In the context of global political, economic, and social change in the latter part of the twentieth century, the rise of transgender activism is not unique. It has precedents in a range of social movements in the post–World War II West, incorporating gendered, sexual, racial, and ethnic identity-based movements, social issues such as environmentalism and patient rights, and others. My focus here is on those movements organized around gendered and sexual identities.

Such activisms are often termed "new social movements" (NSMs), forms of collective action that have reformulated the terms of grassroots political action in the West, if not completely replacing labor- and class-based political organizing in the post–World War II period (see Edelman 2001, Laclau and Mouffe 2001 [1985], Melucci 1996, Seidman 1993). Where labor movements arose out of class conflict, NSMs are seen to arise out of "the crisis of modernity and focus on struggles over symbolic, informational, and cultural resources and rights to specificity and difference" (Edelman 2001: 289), producing new and multiply-positioned social subjects. Central to these politics is a foregrounding of and demand for recognition of group and individual identity. Charles Taylor (1992), referring to such "politics of recognition," writes: "The thesis is that our identity is partly shaped by recognition or its absence, often by the misrecognition of others, and so a person or group of people can suffer real damage, real distortion, if the people or society around them mirror back to them a confining or demeaning or contemptible picture of themselves. Nonrecognition or misrecognition can inflict harm, can be a form of oppression, imprisoning someone in a false, distorted, and reduced mode of being" (25; see also Brown 1995, Fraser 1997).

Critics of identity/recognition politics argue that they cannot account for the complex nature of experience, the ways that "identities" intersect and inflect one another, and the forms of pervasive political and economic inequalities which are often made invisible through the universalisms of identity-based activism (e.g., Boykin 1996, Fraser 1997, Moraga and Anzaldúa 1981, Vaid 1995). The simple recognition of "race" or "gender" as categories of action within identity-based politics does not itself complicate the assumptions of homogenous and unitary identity, one which critics argue is implicitly grounded in the modern, white, male, Western model of the individual, intentional, self-maximizing subject (Alarcón 1990).

Other critics (e.g., Harvey 1993) focus their attention more specifically on the connections between the rise of identity/recognition politics and shifting political-economies from the early 1970s under the sign of neoliberalism, "the post-Keynesian model of the social order that champions unhindered market forces as the most effective means toward achieving economic growth and guaranteeing social welfare" (Maskovsky 2002: 266). From this perspective, identity/recognition politics is a co-option of the progressive left by state-supported business, and an abandonment of labor- and class-based alliances and a meaningful politics of justice in favor of a politics of liberal equality. Indeed, the resonance between identity-based movements and exploitable market niches has been lauded by some gay and lesbian writers as the locus for achieving recognition and rights (e.g., Kirk and Madsen 1989) even as others sound the alarm about reframing citizenship rights as consumer rights (e.g., Chasin 2001, Gluckman and Reed 1997, Maskovsky 2002, Raffo 1997, Sender 2004).[2] The concern for critics of market-as-constituency is the reduction of the political actor to (an implicitly white middle-class) consumer, and the erasure of a broader politics of economic and racial justice at the heart of LGBT politics.[3]

None of these processes is complete or hegemonic, however. Both Judith Butler (1997b) and Lisa Duggan (2003) argue that it is untenable — and ineffective — to classify "redistribution"/economic justice politics and "recognition"/identity politics as distinct entities. Nancy Fraser (1997) moreover points out that identity politics, often derided for their universalisms, originated as a challenge to the universalisms of whiteness, masculinity, and heterosexuality within the post–World War II left and "as such, they have everything to do with justice" (5). Duggan (2003) demonstrates through several case studies how a politics of economic justice cannot be separated from the intensely felt politics organized around identities. Further, both Edelman (2001) and Fox and Starn (1997) are somewhat leery of the appellation "new social movements" attached to the movements that have emerged in the postwar period, since the "new" ignores both the historical nature of many contemporary identity-based struggles but also the ways that collective action has never been simply about class or economic inequalities, as the distinction between "redistribution" and "recognition" implies.

Unsurprisingly, these debates also play out in transgender activism. First, contemporary transgender-identified activists have written extensively on the need to frame transgender politics in terms of a broader justice-based politics (Cartwright 2000, Feinberg 1996) or have explicitly critiqued the limits of identity-based politics (Wilchins 1997).[4] Second, as Meyerowitz notes, there is a long history of activism that could be claimed by contemporary transgender-identified people, much of which was framed in far more radical terms than simple "recognition" (2002: 226ff.; see also Members 1998). At the same time, the demand for recognition has been intimately woven into these politics. The early 1970s gay and lesbian-feminist media cited in chapter 1, for example, indicate that demands for "inclusion" are not new, as self-proclaimed drag queens, transvestites, and transexuals demanded recognition in a broader gay community.

Broad (2002) identifies another (and resonant) tension that complicates an easy definition of transgender activism as a simple recapitulation of recognition/identity politics. She notes how from the earliest transgender activism of the 1990s there have been ongoing tensions between what Bornstein (1998) characterizes as "gender defenders" (those who are invested in transgender as a stable identity) and the "genderfree" (a position which explicitly critiques binary gender as a system of social control) (see also Roen 2002). Broad extends Bornstein's analysis of the "genderfree" to show how these politics complicated 1990s transgender activism from the very beginning with a recognition among activists of the complexity of transgender experience along lines of embodiment, class, race, and sexuality. These complex dynamics are, in effect, also a debate over the constitution of a transgender social movement and what the goals of transgender activism should be: the broader transformation of a system of binary gender (e.g., Wilchins 1997); the assertion of rights for transgender-identified people within an existing structure of legal and medical definitions of sex, gender, and sexuality (e.g., Monro and Warren 2004); or a broader politics that takes into account systemic political, economic, and social inequalities (Currah 2003; see Gamson 1995).

Certainly, none of these are mutually exclusive positions, but despite the critiques of identity politics, movement "fracturings" (Broad 2002), and debates about strategy and goals, the primary focus of contemporary transgender activism has come to be characterized by claims to recognition and "inclusion."[5] Moreover, these claims in 1990s and early-twenty-first-century transgender activism have been reconfigured from the immediate post-Stonewall era. Contemporary transgender-identified activists demand "inclusion" of a *separate* group of people — transgender people — within a broader "LGBT" community, rather than an expansion of the explanatory and identificatory framework of "gay" as 1970s activists had. The 1990s thus ushered in a qualitatively different mode through which these differences could be codified and elaborated, that is, through the very institutionalization of identity categories in the organizations, community centers, and community-derived literatures in the post-1970s era.

Despite these complexities and debates over the nature of transgender activism there are some key moments around "inclusion" that define explicitly self-named transgender activism in the early 1990s. Califia (2003 [1997]), among others, cites the 1991 ejection of Nancy Burkholder, a transexual woman, from the Michigan Womyn's Music Festival, an annual music, cultural, and social event for "womyn born womyn," as a catalyzing moment in this new activism. This event, the subsequent banning of transwomen from the festival, and the protests that followed it (stimulated at least in part by Sandy Stone's "The Empire Strikes Back," published that same year), encapsulate many of the demands over inclusion that followed, but it also recalibrated the stakes of inclusion. After

Burkholder's ejection, a group of transactivists established Camp Trans near the entrance to the festival grounds, which has resulted in an ongoing debate about the status of transgender and transexual people (women and men) at the festival, an issue which has still not been fully resolved.[6] The disputes at Michigan encompass some central tensions in transgender activism as it developed in the 1990s. On the one hand, with the rise of transgender as a category of action and analysis, transgender-identified people and their allies were making claims about the rights of individuals to claim a gender regardless of their genitals or embodied history (e.g., Wilchins 1997). On the other hand, festival organizers and their supporters insisted on the unitary experience of women who had been born female and continued to identify as women throughout their life course ("womyn born womyn") as the criterion for entry to the festival (e.g., Mantilla 2000). Like the early 1970s disputes over FTMs and butch/femme roles (Rubin 2003), this is at its heart a dispute about what counts as "woman." But there is also a difference, for trans activists are not claiming membership in a broader "lesbian" or "gay" community but rather are calling for a specific recognition of the rights of transgender-identified people.

The activism around the murder of Brandon Teena (or for some, Teena Brandon) in 1993 is another central moment in this activism.[7] I will discuss this case in more depth in chapter 6, but as with Michigan, the transgender activism around Brandon Teena's murder encapsulates a new kind of demand: that lesbian and gay people recognize transgender people as a distinct category of person at the same time that their concerns be included in gay and lesbian activism and community making.

To quote Gamson (1995), "for whom, when, and how are stable collective identities *necessary* for social action and social change?" (412, emphasis in original). To this question I would add a few more. What are the stakes of "inclusion" if some, as with many of those whom I discussed in part II, already see themselves as being unproblematically "included" in the category "gay"? Do the "genderfree" politics that Broad (2002) discusses have effects that contest the institutionalization of transgender? And why would transgender-identified people *want* to be included in gay and lesbian organizations if doing so opens up the question of the relationship between these categories of identity?

As I have noted above, these questions also require that we attend to the racial and class politics of "inclusion." In order to try to understand how these politics fall out, I now want to turn to some places and events where the contemporary politics of inclusion play out and consider these latter questions in the light of these developments.

The first thing about the Center: it is a place.[8] The facade of the building on West 13th Street — a converted school built around the turn of the twentieth century — is represented in the Center's logo (or was until it was changed in 2002; see below). Established in 1983, it is one of the oldest of the now numerous lesbian and gay community centers in the country. By 1996, the Center was home to over three hundred groups and programs — from Gay and Lesbian Academics (GLA) to Gay Male S&M Activists (GMSMA); from the Imperial Court to Fat Is a Lesbian Issue (FLAB); and from Center Kids (a program for children of gay and lesbian parents) to aerobics classes for members of Senior Action in a Gay Environment (SAGE). It houses an archive, a library, and, until 1998, the Community Health Project. The AIDS Coalition to Unleash Power (ACT UP) — much depleted from its numbers in the early 1990s — meets here, and Sex Panic!, the pro-sex activist movement of the late 1990s, had its birth at the Center in the summer of 1997. It has a policy department whose staff lobby around local and national legislative issues, and which coordinates an annual "Get Out the Vote" campaign. On the sidewalk outside the Center there are generally groups of people talking, smoking, eating, waiting to go to a meeting, or just leaving one. In the evenings, when most of the group meetings take place, the Center is abuzz with activity, music, demands for silence, suppressed laughter, sometimes angry voices. It threatens to burst at the seams and it's surprising that it hasn't. Center users are diverse along lines of race, cultural background, age, gender, embodiment, language, and so on, and despite the name of the Center — until 2002, "The Lesbian and Gay Community Services Center" — many of those who use its services are bisexual- or transgender-identified. Transpeople in particular come to use the GIP's services — counseling, support group meetings, and so on.

At the bottom of the Center's letterhead is the statement: "Serving the NYC lesbian, gay, bisexual, and transgender communities since 1983." But the addition of this tagline only happened in November 1998, a month after the Center relocated to temporary quarters in the Meat Market. By making this claim, the letterhead achieves a subtle rewriting of an ongoing history in several ways. First, it gives transgender a history stretching back (at least) as far as 1983. Second, marshaling "and transgender" alongside "gay, lesbian, bisexual" implies both a common and uninterrupted history of coexistence while simultaneously differentiating between them.

Not coincidently, the change to the letterhead was a response to a growing call for *inclusion* of bisexual and transgender people in gay and lesbian organizations and spaces. The Center's inclusion of transgender (as a category) and transgender-identified people in its operations and institutional policy casts some light on the ways that such processes take shape at the level of day-to-day decision making in institutional contexts. However, the active inclusion of transgender-identified people in the Center's life — and particularly the establishment of the GIP — has not been uncontested, nor has such inclusion happened easily. Two people at the Center have been particularly important in this history. Under Executive Director Richard Burns, the Center has had the benefit of unbroken leadership since 1987, a fact of bureaucracy not shared by most other such centers. Burns's leadership has had important implications for developing policy both in New York and nationally around many issues, but also around the issue of inclusion. A second player in this history has been Dr. Barbara Warren, former director of Mental Health and Social Services (MHSS) at the Center. She recounted some of this history in an interview:

> There have always been people who are transgender involved in the Center, but they weren't necessarily identified, nor would they identify as such, because they weren't necessarily welcome as such. If they were drag queens, and they were in the Imperial Court for example, they were welcome to do that but even they were on the fringes. It made some gay people, I think gay men, uncomfortable because even though it was a long tradition in the queer community to do drag, that was for the clubs and not necessarily for the "respectable" Center. I don't think that the Center Board or the Center staff ever felt that way, but I definitely think that within the "community" such as it was eleven, twelve years ago, a lot of people were uncomfortable with that. (Interview, March 2, 1999)

Warren's original contact with transgender-identified clients was as the lone counselor of the nascent Project Connect in the late 1980s, a substance-abuse counseling service at the Center which subsequently became one of four programs — including GIP — under her direction. Through a transexual client, Warren began to learn about transexual issues and as word got out that Warren was a sympathetic counselor, people from all over New York soon began seeking counseling for gender-identity issues. Riki Anne Wilchins approached Warren in 1989 to create a social services project specifically geared for transexual people and Warren turned to Burns to assess the possibilities. Warren remembers it as follows:

> So I went to Richard, and Richard's only knowledge of transexuality was Janice Raymond's book.[9] To his credit, he didn't just say "oh, no!" but he said, "This is what I know, and this book is really opposed, and a lot of lesbians say that this is bogus." But he was willing to be educated and he was willing to have the Board get educated. At that point I'd been here a couple of years and they trusted that if I said that this was a population that was in need and that sort of fit, they were willing to be supportive of it. (Interview, March 2, 1999)

The official establishment of GIP's precursor, STA,[10] resulted in some opposition from various lesbian and gay Center users. In particular, there was a concerted effort on the part of a lesbian activist group to oppose the formalization of the program:

> Six months into STA we got zapped, or I got zapped . . . [11] Well, this group spent three days relentlessly calling our number, asking for me, and leaving messages. And the messages were getting increasingly hostile. First they asked about "transexuals at the Center" and then the last messages were "tell the gay man who runs the Center that only a gay man would hire a straight woman who would let in transexuals," you know, "pretending to be women." That was the gist of the messages. But we didn't stand down. We thought they were wrong, and the Board supported us. And it passed. We had some incidents where groups of women who had meetings tried to throw out transexuals that came to the meetings. But we said "You can't do that." We never had a woman-only space here anyway. We always had a policy of inclusion. So, you know, they couldn't really do that anyway, to anybody. (Barbara Warren, Interview, March 2, 1999)

The Center hired Rosalyne Blumenstein in 1994, first as a counselor and later as the Project's director, cementing its commitment to inclusion.

Another Center staff member notes the complexities resulting from these shifts in Center policy, particularly the perceived resistance to "inclusion" by its financial supporters:

There's a lot of work to do for the Center to be more inclusive, but I think the political climate said it was OK [for GIP to be established in 1990]. But how do you make sure everybody has a place at the table when you also have to play with the people that support the very foundation of this institution? It's a very difficult position. Rich gay white men on the Hill have no idea what the GIP does [and] would not want to be connected to anything that's transgender. So it's taking the risk with a multi-million dollar institution, which is really hard. (Anonymous Center staff member, Interview, March 1, 1999)

By "the Hill" the staffer is referencing "Capitol Hill," to index the political power of the gay men (and, to a lesser extent, lesbians) who are the Center's primary financial and political supporters, many of whom she claims are leery of being "more inclusive." This trepidation has indeed played out since the early 1990s around several state and local legislative issues. At the national level it has been most evident in the long-standing refusal of the Human Rights Campaign (HRC), the preeminent gay and lesbian political lobbying organization, to support inclusion of transgender-identified people in the Employment Non-Discrimination Act (ENDA), a case I will return to later.

Several things stand out in these narratives of inclusion and change. First, and self-evidently, "inclusion" is not an uncomplicated achievement. Both Warren and the Center staff member refer to "inclusion" as a progressive move, but both also point to the resistance by people who oppose such inclusion: gay men uncomfortable with drag queens, lesbians who believe transexuals are "pretending to be women," or "rich gay white men" who "would not want to be connected to anything that's transgender." The inclusion of an official program for transexuals in 1990 was also predicated on an "exclusion" of non-transexual women-only groups at the Center. On the other hand, for the anonymous poster writer cited earlier, the work done by Warren, Burns, and others does not represent sufficient inclusion. Moreover, it is instructive to note that Warren mentions only concerns about transexual women and that transexual men apparently did not figure in these early debates over inclusion, another kind of exclusion that some transmen see as an ongoing problem with the GIP.

A second point to note is how these moves toward inclusion resonate with concurrent debates at the Center about gender, race, and "inclusion." The Center is perceived by some people of color as a "white" space, particularly with its location in the affluent Greenwich Village.[12] Center staff and directors are at pains to address this issue, while at the same time they recognize the structural elements of Center bureaucracy, which has mostly white men in director positions and mostly women of color as janitors and maintenance workers. It is also important to note that while "race," "gender parity," and "transgender inclusion" are all issues frequently discussed at the Center — and, as we will see, in other LGBT contexts — they are not generally discussed as interrelated.

The third issue raised by "inclusion" is that of instrumentality: how does inclusion happen? This case is useful in that it highlights how individual decisions shape changes in policy and institutional culture. The willingness of Warren, Burns, and the Center's staff and board to explicitly "include" transgender-identified people in its operations and mission shows how, at a micro-political level, social change occurs. But it is also important to note the larger context within which such change occurs. The Center itself — established in 1983 — has to be understood as an outcome of a decade of activism, an institution that would have been unthinkable ten to fifteen years earlier. Likewise, the founding of the GIP would have been unthinkable prior to the late 1980s and early 1990s, at precisely the moment when "transgender" was crystallizing into its meaning as a collective term. Warren notes that from early in the 1990s,

> it soon became obvious that it ["transgender"] was being used as an umbrella term. I think we were actually the first to use the word in government documents where we were describing things that we were doing. Other people had used it before us to self-describe, on the West Coast. And so we started to use it here officially, putting it in documents and proposals. A little while later [in 1993] we did an interview with a newspaper, [*New York*] *Newsday,* and they printed the word. That was the first time we saw it in print in the mainstream press. (Interview, March 2, 1999)

While I do not want to suggest a causal relationship between the appearance of "transgender" as a category in New York and the establishment of the GIP, the institutional influence of the New York Center was certainly instrumental in its adoption by social service agencies, government funding sources, and mass media in the early 1990s.

But the fourth, and perhaps most interesting, issue raised by "inclusion" is: why would transgender people *want* to be included in such an institution? Concomitantly, why would gay men and lesbians be resistant to such inclusion? And finally, what changed, so that, in Warren's words, the resistance "passed"? The reasons that newly transgender-identified people would want to be included at the Center are simultaneously simple and complex. Simply put, in political terms, for a group marked by gender/sexual difference in mainstream U.S. society which needs to access a range of services and support, an institution such as the Lesbian and Gay Community Services Center is an obvious choice. Further, transgender-identified people argue for inclusion precisely because, as I noted earlier, it is through institutionalization that one's demands are recognized by the state. But also, as I outlined in chapter 1, despite the resistance of (some) gay and lesbian people, many gay-, lesbian-, and transgender-identified people see a historical relationship in their common social ostracism even as they have been sorting out the differences between themselves.

Finally, I will make a related observation which is linked to these questions in a direct way, though it may not be evident at first: the oddest thing to me about the Center is that I have very few field notes about it. Most weeks during my fieldwork, I would drop in at least once a day. The Center was my base during fieldwork, the place where I had access to resources, conducted interviews, picked up condoms for my outreach work, and where I could type up field notes. I have many notes on the GIP, but very few notes about the Center itself. Looking back, the reason is obvious: the Center was a "lesbian and gay" center, and while the GIP was located there, that hardly seemed to matter to me at the time. Yet, as I am arguing, it is in "gay and lesbian" contexts that "transgender" as a category has formed much of its shape and meaning.

This brief history of "inclusion" at the Center serves to show how social change happens historically in the small-scale and day-to-day operations of organizations like the Center. Next, I want to explore the emotion and instrumentality of "inclusion" at a particular moment, the 1996 National Gay and Lesbian Task Force (NGLTF) Creating Change conference.

CREATING CHANGE: BELONGING AND EXCLUSION

The first thing about Creating Change: it is not a place. Rather, it is an annual five-day gathering of several thousand lesbian and gay ("*and*" as we will see, "bisexual *and* transgender") activists under the auspices of the NGLTF, the most significant national organization for gay and lesbian ("*and* bisexual *and* transgender") grassroots activism. Creating Change is a moveable feast, meeting every fall in cities as varied as Washington, D.C., San Diego, Pittsburgh, and Oakland and transforming look-alike conference hotels into hotbeds of activism, strategy sessions, workshops, and panel discussions.

At five on a Wednesday morning in November 1996, I was whisked off to D.C. by bus with every full-time member of the Center staff, from Richard Burns, the executive director, to Flo, the new maintenance worker. I went because Barbara told me "you should see it" and because I could get a free ride on the bus. I justified it as fieldwork because I knew several transgender activists would be there. But even as the bus pulled out, I was regretting the days I would be giving up for doing my "real" fieldwork: outreach, bars, clubs, and the Meat Market. We were leaving on Wednesday to make the pre-conference "race institutes," a day where white people and people of color would break up into workshops in order to discuss issues of race, racism, and racial exclusions in the gay and lesbian ("*and* bisexual *and* transgender") community. Given recent racially charged confrontations at the Center, it was considered vital that the entire staff be able to attend these workshops. Upon arriving at the hotel, I joined the white people. When we entered the room where the institute was already underway, those present broke into applause. It seemed that we had Arrived, and the sense of belonging was overwhelming.

These two themes — the sense of belonging and the anger over exclusions — pervaded the entire five days. Indeed, "inclusion" of people of color and of bisexual and transgender people in the national gay and lesbian movement was central to workshops, informal conversations, and public activism. Bisexual and transgender activists were out in force, and many gay and lesbian activists were speaking up for them too. For example, on Thursday morning there was a Community Centers Institute, a workshop for people who run community centers around the country, attended by about seventy people. The workshop was facilitated by Richard Burns, and on the table for discussion was a proposal to create a National Association of Lesbian and Gay Community Centers. Conversation in the room turned quickly to the question of "inclusion." Why isn't it called the National Association of Lesbian, Gay, Bisexual, and Transgender Community Centers? someone demanded. Burns pointed out that it would be unfair to include the "B" and the "T" if centers weren't actually providing space and services for these groups. Yet, when asked which centers represented in the room did provide such spaces and services, every single hand went up. The conversation went back and forth, getting rather heated at some points, but nothing was resolved. This was just the beginning of the calls for "inclusion" that weekend, but at the same time, while transgender and bisexual inclusion animated this discussion, the question of racial "inclusion" — so prevalent in the previous day's race institutes — was never mentioned.

Saturday was the biggest day of the conference and the most fraught. At 9 a.m., there was a networking meeting of transgender activists. An informal coalition had been made with the bisexual activist caucus, and we joined them at ten to discuss the battle plan for the day. Several activities were planned: one was a picket of the Human Rights Campaign's (HRC) booth to protest their refusal to include "gender identity or expression" as a protected category in ENDA. But most significantly — the *coup de main* — was a plan to commandeer the podium prior to the Saturday afternoon plenary session in front of 2,500 activists, where a statement was to be read.

Just before noon, people began to file into the hotel ballroom for the plenary address by Carmen Vazquez, director of public policy at the New York Center and a well-known Puerto Rican lesbian and socialist activist. A few minutes before Vazquez was due to speak, two people stepped up to the podium — one bisexual- and one transgender-identified. Each of them spoke briefly about the myriad ways that they had felt excluded over the past few days because of participants' failure to use language "inclusive of bisexual and transgender people." Meanwhile, Phyllis Frye, the founder and executive director of the International Conference on Transgender Law and Employment Policy (ICTLEP), was going around the vast ballroom attaching signs which read "*and* bisexual *and* transgender" to each "National Gay and Lesbian Task Force" banner or poster.

Then, after a dramatic pause, the speakers asked everyone who was bisexual- or transgender-identified to come to the front of the hall. To rousing applause, about two hundred people, many wearing Transexual Menace t-shirts, stood up and walked forward, hugging, punching the air, and carrying signs proclaiming "*and* bisexual *and* transgender." Then the two speakers asked everyone present who had used language inclusive of bisexual and transgender people during the conference to stand up. Almost everyone in the room sprang to their feet, and there was more applause. Finally, to those who remained seated, one of the speakers asked them to stand if they pledged themselves to being inclusive of bisexual and transgender concerns in their future work. The entire room was on its feet, applauding wildly.

There is something visceral and immediate I am unable to capture here about the emotional impact of these days' events, the sense of belonging as much as the anger over exclusion. Yet the emotion is central, for it points to the ways in which the politics of identity becomes so very charged around the negotiation of identity boundaries. Following the above events, in 1997 NGLTF changed its mission statement (though not its name) to "include" bisexual and transgender people, and bisexual- and transgender-inclusive language seems to have become the order of the day in progressive organizations.

So, with all this rousing support and these changes, why, one might ask, does the activism around this issue continue? One reason is foregrounded by the Center staff member I quote above: while 2,500 left-leaning grass-roots activists might be all for "bisexual and transgender inclusion," such ideas do not always play well with other segments of the (firmly) gay and lesbian community. I can draw out several ways in which "inclusion" and a certain kind of "progress" can be traced from the stories I tell above: in having the Gender Identity Project at the powerful New York Center; in "transgender" being included at the foot of the Center's letterhead or in NGLTF's mission statement; or in the willingness of HRC staffers to hear the concerns of bisexual and transgender activists at Creating Change as we picketed their table.

However, like the history of "sorting out" of gender/sexual-variant identities, this kind of direct action and its outcomes also has a history. The Lavender Menace takeover of the podium at the Second Congress to Unite Women in May 1970 is one such example. There, the demand by lesbian protestors was for the women's movement to acknowledge and incorporate the particular concerns of lesbians, which, to that point, had been studiously ignored. But, like the demands of the early 1970s drag queens, transvestites, and others, the Lavender Menace zappers were demanding a reorientation of the categories that formed the basis for activism—that of "woman" in the latter case and of "gay" in the former. At Creating Change, however, while demands for inclusion were broadly invoked and the tactics not new, the goals were qualitatively different. Transgender activists were arguing for the inclusion of a new *category* which is animated by a claim that non-normative gendered identities and sexual orientation are separate issues.

These dynamics are shaped by both historical and contemporary concerns. The demands for inclusion are mounted against the perceived intransigence of accommodationist gay and lesbian leaders. Like post-Stonewall leftist activists who opposed the accommodationist tactics of the homophile movement, transgender activists see in resistance to "inclusion" a fear that it would set back the gains that the gay and lesbian movement has made. This indeed was HRC's reasons for not including "gender identity or expression" in ENDA, and it is not an insignificant fear, for "transgender" is also available to socially conservative groups as a new discursive tool to characterize the gay and lesbian movement as deviant, anti-family, and un-American.

What was most striking about the events at this conference, though, was the relative disconnection between the concerns of transgender and bisexual activists and the anti-racism activism evident in the first two days. While activists debated the concerns of both people of color and transgender/bisexual activists throughout the conference, these concerns were not generally linked. Carmen Vazquez's plenary, coming right after the event described above, was one moment where they were: Vazquez made an impassioned plea for a lesbian and gay politics which would be transformed by acknowledgment of its deep roots in, and shared concerns with, communities of color, working-class communities, and the histories of transgender- and bisexual-identified people. On the heels of the calls for inclusion, Vazquez's speech received its own ovation. Yet, other than here, "race" and "class" at Creating Change seemed most often to be understood as discrete categories of analysis and social action. In both talk and practice, they resided alongside "sexuality" and "gender" as a kind of difference, issues that were essential to engage and discuss in the lesbian and gay movement, but not disruptive or transformative of the primary category that organized the conference — "sexuality" — as Vazquez had so forcefully demanded.

In the next section, I look at how these issues play out in legislative advocacy some years after the events described above. While the social field I invoke next is the level of national legislation, it engages this question of "inclusion" in gay and lesbian organizations — and the place of race and class in their politics — because of the players involved. In the debates over transgender-inclusive language in legislation, "inclusion" indexes a progressive move but simultaneously performs the institutionalization of a "difference" model of democratic representation which leaves categories of action and analysis unexamined.

HATE CRIMES AND CATEGORY CRISES:
GENDERPAC AND THE HUMAN RIGHTS CAMPAIGN

The first thing about the Gender Public Advocacy Coalition (GenderPAC) and the Human Rights Campaign (HRC): they have an uneasy relationship. HRC's position on ENDA in particular has caused enormous bad feeling among transgender activists, and when GenderPAC was founded in 1996, the amendment of the pending bill was seen as a priority. On the other hand, since GenderPAC's founding HRC had facilitated its access to members of Congress and aided GenderPAC members with advice on lobbying, while (until 2003) standing by the position recounted above: that gay and lesbian identities and transgender identities are separate, and that the inclusion of "gender identity or expression" in the ENDA bill would not only scuttle it but would also contradict this very distinction.

But in March 1999, a few GenderPAC members — including me — were invited by HRC to a reception in Washington, D.C., in honor of the sponsors of ENDA and the just-introduced Hate Crimes Prevention Act (HCPA). HCPA was a bill promoted by the Hate Crimes Coalition, an umbrella group of civil rights organizations which includes among others HRC, the American Civil Liberties Union (ACLU), the National Association for the Advancement of Colored People (NAACP), and — perhaps unthinkably a few years earlier — GenderPAC. With the publicity given to the then-recent murders of Matthew Shepard in Wyoming, James Byrd in Texas, and Billy Jack Gaither in Arkansas, those behind the HCPA bill were cautiously optimistic that it had a chance of passage. Shepard and Gaither were both gay men whose murders were widely publicized as homophobia-inspired hate crimes, while the murder of Byrd — a black man in Texas dragged to death behind a truck by a group of white men — spurred anti-racism activism around hate crimes legislation. The linkage of these three murders highlights the coalitions between groups working on issues of race and sexuality, as well as gender, religion, and ethnicity. The bill was aimed at bringing together and strengthening existing federal hate crimes legislation and contained the phrase "actual or perceived . . . gender" as a category which would be covered, wording that is noticeably absent from ENDA.[13] As with the grassroots activists at Creating Change, national activism and advocacy around hate crimes bring together people around diverse issues, but linked by a common experience of social injustice. As with Creating Change, though, this coalition simultaneously marks a recognition of similar goals but also of an implicit claim to the differences between them.

Riki Anne, Carrie, Julia, and I — conservatively dressed, and somewhat nervous — traveled to Washington on the train, planning what we were going to say to the HRC staffers, the legislative assistants, and, if we got the chance, members of Congress themselves. It was agreed among us that we should stress the point that GenderPAC was focused on protecting *all* people whose gender expression varies from the norm, not just those identified as transgender, a central point in GenderPAC's policy (and one I will take up in chapter 6). Once in D.C., we were met by Dana Priesing, another GenderPAC member, and headed straight to the Longworth House Office Building. The passages of the congressional office buildings are long, high, and cool, and you can hear the echo of your footsteps return to you as a pleasant complete sound, like the closing of a book. You can almost smell the power here, and it is intoxicating. Once we found the large reception room, we set off to mingle and push HRC members and legislative assistants on the importance of including language that would bring transgender-identified and other gender-variant people into ENDA, just as it appeared in HCPA.

The five of us wandered around the room meeting the movers and shakers, reminding them of the less publicized but equally grisly killings of five transgender-identified women in the first few months of 1999 alone. I talked about Vianna Faye Williams, whose murder I will discuss in chapter 6. An HRC staffer assured me that the lawmakers' intent that HCPA should include transgender-identified people would be spelled out during the legislative debates, an important step in guiding judges' interpretations of the legislation's scope. It seemed that HRC had fewer concerns around the inclusion of such language in HCPA than in ENDA.

Later, Senator Edward Kennedy came to the podium and gave a speech to rousing applause; he was followed by several members of the House of Representatives. Representative Barney Frank, one of only a few openly gay or lesbian members of Congress, spoke at length about bipartisanship and of the importance of recognizing that "gay, lesbian, bisexual, and transgender" people are targets of hate crimes. Then, in front of Senator

Kennedy, the Representatives, and everyone else, Elizabeth Birch, the executive director of HRC, extended a special note of thanks to the "transgender activists" who had attended and mentioned Riki and Nancy Nangeroni (another GenderPAC activist) by name. We looked at one another over the heads of the assembled dignitaries with raised eyebrows.

This recognition was a double-edged sword for Riki, however. On the one hand, the recognition of GenderPAC was a significant achievement. On the other, by classing hir as a "transgender activist," it undercut the broader politics of gender variance s/he aims to engage where, as s/he argues, it is not only transgender-identified people but gay, lesbian, bisexual, and heterosexual people who are frequently discriminated against on the basis of gender-variant expressions. As we will see in the next chapter, this political stance has produced its own dynamics, with transgender activists claiming that Riki is, essentially, *excluding* transgender people by refusing to frame hir politics through that category.

Here, though, I want to make another point: "actual or perceived gender" can be strategically included in HCPA partly because the bill has more chance of passage but also because it stands alongside "sexual orientation" with other categories of social difference: race, ethnicity, religion. By the same logic, they can be just as strategically excluded from ENDA because transgender people, like Jews or African Americans, are conceived of as a distinct group. Moreover, even though the legislative phrasing of "actual or perceived gender" aims to account for a broader range of violence than simply violence against transgender-identified people, the citation of this category in reference to Riki as a "transgender activist" reasserts the difference of a coherent group. If "transgender issues" are perceived to be analogous to — but not the same as — gay and lesbian issues, then the effect of the discourse of "inclusion" works just as well to exclude: to exclude transgender-inclusive language from some bills and to produce clear lines between transgender-identified and gay/lesbian people. More significantly, it works to exclude the idea that gender variance (or race, or class, or religion) impacts on "sexuality." And finally, the disaggregation of race (or religion, ethnicity, etc.) from sexuality or gender brackets those concerns both in legislative and policy contexts.

In the next section I look at how, outside the rarefied halls of Congress, race, gender, sexuality, age, class, and other social differences can come to collapse into one another in ways that cannot be accounted for by discrete legislative, activist, or social service categories.

In the intervening years since the events described above, these questions have become broadly debated and have been acted upon. Despite the historically complex relationship between the women's movement and transexual women, in 1997 the National Organization for Women (NOW) passed a resolution recognizing that transexual women have a place in NOW. In New York City and other jurisdictions around the United States, legislation has been enacted to extend hate crimes and nondiscrimination laws to include transgender and gender-variant people. Moreover, in December 1998, the HRC issued a statement that "strongly supports public and private initiatives that counter discrimination based on real or perceived gender identity." The statement continues: "[HRC] is committed to a mutually beneficial relationship with the transgender community. It is our hope that such a relationship will help inform and craft a shared vision of a world that honors and respects all people regardless of sexual orientation or gender identity" (In Your Face 1998).[14] In 2001, HRC added "transgender" to its mission statement, and in 2003, the organization finally agreed to add transgender-inclusive language to ENDA, even though it continues to support the non-inclusive version that is still before the House (but see page 258 n. 9). Again, the focus on inclusion is evident in all these shifts and marks significant progress for the political vision of the organizations involved. But as I have argued above, inclusion is not an uncomplicated move, nor a simple story of progress.

Before I consider these shifts, I want to return once more to New York and the first ethnographic site in this chapter. At the end of 1998, the Center moved to temporary quarters on Little West 12th Street to allow for renovations at its nearby 13th Street site, and directly into one of my other primary field sites, the Meat Market. Greenwich Village and the Meat Market lie within the city's sixth police precinct, supposedly tolerant of non-normative genders and sexualities because it has had to accommodate a large and powerful gay and lesbian population since the Stonewall riots of 1969.

In November 1998, just as the Center was moving into its new premises *New York* magazine reported on protests by white, middle-class residents of the abutting, highly valued residential neighborhoods (Horowitz 1998). Residents — while trumpeting their own "tolerance" — were demanding a police crackdown on fem queen prostitution in the Meat Market, linking it with a rise in crime and an impact on their "quality of life" (see Chesluk 2004). Certainly, there were a number of highly publicized murders involving transgender-identified people in the Meat Market in late 1998, highlighting and linking the issues of crime and prostitution both for local residents and for the wider New York population. While residents denied it, Center staffers linked the publicity accorded this issue to the (transgender-inclusive) Center's move to the Meat Market. Center staffers accused protesters of hypocrisy since the gay and lesbian community in Greenwich Village — the site of Stonewall itself — had spent decades resisting and protesting police harassment of sexually oriented activities, both public and private. Moreover, the fact that residents specifically targeted transgender-identified sex workers of color resulted in further accusations of both racism and transphobia by local activists. The town hall meeting discussed in chapter 2 was in fact partly a response to residents' protests. Several members of the audience argued that it was the Center's "inclusion" of transgender-identified people that had given rise to residents' fears and the mobilization of police action against the Meat Market girls. Thus, "inclusion" was linked in many ways to the presence of sex workers and people of color in the "tolerant" Village, issues which became fraught as they bumped up against the complex relationships among political and economic structures, property ownership, race, crime, publicity, and perceptions of what kinds of sexual activity are considered acceptable.

The issue of sex work in the Meat Market has not been resolved, as one might expect. In early May of 2002, Village residents — through an organization rather dramatically called Residents in Distress (RID) — organized a protest, symbolically in the same park opposite the Stonewall Inn where the gay and lesbian ("*and* bisexual *and* transgender") movement is claimed to have been born. The few RID members were outnumbered at least fifteen to one by counterdemonstrators including Melissa (by now an elected Democratic Party county judicial delegate), staff and clients of several social service organizations (many of them study participants during my fieldwork), members of the New York Association for Gender Rights Advocacy (NYAGRA), city politicians, myself, and students from a class I was then teaching at NYU entitled "Transgender Histories, Identities, and Politics." RID members were certainly not all gay and lesbian but nonetheless were representative of a white, middle-class gay and lesbian elite in the eyes of the counterdemonstrators. The larger counterdemonstration was far more diverse with young, African American or Latina, and many transgender-identified people in attendance, all crammed into the tiny triangular park.

The event turned into something of a shouting match, with a city council member attempting to mediate between the two sides. In this deeply symbolic site, claims about inclusion and exclusion flew to and fro, animating both contemporary concerns and reiterating historical battles that had taken place on this same ground over respectability and "flamboyance," peace and noise, privacy and publicity, accommodation and confrontation, but this time inflected more clearly by class and racial differences. More than once that evening, a counterdemonstrator pointed to the Stonewall Inn and shouted the claim that "transgender people" had started the revolution that had enabled gay and lesbian people to become politically connected property owners. While RID did not explicitly frame its claims in terms of transgender-identified people or people of color, their complaints about noise, sex work, and drug use in the Village were seen as code words for transgender-identified youth of color. The counterdemonstrators were particularly incensed since the city council had only a few days before passed Intro. No. 24. Commonly referred to as the "transgender rights bill," this legislation had extended the meaning of "gender" in the city's human rights ordinance to include "actual or perceived sex, and shall also include a person's gender identity, self image, appearance, behavior, or statement, whether or not that gender identity, self image, appearance, behavior, or statement is different from that traditionally associated with the legal sex assigned to that person at birth." In short, while not using the term "transgender," the legislation was expressly intended to extend local anti-discrimination law to cover transgender-identified people, and the city had even produced a postcard as part of a public awareness campaign, advertising the bill's provisions (see figure 6a and b).[15] The RID demo seemed to fly in the face of this victory, and it was perhaps the propinquity of these events that turned the debates that evening, time and again, to the question of "inclusion" and "exclusion" of transgender-identified people from the Village and from history.

However, like the debates over the Center's relocation in 1998, the RID demo condensed a series of much broader issues: real estate values and class- and race-inflected social values, policing and freedom, urban renewal and the ideals of democratic use of the city's spaces. If the issue of "prostitution" was the express concern for RID, it was one undergirded by a broader social imaginary of historical and contemporary gender vari-

THE TERM "GENDER" SHALL INCLUDE ACTUAL OR PERCEIVED SEX AND SHALL ALSO INCLUDE A PERSON'S GENDER IDENTITY, SELF-IMAGE, APPEARANCE, BEHAVIOR OR EXPRESSION WHETHER OR NOT THAT GENDER IDENTITY, SELF-IMAGE, APPEARANCE, BEHAVIOR OR EXPRESSION IS DIFFERENT FROM THAT TRADITIONALLY ASSOCIATED WITH THE LEGAL SEX ASSIGNED TO THAT PERSON AT BIRTH

NYC COMMISSION ON HUMAN RIGHTS, 40 RECTOR ST. 212.306.7450

MICHAEL R. BLOOMBERG, MAYOR   PATRICIA L. GATLING, COMMISSIONER

BI-GENDERED CD CROSSDRESSER DRAG KING DRAG QUEEN FEMME QUEEN FEMALE-TO-MALE FTM GENDER BENDER GENDER BLENDER GENDER GIFTED GENDER QUEER MALE-TO-FEMALE MTF NEW MAN NON-OP NON-OPERATIVE TRANSEXUAL PASSING MAN PASSING WOMAN POST-OP POST-OPERATIVE TRANSEXUAL PRE-OP PRE-OPERATIVE TRANSEXUAL SEX CHANGE SHEMALE TG THIRD SEX TRANNIE/TRANNY TRANS TRANSBUTCH TRANSEXUAL/TRANSSEXUAL TRANSGENDER TRANSGENDERIST TRANSIE TRANSPERSON TRANSEXED TRANSEXED MAN TRANSEXED WOMAN TRANSEXUAL MAN TRANSEXUAL WOMAN TRANSVESTITE TRANS-WOMAN TS TWO-SPIRIT

QUESTION: **WHO IS THE TRANSGENDER COMMUNITY?**
ANSWER: Transgender = an umbrella term used to group the gender different communities.

QUESTION: **DOES THE NYC HUMAN RIGHTS LAW PROTECT TRANSGENDER PEOPLE?**
ANSWER: Yes. Transgender people are protected from discrimination in employment, housing, public accommodations (providers of goods and/or services, such as restaurants, medical offices, hospitals, theatres, etc.) and bias-related harassment. The definition of "gender" adopted in the Law is on the reverse side of this card and was written to clearly include people who are or who are perceived to be transgender.

QUESTION: **IF I HAVE BEEN DISCRIMINATED AGAINST, WHERE DO I CALL?**
ANSWER: Call to set up an intake appointment to speak to an attorney at the Commission **212-306-7450**.

GENDER IDENTITY PROJECT NYC LGBT COMMUNITY CENTER 212-620-7310 www.gaycenter.org

MANHATTAN DISTRICT ATTORNEY'S OFFICE - KATIE DORAN, ADVISOR FOR THE GLBT COMMUNITY 212-335-9021

NY ASSOCIATION FOR GENDER RIGHTS ADVOCACY (NYAGRA) 212-675-3288 x266 www.nyagra.tripod.com

SYLVIA RIVERA LEGAL RESOURCE PROGRAM - URBAN JUSTICE CENTER 646-602-5699 www.urbanjustice.org

LAMBDA LEGAL DEFENSE & EDUCATION FUND 212-809-8585 www.lambdalegal.org

MICHAEL CALLEN-AUDRE LORDE COMMUNITY HEALTH CENTER 212-271-7200 www.callenlorde.org

NYC GAY & LESBIAN ANTI-VIOLENCE PROJECT 212-714-1184 www.avp.org

WEST VILLAGE TRANSLEGAL CLINIC C/O LESBIAN & GAY LAW ASSOCIATION (LEGAL) NYC LGBT COMMUNITY CENTER 212-620-7310 www.gaycenter.org

LESBIAN & GAY IMMIGRATION RIGHTS TASK FORCE 212-818-9639 www.lgirtf.org

NYAGRA www.nyagra@nyagra.com

POSITIVE HEALTH PROJECT 212-465-8304 www.positivehealthproject.org

FIGURE 6a and b: NYC Commission on Human Rights postcard publicizing the "Transgender Rights Bill."

FIGURE 7: Postcard advertising the reopening of the Lesbian, Gay, Bisexual, and Transgender Community Center.

ance associated with publicity, blackness, poverty, disruption, and danger. Thus "transgender inclusion" became a flashpoint at this demonstration in the same way that gender-variant "flamboyant" behavior or "male-identification" had in the late 1960s and early 1970s, even as all these figures stood for far more. When a RID representative made general claims about drug use and residents' fears of being attacked, counterdemonstrators yelled back that they were "stereotyping transgender people." And when RID heatedly denied charges of racism, counterdemonstrators called out the names of black and Latina sex workers and fem queens who had been murdered in the Meat Market or nearby.

That evening remains for me a particularly dense node in the dynamic I am considering here. The presence of myself and my students, the location opposite the Stonewall Inn, the recent passage of Intro. No. 24, the presence of a city council member who was one of its sponsors, the presence of fem queens and social service agency representations . . . all point to how transgender as a category of political action has enabled a transformation — but also a reduction — of debates over class, racial, gendered, and sexual difference in the United States through the overdetermined mode of "inclusion."

Two months later, in late June of 2002, the Center returned to its newly renovated home on 13th Street. At the public opening, the Center's new logo and name were officially adopted. The image of the Center's facade had been replaced by a startling orange sunburst, its shard-like rays representing diversity in inclusion (see figure 7). From now on, announced Richard Burns, the place would be known as "The Lesbian, Gay, Bisexual, and Transgender Community Center." Just as at Creating Change, the audience erupted in applause and roars of approval.

INCLUSION AND DIVERSITY

The various shifts in this chapter—discursive as well as historical and geographical—mark a set of debates around various claims to "inclusion." On the one hand, organizations like the Center, NGLTF, HRC, and even NOW have included—in a variety of ways—the demands of transgender-identified activists for recognition in their organizations. On the other hand, acts perceived as exclusions are performed by the same or other organizations or by protestors who, for a wide variety of reasons, oppose aspects of what "inclusion" implies. Finally, different kinds of "inclusion" resonate with and against one another.

Yet these dynamics are not necessarily diametrically opposed, nor are they self-evidently one thing or another. The anonymous person who posted the sign on the Center's notice board clearly felt excluded despite all the attempts to make him or her feel included. The residents who were protesting sex work in the Meat Market were balancing the exclusions they wanted—sex work, crime, perhaps even poor people of color—with the image of tolerance and inclusion for which the Village has had a reputation. And HRC's informal—and important—inclusions of GenderPAC in the shadowy insider world of Washington politics, its public recognition of transgender leaders and issues, and even its change of heart on transgender-inclusive language, are the flip side of the firm adherence to the claim that transgender people have different political and social histories, goals, and needs from gay and lesbian people, a position, indeed, shared by most transgender activists.

As noted earlier, critics of identity-based politics argue that the reduction of social issues to single-entity interest groups ignores the intersections of a range of social differences we name through categories like gender, sexuality, class, race, age, and so forth. From this perspective attempts to represent these domains within identity-based groups do not challenge the boundaries of groups themselves but rather augment the central concerns of a group. And indeed, racial injustice, class differences, or gender politics are incorporated in mainstream gay and lesbian activism through the trope of inclusion, rooted in a model of diversity. This has become the mode through which people of color, non-U.S. gay men and lesbians, working-class gay men and lesbians, or — increasingly — transgender-identified people are represented in a movement based on assumptions of whiteness and middle classness. As Warner (1993) notes, the "rainbow theory" of the liberal left is a pluralism that reifies such identities and one that "reduces power to a formalism of membership" (xix). Likewise Homi Bhabha argues that "diversity" is the "*containment* of difference" (Rutherford 1990: 208, emphasis in original) whereby very real social differences within the categories of "diversity" politics are muted. In terms of gay and lesbian activism, Duggan (2003) locates this focus on "diversity" precisely in the rapid shift in early 1970s gay and lesbian politics from an emphasis on a radical social movement focused on social change, economic justice, and sexual liberation to one of "equal rights" which worked within existing political structures, a shift in emphasis highlighted by HRC's legislative and political agenda. Indeed, HRC's statement that it "is committed to a mutually beneficial relationship with the transgender community" indicates precisely this view of a "transgender community" as a distinct and separate entity.

"When something is firmly classed as anomalous, the outline of the set in which it is not a member is clarified," writes Douglas (1992 [1966]: 38). The high emotion of telephone zaps, podium hijackings, hate crimes legislation, street protests, and so on speaks to the danger that Douglas recognizes in category crisis. This danger lies in the broader cultural and historical associations of non-normative gender expression with excessive sexuality, sex work, fetishism, and the concomitant associations of street life, blackness, and poverty. These are the very associations that mainstreaming gay and lesbian activism has worked so hard to delink from the "set" of homosexuality even as it engages racism, poverty, and gender parity as *equivalent* concerns. The significant point, though, is that while the debates over the status and membership of gender-non-normative people in gay and lesbian politics and social formations have a long history, the conceptualization of a "set" named "transgender" has produced a qualitatively different situation in the early twenty first century from that which existed even in the early 1970s. While demands for "inclusion" animated much debate in the pre- and immediate post-Stonewall era, those demands were, implicitly, to be recognized as a part of a "set" called "gay." "Transgender" not only allows transgender-identified people to organize and name themselves, or to demand *inclusion,* but it can serve — and has done so — to justify *exclusions* based on precisely the same claim that transgender-identified people *are* ontologically different from gay and lesbian people.

I would argue that for all the resistance to "inclusion," mainstream gay and lesbian organizations have come to *depend* on transgender not simply to define themselves as a discrete set, as Douglas suggests, but because transgender incorporates, and thereby removes from the category "gay" (and in different ways, from "lesbian"), gender-variant behavior or identities. That is, not only does transgender provide a foil against which "gay" — implicitly white, middle class, respectable, private, dependable, and most deeply, male — can define itself but it allows any gender-variant behavior — even from those who identify *as* gay — increasingly to be moved into the category transgender. Ironically, for all the fears of gay and lesbian activists that transgender people will scuttle their movement, it is the acceptance by both gay and lesbian *and* transgender people of the ontological distinction of their identities that reinforces the racialized and class-inflected diversity politics of mainstream gay and lesbian politics. While many activists and scholars challenge the "diversity" model of gay and lesbian politics and insist on a politics which would be transformative of racial, class, and political relations (e.g., Chasin 2001, Duggan 2003, Maskovsky 2002), in institutional contexts these critiques are reduced again and again to simple "inclusion."

Thus, it becomes impossible to address the concerns of those people whose lives have been transformed by neoliberal economic and political restructurings and the associated reduction of politics to group representation. In the case I am most concerned with, the Meat Market queens are doubly disenfranchised by these processes. On the one hand, they are subject to the most brutal logics of the corporatization of public space, transformed modes of racism, the restriction of state support, and "quality of life" policing, compounded by their poverty and racial identification. On the other hand, the forms of identity-based politics which have hijacked the terms of racial, social, and economic justice cannot account for them either since, as I showed in chapter 3, their claims to selfhood are unintelligible through the neat distinctions of "LGBT" politics. Even as transgender issues are "included" in gay and lesbian organizations, the terms of that inclusion require a coherence to the categories that the Meat Market fem queens confound. But the challenge that they mount to the politics of inclusion is not simply one of naming or representation. Rather, their understandings of self contest the very basis of those politics, namely, the ontological distinction between gender and sexuality and the conceptualization of these categories as equivalent to, but separate from, race, class, culture, and so on. In this way, "LGBT" politics — and discourses of inclusion and exclusion — is as much about the politics of race and of class as it is about the politics of gender and sexuality, though in ways that Creating Change conference-goers or other activists rarely engage.

In the next chapter, I will extend this analysis through examining one of the central concerns of contemporary transgender activism — violence suffered by transgender-identified people. If the logic of inclusion produces exclusions of a different order, the activism around violence is complicated by yet another set of problems.

6

The Calculus of Pain

Violence, Narrative, and the Self

Academics, shrinks, and feminist theorists have traveled through our lives and problems like tourists on a junket. Picnicking on our identities like flies at a free lunch, they have selected the tastiest tidbits with which to illustrate a theory or push a book. The fact that we are a community under fire, a people at risk, is irrelevant to them. They pursue Science and Theory, and what they produce by mining our lives is neither addressed to us nor recycled within our community . . . Our performance of gender is invariably a site of contest, a problem which — if we could but bring enough hi-octane academic power to bear — might be "solved." — RIKI ANNE WILCHINS, *Read My Lips*

In the previous two chapters, I have critically investigated the institutionalization of transgender as a category, arguing that it cannot be understood unproblematically either as a tool for social change or as a descriptor of gender variance transhistorically or cross-culturally. But it is also self-evident that the activism, scholarship, and broad social movement organized around this category have had important effects on transgender-identified people's lives. One of the recurring themes of my research was a demand that, whatever my critical goals, I concern myself with the lived realities of study participants' lives, and in particular that I pay attention to the multiple and often horrifying ways in which transgender-identified people experience violence.

The epigraph above captures this demand forcefully. Both in hir writing and in the long hours we spent together, Riki Anne Wilchins queried my motives, challenged me to become involved in transgender activism, and debated with me the ethical obligations of social scientists who study disenfranchised people. Marcus's (1998) notion of "complicity" as the central mode of contemporary ethnographic fieldwork captures how I became entangled as simultaneously a researcher, an outreach worker, and an activist, as well as how my dissertation research was refracted through other kinds of knowledge production. Indeed, I helped Riki edit the book from which the above quotation is taken, we co-authored a paper (Valentine and Wilchins 1997; see below), and much of my fieldwork was spent going to demonstrations and working on behalf of various transgender organizations. And, as I spent long hours in the Meat Market watching the girls dodge thrown bottles or insults, as others told me about being chased and threatened, or when I learned of another study participant who had been killed, the demands of my activist informants meshed with a deeply felt anger and desire to act. As I became involved in social service outreach and activism I accepted that, whatever else I thought to be true about "transgender," it was nonetheless a useful and potent category of social action.

Yet it is at these critical points (critical here in the sense of important) that it is vital to maintain a critical eye (and here I mean it in the sense of paying close attention). A key theme began to emerge during this work as I heard many divergent experiences and practices described to me as violent, including my research itself. In turn, I had my own analysis of violence and its causes, which often did not coincide with my study participants'. As such, I began to think about "violence" as something which also needed to be investigated, but not simply because I wanted it to stop, nor simply to generate theoretical observations about it. Rather, it was because I came to believe that thinking critically about violence — how people experienced it, what it meant to different people, and how it was mounted as a claim — was central both to understanding the politics of transgender as a category but also to developing effective strategies against such violence.

This chapter is, therefore, about violence: the day-to-day experience of violence endured by transgender-identified people but also how this experience is turned into stories about violence for the purpose of mounting claims against its perpetrators. In part, it is a continuation of the previous chapter, engaging transgender activism at the level of legislative advocacy and how particular understandings of transgender become institutionalized. But it is also concerned with violence as a category itself, how it can escape the boundaries of state-defined violence even as narratives of violence do not always account for the violence of the state. It is about how violence can come to describe many different kinds of practices — even holding particular political positions or doing ethnographic fieldwork — that are not always easily identifiable as violent. And it is about how addressing such violence may produce its own violations. Second, since my concern with violence arose out of demands that I address violence in transgender-identified people's lives, this chapter is simultaneously also about the ethics and responsibilities of those who study marginalized populations, the complex choices we face, and the relationship between ethics and critical scholarship. Finally, and most importantly, this chapter is also about the relationship between the institutionalization of discourses around violence and the institutionalization of transgender as a category, for they are complexly linked.

My dual use of "critical" above highlights the range of dense and intersecting meanings incorporated by violence: the critical importance of addressing violent acts, the critical role that stories play in doing this work, but also the job of maintaining a critical perspective on these social facts. As such, this chapter could be read by some as being critical in a third sense — that of being disparaging or dismissive of those who experience violence and tell stories about them. This is not my goal. Rather, I argue that it is essential to maintain a critical stance toward (or keep a careful eye on) the ways that violence becomes socially relevant precisely so that we are *able* to act carefully and effectively against violence.

The reason I want to keep my critical/critical eye on these points is central to the concerns I have raised throughout this book: how does the telling of stories about violence produce its own kind of violences and violations? And what happens when certain people get drawn into a discourse about "violence against transgender people" when they do not understand themselves in those terms?

I will start with a murder.

The last time I saw Vianna-Faye alive was on a Saturday night—early Sunday, really—in November 1997. She saw me from inside her car and jumped out waving. Get in, she said, and we'll drive around. We cruised the cool, dangerous streets of the Meat Market in her car, talking as she kept one eye on the cars crawling past, alert for the possibility of a date, someone who would pay for sex. This car was paid for by sex work, and the money she had saved by working these streets would pay for her sex reassignment surgery.

Despite the fact that Vianna-Faye fit GIP's description of a transgender person, she did not use the term "transgender" to talk about herself. If I pushed her, she would sometimes say she was a fem queen, but far more often, unlike her peers in the Meat Market, a woman. Vianna-Faye was different from most of the girls out here in other ways too. She had begun her transition later than most of them, in her twenties, after immigrating to the United States from Jamaica, and while she was, in the racial imaginary of the United States, a "person of color," she held onto her specifically Jamaican identity. Moreover, and again, unlike most of the other girls, she had definite plans for surgical transition. That evening, Vianna-Faye told me that she finally had a date—not a trick, but rather for an appointment for SRS—on January 14, 1998, in Montreal. She planned to kick sex work and get a job. After transition, she said, she would be able to move on, get a real job, and stop being "Felicia" (her "street" name) forever. This life was almost over.

It's odd what you remember about your last hours with those who are now dead. I remember being nervous about being in her car: what if the cops stop us? How would I explain that I'm an anthropologist, not a client? What happens if I get arrested, or worse, beaten? It's been known to happen. And I remember that she took six packets of sugar in her coffee; I hadn't brought enough when I had jumped out on 14th Street to get us a snack. She had to go back into Dizzy Izzy's Bagels to get some more while I sat listening to the radio. When she climbed back in, I stirred the sugar into her coffee. Feeling suddenly generous I said: "When you get home from Montreal, I'll bring you chicken soup." She looked at me briefly. "Really?" she asked. "Yes," I said, with more conviction, "chicken soup is good when you're healing from anything." "OK," she said. "I'll hold you to that."

But she never made her appointment. On Christmas Eve 1997, the day I officially ended my fieldwork, she was murdered in her apartment in Jersey City, apparently by a twelve-year-old boy who was a neighbor. She was found in her nightgown, with multiple stab wounds to her back, neck, and chest.

I found out about her death almost by accident. A few weeks later, now that fieldwork was over, I could return to the Meat Market in another guise, a civilian again, going to a bar on 13th Street. Walking over with my friend Raeph, we bumped into Alexis.

"Did you hear Felicia was killed?" she asked, lighting a cigarette. It took me several seconds to register.

"Vianna-Faye?" I asked in disbelief. Yeah, said Alexis, who proceeded to give me the details. And, she continued, she used to be Felicia's roommate, and she still had a key, and the cops said she could have her stuff and wasn't that cool?

I didn't know whether to cry, to yell at her, or to dispute the ludicrous idea that the police would give her such carte blanche with a murder victim's belongings. Instead, I said goodbye and walked on in a daze. It was while I was clutching my beer in the bar, not much company for Raeph, that I realized with a dual sense of horror and certainty that I had an ethnographic story to tell about violence against transgender people.

THE USES OF VIOLENCE

As "transgender" has become a useful category for talking about gender variance, so violence is a useful category for activism and moral argumentation: what could be more self-evident as an embodied experience? And who can tell the anthropologist to get off his high horse when he talks about a friend, murdered?

In a 1995 article in *Current Anthropology*, Nancy Scheper-Hughes argues for the "primacy of the ethical" in anthropological practice, that is, the moral imperative for anthropologists to act on the suffering and violence they witness in the course of their research. She describes her intervention in the community-led rough justice meted out against three young men accused of theft in a South African squatter camp near Cape Town. Flouting the wishes of some community leaders, she arranged medical attention for the youngest offender, whose flogging had brought him close to death. Scheper-Hughes argues that her ethical responsibilities—as an anthropologist and as a human being — meant ignoring the demands that she not intervene. She writes: "To speak of the 'primacy of the ethical' is to suggest certain transcendent, transparent and essential, if not 'precultural' first principles . . . I will tentatively and hesitantly suggest that responsibility, accountability, answerability to 'the other' — the ethical as I would define it — is precultural to the extent that our human existence as social beings presupposes the presence of the other" (419).

Scheper-Hughes calls for a "barefoot anthropology," which eschews the view of an "imagined postmodern, borderless world" (417). In her account, a focus on the transnational, the borderless nature of cultural and financial flows, and postmodernist concerns with the diffuse and complex nature of power has distracted anthropologists from the local and specific and from evidence of profound suffering. As an alternative, Scheper-Hughes calls for a "new cadre of 'barefoot anthropologists'" who "must become alarmists and shock troopers — the producers of politically complicated and morally demanding texts and images capable of sinking through the layers of acceptance, complicity, and bad faith that allow the suffering and the deaths to continue" (417).

In many ways, I find Scheper-Hughes's call for an ethically oriented "barefoot anthropology" to be galvanizing. Since Vianna-Faye's death, several more of my study participants have been murdered; far more have been subject to verbal and physical harassment. These stories are not uncommon: a 1997 survey by GenderPAC found that almost 60 percent of transgender-identified people surveyed had experienced some form of harassment or abuse directed at them because of their non-normative expression of gender (GenderPAC 1997). Since the early 1990s, transgender-identified activists and advocates have begun to use these stories to appeal to state bodies, demanding legislative action to address such violence, a process I have participated in. Indeed, the evidence of violence against transgender-identified people has been a central impetus to the development of the kinds of activism I discussed in chapter 5. In particular, the activism that arose after the murder of Brandon Teena is noted by several authors as a crucial moment in the consolidation of anger and action around these issues (see Califia 2003 [1997], Cartwright 2000, Wilchins 1997).

Yet, for all this irrefutable evidence, I cannot accept Scheper-Hughes's claim for "precultural" ethical stances on such facts of violence, for, as scholars such as Arthur and Joan Kleinman (1996) and Allen Feldman (1991) have shown, violence, suffering, and pain are not simple or self-evident categories of experience. These scholars argue that violence must be understood as a complex cultural category, drawing in both the visceral reality of murder and violation but also a set of representations, discourses, and stories *about* such social realities. Moreover, others (Krohn-Hansen 1994, Riches 1986) have pointed out that "violence" itself is notoriously hard to define. These authors themselves find it difficult to define what violence is: on the one hand it is sensual and obvious; on the other, it depends on its definition and narration by its victims to become real *as* violence. Daniel, who argues that violence is the counterpoint to the "omnibus" (1996: 195) concept of culture with which anthropologists work, captures this dynamic best: "The point is this. Violence is an event in which there is a certain excess: an excess of passion, an excess of evil. The very attempt to label this excess (as indeed I have done) is condemned to fail . . . Everything can be narrated, but what is narrated is no longer what happened" (208).

Yet, for violence to be comprehensible, for the "excess of evil" to be made sense of, for such acts to be conceived of as constituting a social problem, it is necessary to produce stories about them. Feldman argues that violence is never simply an event or practice but is also necessarily about how the event becomes narrated, represented, and contested with counterstories (see also Axel 2001, Knox 1998). Writing of how paramilitaries in Belfast speak of interrogation, he notes: "the oral history of interrogation recounted by paramilitaries is a cultural tool kit, an empowering apparatus that paramilitaries take into the theater of interrogation in order to mediate, and possibly invert, the interrogator's scenario of violence" (1991: 14).

Feldman's "tool kit" maps onto how many transgender-identified activists draw on experiences of violence in constructing meaningful stories about themselves, about their survival, about the experiences of others, and how such narratives are used in appeals to the state (see Butler 1997a). However, while scholars like Feldman point to the centrality of narration, sensemaking, and representation in considering violence, they tend to focus on moments of violence that seem to resist analysis or that seem to be — surely must be — understandable cross-culturally as quite evidently violent: brutal interrogations, beatings, murders, massacres, torture. I have started this chapter with a similar kind of horrifying and very real story.

But I want to consider how violence is capable of drawing a much wider range of practices and experiences into its purview, to show how "violence," as Daniel argues for "culture," also has an omnibus character.

Indeed, I found that "violence" can incorporate not only physical abuse and murder but all practices that may be perceived as impacting negatively upon a life, including the practices of ethnography itself. The violence of representation and of physical harm, of emotional and physical scarring, are hard to consider apart precisely because they can be experienced and narrated simultaneously.

These violences, large and small, have been increasingly part of the process whereby the idea of transgender has been constituted. This is not to say that transgender identities are formed, or that transgender activism is conducted, exclusively in relation to violence, nor should my claims here be read as arguing that transgender-identified people necessarily experience violence more than other groups or individuals. Moreover, I am not suggesting that violence is the sole or even the central feature of all transgender-identified people's lives. The GenderPAC study cited above shows, conversely, that 40 percent of the transgender-identified respondents report *not* experiencing harassment, violence, or abuse. The point I am making is that whatever the statistics, in contemporary political activism, violence has become a central "tool kit" in drawing the attention of the state — and others — to the lives of gender-variant people. As Moran and Sharpe (2002) write, in discussing community-based surveys of violence against transgender-identified people, " The sites and techniques of mapping violence, the methods of reportage deployed by activists and the police practices of recording violence are . . . all process [sic] through which transgender identities and politics take shape" (270).

My use of "violence" in this chapter is thus uncomfortably situated (as is my use of "critical" and "transgender"): I am using it in its most evident, least theorized sense, to refer to the mind-numbing, monthly reports I receive of another decomposed body unearthed, another study participant or friend dead, another story of a thrown bottle or a catcall. This is the sense that Daniel, Scheper-Hughes, Riches, and others engage, and the kind of violence I implicitly invoke in telling the story of Vianna-Faye's murder. I am also using it to refer to the ways that transgender-identified people recognize certain discourses and representations to be linked to practices of physical violence; and by including catcalls and murder in the category of "violence" I am also doing some of this work. I also think about "violence" as a series of discourses which are being used to help constitute transgender experience, to make it something that people should care about, write books about, legislate about. But finally, to return to Vianna-Faye's story, I want to look at how "transgender" as the vehicle for activism (as I am arguing for "violence") posits coherent and readily identifiable states of identity to the exclusion of other ways of conceptualizing gendered/sexual identity. As such these practices and discourses perform *another* set of unintended representational violations which resonate with larger structural violences.

My analysis of violence lies in the territory between representation and physical violence — *discourse as violence* — and how such facts are mounted to make a series of claims — *violence as discourse*. Like Scheper-Hughes and Daniel, I am impassioned by the evidence of violence to write about it. But, like Feldman, I am compelled to think critically about violence precisely because I believe that such a focus is *necessary* for effective and politically engaged work by anthropologists and others. Ethical action from this perspective is shaped by competing claims about what is moral and what is not, and about what does or does not constitute violence and harm. I will argue that an investigation of these complexities — and the diffuse nature of power, the ambiguity of social practices, flows of discourse, and symbolic capital — must be the starting point for effective and ethical action.

VIOLENCE AS DISCOURSE: GENDER LOBBY DAYS

The visit to Capitol Hill in 1999 described in chapter 5 was one outcome of an already well-established tradition of transgender legislative activism in the 1990s. In 1995, Phyllis Frye of the International Conference on Transgender Law and Employment Policy (ICTLEP) and Riki Anne Wilchins had organized the first National Transgender Lobby Days in Washington, D.C. On an early May morning in 1997, I was in front of the Capitol building in Washington, D.C., with about sixty activists, most of them white, for the second Lobby Days event, this time sponsored by GenderPAC, which had been founded six months earlier in November 1996 with a mission goal of "gender, affectional, and racial equality." Our goal that day was to highlight the concerns of gender-variant and transgender-identified people for members of Congress. Those present included transexual men and women, cross-dressers, and others who refused gendered identities, as well as a couple of staffers from the Human Rights Campaign (HRC), there to offer expertise and advice about lobbying.

GenderPAC and its members had wanted to focus their lobbying efforts on amending the Employment Non-Discrimination Act (ENDA), which, as explained in chapter 5, would criminalize employment discrimination based on sexual orientation, but not on the basis of "gender identity or expression." However, HRC had persuaded GenderPAC officers that a more productive strategy would be to lobby for the inclusion of "gender identity and expression" in the Hate Crimes Statistics Act, the same bill we were invited to celebrate just two years later. More to the point, HRC was not willing to support GenderPAC's position on ENDA. The focus on hate crimes had been an initial strategy of gay and lesbian lobbyists, they argued, and had made possible more complex legislative negotiations around gay/lesbian issues. While HRC's position on ENDA still angered those gathered before the Capitol building that morning, GenderPAC officers had grudgingly conceded that "hate crimes" would be the official theme of Lobby Days. While we did not know it at the time, this decision by GenderPAC's officers would have complicated results.

The issue of hate crimes had already become a focus for transgender activists in the early 1990s. Since the first Lobby Days in 1995, GenderPAC had produced *The First National Study on Transviolence* (GenderPAC 1997; see Moran and Sharpe 2002). Using this report, we hoped to persuade members of Congress to sign on to a letter to the Department of Justice (DOJ), requesting that the Department hold a meeting with Gender-PAC representatives. At the pre-lobby conference the night before, Riki had told the assembled group: "Violence is a perfect issue, like motherhood. No one can be against motherhood and no one can be for violence."

Nervously, we split up into small groups and set off to call on the offices of our congressional representatives. Riki, Rosalyne, and I made the rounds of New York State representatives, ending up some time later that morning in the offices of Representative Jerrold Nadler, a vocal supporter of the gay and lesbian community. As his legislative assistant flipped through the GenderPAC report, we gave details of murder victims that we knew by heart and whose stories — in short paragraph form — were included at the end of the report: Deborah Forte ("Ms. Forte suffered three stab wounds to the chest — each half a foot deep, and in addition a number of slash wounds across her chest, a smashed nose, multiple severe blows to her head and face, and signs on her throat of partial strangulation"); Chanell Pickett ("strangled to death in Watertown, MA early on the morning of November 20, 1995"); Brandon Teena ("On Christmas day 1993, Brandon Teena was raped and assaulted at a Christmas party by two men . . ."); and a host of others.

"Now this is something we can work with," the assistant said, nodding. By the end of the day, sitting in the Rayburn Office Building cafeteria, we were all somewhat dazed: twelve members of Congress had signed the letter. None of us had anticipated this level of success.

"We're two years ahead of schedule," Riki kept saying, shaking hir head in wonder.

GenderPAC got its meeting with the DOJ (a very productive one). In short order, it was invited to join the Hate Crimes Coalition, and through its work the Hate Crimes Prevention Act was introduced in 1999, defining as a crime the willful bodily injury of any person "because of the *actual or perceived* religion, *gender*, sexual orientation, or disability" (U.S. Congress 1999, my emphasis) of that person. This means that the provisions of the bill could potentially cover transgender-identified people.

In chapter 5 I laid out some of the basic critiques of the politics of inclusion. The same problems are apparent here, for the lives of people such as Brandon or Vianna-Faye become evened out, represented as "transgender people" without attention to the complexity of their social identifications, their capacity for agency, or the circumstances of their murder (see Hale 1998). But this critique requires a further complication in this case. While GenderPAC was founded primarily through a coalition of transgender activist organizations in 1996, its subsequent policy has indeed attempted to straddle the divide between a "politics of recognition" and a broader progressive politics which eschews identity categories. GenderPAC has moved away from describing itself as a "transgender organization" because its staff and members hold that such an appellation ignores how all people are potentially subject to violence because of variant expressions of gender, and how race, class, and homophobia also structure such violence.[1]

These choices, though, have their own complexities and outcomes. As Broad (2002) argues, transgender activism has since its inception as a social movement been fraught with debates over whether "transgender" is a stable category of social action, or whether differences of race, class, and sexuality contest this stability. This dynamic came to a head in early 2001 with mounting anger among transgender activists over GenderPAC's refusal to represent itself as a specifically transgender organization and its perceived abandonment of its transgender constituents. Several board members resigned in 2001, prominent activists coauthored a letter denouncing GenderPAC, and many joined new organizations such as the National Transgender Advocacy Coalition (NTAC) which were established to take over the work they understood GenderPAC to have abandoned. Critics of GenderPAC range from those who claim that GenderPAC has been "bought off" by HRC to protect ENDA to more sophisticated analyses which recognize that while a broad vision of politics is necessary, political realities require a simultaneous engagement with identity categories (Cartwright 2001, Park 2003). From this perspective, GenderPAC's unwillingness to attack ENDA during Lobby Days 1997 was its first betrayal of the transgender community.

Moreover, other activists have made a direct link between GenderPAC's politics, its use of murder narratives such as those discussed above, and what they see as a further violation of transgender-identified people by GenderPAC: "Is it morally right for GenderPAC to use [the stories of] Transgender and Intersex victims to raise the bulk of their funds, yet only use a tiny portion of those funds to work for issues that affect those same individuals? Would this not make our dead brothers and sisters victims a second time?" (Helms 2000). In other words, the very use of an alternative form of political organizing and theorization of gender variance can itself be seen as an exercise in violence.

The fallout from Lobby Days 1997 encapsulated a range of issues that I faced as both an activist and ethnographer. As I learned of Vianna-Faye's death, or of another friend who was chased down the street, the endless debates over GenderPAC exhausted and infuriated me. But, again, these are the very moments when the critical eye is necessary (and the moments when it is least likely to be focused), because engaging in carefully positioned and effective advocacy is intimately connected to understanding a range of complex conceptions of violence and suffering — and what that violence constitutes. And this also complicates the position of the anthropologist who is engaged in these debates and dynamics as a social actor as much as a researcher. As Edelman (2001) notes,

> social movements are often notoriously ephemeral and factionalized . . . , manifest major discrepancies among leaders and between leaders and supporters . . . , and — probably most importantly — rarely attract more than a minority of the constituencies they claim to represent. . . . To which faction or leader does the ethnographer "commit"? What does that commitment imply about hearing dissenting or uninterested voices or grasping alternative histories, political projects, or forms of cultural transformation? (310–11)

Indeed, how does one "take sides" — and more importantly, act — in disputes between different groups with divergent, if valid, analyses of what action is required? The demand that anthropologists act on behalf of their study population and against the facts of violence, then, is deeply complicated by the terms by which that population is defined, who defines it, and what strategies are seen as valid. Moreover, as I will discuss next, anthropological practices, even those motivated by good intentions, can themselves be seen as violent.

DISCOURSE AS VIOLENCE I: WORKING FOR THE FBI

December 1996: There were already about twenty-five members of the GIP's transgender support group in the overheated room when I came in, regrettably late. I had been initially invited to the group in October by Melissa to give a presentation about my work. In the October meeting it had been immediately apparent that while Melissa vouched for me, my presence was not altogether welcome. As a support group this venue was supposed to be a safe space for transgender-identified people, and so I did not strictly have the right to be there. After some discussion, the group had agreed that I was welcome to take notes but that I could not tape record the session.

This December evening was the final meeting of the group before the Christmas break, and everyone was taking turns summarizing their experiences over the fall. There were several people present whom I had not met in the October meeting, but as the group had already started, I simply sat down next to Nick, the other group facilitator, and — in retrospect, without consideration of the ethical issues — pulled out my notebook. When my turn came, I identified myself as a non-transgender-gay-identified man and as an anthropologist working with the GIP. I thanked the group for the opportunity to listen and learn from their experiences. I finished, and the next person began to talk, but as I dutifully wrote down her reactions, one of the people I hadn't met previously — Jillian — suddenly burst out: "Would you mind not taking notes in a confidential meeting!"

All hell broke loose, in a kind of controlled way. Nick asked her to rephrase the request in a more polite manner. Melissa and Cindy jumped to my defense. I apologized, explaining that I had received permission to take notes on a prior occasion, that all members would remain anonymous, that she could see my notes, and that I would stop writing. Jillian was not mollified, however. She said that she would rather pay "my two dollars" than have me in the room, drawing a connection between the free services of the group and "government funding" which, she argued, made my presence possible.[2] Later, after the group had ended, she told me that "people from the FBI" wanted to take notes on groups such as this, and I was suspected as part of this policing. She was tired, she said, of having notes taken down about what she says and who she is. After some fifteen minutes of explaining my project and convincing her I was not an FBI agent, we parted, if not friends at least not enemies.

Jillian's was not the only negative reaction I encountered during my fieldwork. The perception of anthropology as simply another arm of the sciences which have sought to pathologize, exoticize, and objectify gender variance is understandable in a field of discursive and practical relations which have always placed gender variance as the thing to be explained. Jillian's reaction speaks to how the practices of ethnography, and more broadly of representation, can be seen harmful in and of themselves. Such academic and clinical investigations are indeed the target of Wilchins's words at the head of this chapter.[3] Wilchins posits the same link Jillian implicitly makes between my practices of note taking and the power of the state in the person of an FBI agent: that representations are or can be inherently violent and harmful.[4]

The linkage of representations and violence is even more complex, though, when one considers the work of some feminist theorists who see the mere existence of transexual women or cross-dressers (though less often transexual men) as a form of violence against a self-evident, essentialized category of women (Jeffreys 1996, McNeill 1982, Raymond 1994 [1979]). In this view, propounded most famously by Janice Raymond in *The Transsexual Empire*, transexuality (especially MTF transexuality) is an outcome of a patriarchally enforced gender binary which violently oppresses women and dupes transexuals into undergoing SRS.

This contention was at the heart of my first encounter with the direct action group Transexual Menace, one in which these positions were compacted into a dense and emotional encounter between Janice Raymond and Menace activists. In October 1994, two years before I officially began fieldwork, Raymond was in New York at the now-defunct Judith's Room feminist bookstore on Washington Street (some three blocks from where I would one day meet Vianna-Faye) to read from her new book on reproductive technologies. The majority of those present, however, were white, middle-class transexual women who wanted to challenge her in person, especially because *The Transsexual Empire* was about to be reissued by Columbia University Press, substantially in the same format as the original.

It was a tense evening. After Raymond's reading from her new book, a question and answer period about *The Transsexual Empire* became an acrimonious exchange. "Why would you want to have surgery?" she asked some of the transexual women present. "Don't you understand that you are buying into a binary system of gender which is ultimately oppressive?" People responded by arguing that their experiences of womanhood were not creations of doctors or of an abstract patriarchy, and that they themselves had experienced ostracism and oppression because of their transexual and transgender identities.

This was also the first time I met Riki Anne. S/he challenged Raymond's analysis by drawing Raymond's attention to the way Raymond herself was implicated in the same system of binary gender by presenting as—and insisting on the identity of—woman. Quoting Judith Butler, and keeping hir voice even, Riki stumped the writer several times. When Raymond asked hir why s/he had had surgery, Riki replied: "How do you know what my genitals look like?" Hir point—that all gender, all genitals are the product of systems of meaning—was lost in the heat of the debate. At the end of the evening, Riki read a prepared statement, from which I have excerpted the following quote:

> It was only a few months ago, responding to a party invitation at the Gay Community Center, that I neglected to read the footnote: "No Transvestites, No Men and No Transexuals." When I called the lesbian in charge, she told me I was really just a transvestite who had mutilated himself and hung up on me. Ideas have effects. It is clear that as transgendered men and women, we face two kinds of violence each day: One is the larger violence, that perpetrated by straight society on our bodies, which has taken from us people like Brandon Teena and Marsha P. Johnson. . . . [Our] invisibility is facilitated by the smaller violence, that perpetrated by writers and theorists like you who, by their insistence that our men are really women, or that our women are really men, or that we are crazed masochistic he-shes or self-mutilating cross dressed she-males, serve to lend the gender bashing of transexual men and women a social, and respectable, face to show the world.[5]

In critiquing Raymond's perspective, I find it easy to sympathize with Riki's position. I can argue that Raymond's interpretations ride roughshod over the complex details of people's lives, ignore the subjectivities of transexual people, and, moreover, that her firm insistence on the category "woman" shores up binary gender in ways quite different from those she argues are enacted by transexual women. On the other hand, for Raymond and her audience, the presence of Transexual Menace members (and probably myself) at the reading was a fulfillment of Raymond's claims in *The Transsexual Empire*. By asserting their rights as women in a women's bookstore, and by confronting Raymond, Transexual Menace members were only reinforcing for her what she already believed about the patriarchal violence — visceral and representational — enacted by transexuals and transgender-identified people against (non-transexual) women. For Transexual Menace members, on the other hand, the power of Raymond's book, its status as a reference text on the politics of transexuality, and its effects in the world (evident, for example, in Richard Burns's response to Barbara Warren, which I discussed in the previous chapter), is itself an exercise in violence.

If for Raymond, Wilchins's presence at Judith's Room represented a usurpation of women's space by a man, then for Wilchins, Raymond's insistence on an essentialized category of "woman" violated hir own attempts to construct meanings about hir body not constrained by binary gender. Similarly, Jillian's perception of me as a note-taking FBI agent speaks to a broader concern with the links between representation and power. In all cases, representation in and of itself is linked to social power and the certainty of power's effects in the form of violence. My point here is not to adjudicate who was "right" in this debate. Rather, I want to show how "violence" can be drawn on in myriad ways and that representations and even personal identification itself can be posited as violent acts.

But Wilchins's claims also produce another point of entry for critical thinking about violence and representation. In invoking Brandon Teena's name, Brandon was also brought into this room implicitly as a "transgender man." Riki saw it as vital to claim Brandon as a man, even as others have claimed him (her) as a butch lesbian (see Hale 1998). As I will discuss below, calling Brandon — or Vianna-Faye or a range of others — "transgender" is itself a representational step that has consequences beyond simple representation.

As I have argued, there is a clear relationship between representation and violence, and I do not seek to deny this. Further, regarding Wilchins's,

Raymond's, and Jillian's competing claims, choosing to have sex reassignment surgery, taking notes in a meeting, representing someone as a transgender man, or writing a book are clearly qualitatively different from murdering someone. But all draw on a similar epistemology and causality: that representations or ideologies have effects in and of themselves; that representations are linked in a causal way to institutions of power beyond the control of the individual; that individuals are bound to enact the demands of hegemonic representations; and that those who are acted on are victims. As Butler (1997a) notes, it is precisely because identities are produced through discourse that discourse has the power to harm.

What complicates this relationship between representation and violence even further, however, is the way that such analyses bend back on themselves and work against one other. For if Wilchins sees hirself as constrained by identity labels, such a view is not always seen as liberatory to others. As I noted above, GenderPAC's shift away from an identity-based politics under Wilchins's leadership has resulted in harsh denunciations and literal accusations of violence. But even Wilchins's analyses of hir personal embodiment and identity are sometimes seen as personally threatening to the very people s/he argues for in hir activism.

DISCOURSE AS VIOLENCE II: FOUCAULT FROM A FAUCET

Cindy, along with Riki, is one of the people to whom I was most indebted in my fieldwork. We first met in a GIP support group in October 1996 and quickly became firm friends and e-mail buddies. At the time I met her, Cindy was just beginning to transition, was still married (with two children), and was deeply depressed by her situation even as claiming her identity as a woman was liberating for her. Her history—of child abuse, rape, drug addiction, alcoholism, suppression of feelings—is one that is all too common among transgender-identified people. Her personal narratives abound with images of life held onto against enormous odds. I was immediately impressed by Cindy's courage and conviction, sometimes exhausted by the intensity of her experiences filtered through e-mails and conversations, but always ready to learn something new from her.

Shortly after the support group meeting I describe above, I promised to e-mail Cindy a paper I coauthored with Riki, a version of which was published in the journal *Social Text* a year later (Valentine and Wilchins 1997). Part of the motive for sending this paper to her was that she had asked to see it; another part was that, as I had said to her, her courage and drive reminded me of Riki's and I wanted the two of them to be friends.

The title of this paper, "One Percent on the Burn Chart," refers to the percentage of the body's surface area represented by the genitals in assessing burns in a trauma unit and is intended to draw attention to the fact that, for such a small piece of the body, it carries an enormous amount of cultural weight. In the paper, Riki and I drew on Butler's (1990) famous observation that *all* gender identities and performances are enactments of unrealizable, hyperbolic gender. The point we were making was that the theoretical focus on gender or embodied variance — be it transexuality, cross-dressing, or intersexuality — draws attention away from precisely this observation. In the article, we discussed a workshop that Riki does, called "Our Cunts are Not the Same: Transexual Sexuality and Sex-change Surgery." Here, I quote from the published version:

> During a practical session in this workshop, s/he [Riki] invites the people present to don latex gloves and examine hir vagina. Despite requesting participants to think of hir genitals as they are, and not as they are in relation to something else, the comment s/he gets most often is: "it's just like mine!" Riki remarks that this comment illustrates, above all, the need these participants have to integrate that "one percent on the burn chart" into a coherent idea about sexed and gendered bodies. The alternative, which forms the backbone of hir gender activism, is to seek an entirely different ordering of sex, gender, and genitals, for instance, "just your average, straight white guy with a cunt who really digs lezzie chicks like me," as s/he signs hir email. (Valentine and Wilchins 1997: 218)

I sent this off to Cindy on Christmas Eve, 1996 — a year to the day before Vianna-Faye would be murdered — via e-mail. Later that evening I received an e-mail from Cindy, from which I quote the following:[6]

> To me, my life has been a horror show. It maybe cute for a middle class punk like Riki Anne Wilchins to fuck with a speculum in front of geeks and gawkers. She can always go back to making a wonderful living with her computer talents if she doesn't sell enough tickets. My emotional reaction is that I'm deeply offended if I'm at all considered to be like Riki. Maybe I could have done more to help others but things were never quite as cushy for me. I haven't existed for twenty years. I don't earn very much money. I couldn't tell Foucault from a faucet. But now I am back and this is supposed

to be the best that people who are supposed to be like me have to offer? . . . .
It makes me cry. . . . I feel so disappointed, so angry. [. . .] I don't know
David, but I've been attacked by someone who calls themself a male lesbian
[. . .] I've been attacked by someone who ultimately says, through public
discourse and self-definition, I, Cindy, am a man. This occurs because of her
position in "the community." If she defines the terms of the debate, then I
want no part in the arguments.

In that way, Riki's words, Riki's definitions rape me because they undermine the credibility of my take on myself and Wilchins has "power over"
me. (Wilchins has obtained a higher level of credibility by virtue of curricu-
lum vitae, past actions. Wilchins words count more than mine because Riki
has a standing. Anything I do or say as an unknown individual would be
measured against Wilchins ideas plus credibility. Wilchins will be quoted, I
will never be.) And if Wilchins can rape me by having power over me, then
Wilchins is indeed, very much a man. Assertions can be violent and debilitating in that they always make one size fit all.

Needless to say, a flurry of e-mail correspondence followed this. I assured Cindy that my intention — and, I assured her, Riki's — was not to
deny her the right to identify as a woman, to undergo surgery, and to claim
the gender and the life she desired (as she subsequently has). Cindy was
angered by our analysis because she perceived it as an attack on her desire
to live as a woman — and that such a transition would be re-read, re-repre-
sented, as nothing more than a falsity. In this way, Cindy's analysis mirrors
those critics of deconstructive methods and theory which see the outcome
of deconstruction as a world without meaning or distinction.

But most important for my purposes here — the analysis notwithstanding
— is to note how both Riki and I (implicitly) are implicated as rapists and
attackers. Our representations, Riki's perceived power in shaping the politics of transgender activism, and my position as an anthropologist are all
seen by Cindy as evidence of violence against her desire to transition and
to claim the identity of woman. Like Raymond's analysis of transexual
women — or Riki's critique of Raymond's book, or Jillian's demand that I
stop taking notes, or critics of GenderPAC's politics — Cindy's interpretation of our paper posits a direct relationship between ideology and representation on the one hand, and violence and power on the other. Moreover,
her reaction indicates how even well-intentioned, carefully considered
positions can be read as exercises in violence, even rape.

The density of this story, the ways that representations and experiences of violence double back on themselves, underlines my central point: in making claims about how gender-variant and transgender-identified people experience violence, "violence" is neither an easy nor a self-evident category, and the ability of an anthropologist or any social actor to counter such violence is deeply complicated by the interpretation of what counts *as* violence.

SELF/OTHER/VIOLENCE

Drawing on the above stories, I want to make two interrelated points. First, these stories show how violations do not reside simply in external acts but in the interpretive processes whereby those acts both produce and work against a sense of self. By this I mean that the concerns of Gender-PAC critics, Jillian's reaction to my notetaking, Cindy's interpretation of the article, Raymond's claims against transexual women and vice versa all locate violence in representational acts which violate deeply felt understandings of the self but which, in the same moment, confirm the abjection of that self. Second, though, I am also interested in the ways in which other interpretive processes — institutional and social — also engage these practices and perceptions of self and make them make *social* sense. For identity is not something that simply arises from the self and its experience but is the product of an ongoing process of meaning-making which draws on, and is drawn into, institutionalized categories of selfhood.

And it is here that my sense of dis-ease in the moments I recount above comes together with the critique I am developing around the invocation of "violence," for what other violations may be enacted when people are drawn into institutionalized categories which do not necessarily make sense of their selves? What if the structural conditions which produce violations for located social actors are not part of the narrative of violence told on their behalf? Here I turn to two people (both dead) who have figured in this chapter: Vianna-Faye Williams and Brandon Teena.

Brandon Teena's story is one of the most often-told and invoked tales of violence against transgender-identified people. A white, working-class, female-born Nebraskan youth who had lived at least part of his (or in some accounts, her) life as a man, Brandon became romantically involved with a woman, leading to his outing as a female-bodied person and rape at the hands of two local men, John Lotter and Marvin Nissen. Brandon's reporting of the rape produced no action on the part of the police; rather, Sheriff Charles Laux interrogated and derided him. Even more shockingly, the police informed Lotter and Nissen of the rape report. Shortly after this, on New Year's Eve 1993, Lotter and Nissen murdered Brandon, his girlfriend, and a friend who was with them.

The vigils and demonstrations that took place around the trial of Brandon Teena's murderers, and the media response to it, were one catalyst for the transgender activism that arose in the 1990s. Activist responses to two published accounts of Brandon's murder are instructive here. In 1994, Donna Minkowitz wrote a story in the *Village Voice* detailing the murder, characterizing Brandon as a confused teenager, a lesbian, and referring to the youth as "she" (Minkowitz 1994). This article precipitated an outraged reaction from transgender activists and a demonstration to demand a published correction of what activists argued was the paper's misrepresentation of Brandon as a woman. Part of the anger directed at the *Voice* was a claim about violence—that in characterizing Brandon as a woman, the paper was further violating Brandon's dead body (see Califia 2003 [1997]: 230–32).

Similarly, John Gregory Dunne's (1997) *New Yorker* article about Brandon's murder was roundly condemned by activists I spoke to after its publication. Apart from his use of "Teena" and feminine pronouns, Dunne frames the murder in terms of the rough violence and anomie of rural working-class America. Though I found his argument compelling at some levels, my informants uniformly argued that his article dismissed Brandon's gender identity, and that by making it a story about class, Dunne displaced the real story of the murder: violence against transgender people (see Halberstam 2003).

Yet, as Jacob Hale notes, it is not at all clear how Brandon identified at the time of his death. Outlining the variety of ways that Brandon identified, Hale notes, "To do more than speculate about this [Brandon/Teena's identity] is to collude with the foreclosure of future self-constructions that was so abruptly enacted by murder" (1998: 318). Hale notes further that the "insistence by others on consistently gendered pronouns that do not reflect one's own subjectivity and agency can be as much a technique of objectification as Sheriff Laux's 'You can call it an *it* as far as I'm concerned'" (1998: 319, emphasis in original).

In using "he" for Brandon, I am doing something of the same order, based on the conviction of others that he did indeed identify as such. At the same time, Hale's analysis forces me to recognize my complicity with this process, and how this story — this categorization — displaces the complex ways that a murder comes to happen. Moreover, it is important to note that Hale, too, draws a link between representation and violence, arguing that the insistence on male pronouns for Brandon is a "collusion" with the foreclosures performed by murder.

Knox (1998), in her study of murder in U.S. society, argues that murder is never a self-evident act. Rather, she claims, murder is always subject to a re-authoring, a re-telling which fits the messy moments of death into a narrative about motive, frame, and desire. This becomes apparent to me even in the story I started out with, the story of Vianna-Faye's murder. Certainly, of all the people I met in the Meat Market, Vianna-Faye embodied most closely the model of "transgender" I have described throughout. Unlike most of the fem queens in the Meat Market, she rejected the category "gay" as being relevant to herself and insisted on the vital distinctions between herself as a woman and myself as a gay man, even though she also sometimes used "fem queen" about herself. Yet, at the same time, she resisted "transgender" as a category of identification precisely because she felt that it detracted from her identity as a woman.

Even more importantly, though, it is not totally clear why Vianna-Faye was murdered; the twelve-year-old boy's motives in killing her are not available. Some reports mention robbery as the motive; as she was a Jamaican woman, racism may have been a factor. She was murdered in her own home, not on the streets of the Meat Market, and there is no evidence that her gender identity or her line of work contributed to her murder, though it is equally possible that it did. But her story, as well as Brandon Teena's, has become unproblematically narrated in activist discourses and practices as one of "violence against transgender people." Again, these are discourses and practices in which I have participated, as I did at the event to mark the introduction of the Hate Crimes Prevention Act. And who is to say that this is not valid? That perhaps it was the boy's knowledge of her gender variance that made her a target, that fueled a socialized rage against difference, that brought together a desire for easy gain and the disposal of a gendered anomaly? The ambiguity persists, even though she has become a story to be narrated, another grim story of death to add to the rolls of those who are gone because of "violence against transgender people."

I will ask the same question here that I have asked before: does it matter, in the end, how Vianna-Faye or Brandon or a sickeningly large number of other people, now dead, are represented, as long as their stories are told? Does it matter that Brandon might have sometimes seen herself as a lesbian, sometimes himself as a man, sometimes as some other kind of self? Or that Vianna-Faye rejected the explicit definition of "transgender" as something of relevance for herself? If race or class or age or immigration status or region factor into these murders, does it matter if they become represented simply as victims of violence against transgender people? I would say yes, it does.

NARRATING THE SELF/OTHER TO THE STATE

And it matters not simply for the sake of accuracy, nor for the sake of critical inquiry. To return to Taylor's formulation, a "politics of recognition" is not simply about the recognition of a group but about the recognition — or identification — of people as belonging to a group in the first place. Up to now, I have been telling two kinds of stories: first, the way that violence is far more complicated than murder or a beating; and second, the way that violence comes to be narrated through a category — transgender — which seems to make sense of that violence. But in arguing that these critical insights matter, three more questions need to be asked: what of the people who reject their identification — that is, their identification by others — in a category, or whose understandings of categories is different from those who identify them? How useful is a politics that seeks to represent them as such? And if this is indeed a problem, what is to be done about it? I will attempt to answer the first two questions here and will leave the last until the end of this chapter, though I will take it on most fully in the conclusion.

In answer to the first, again I am drawn to the thrown bottles and the dark threats of the Meat Market, of the little and big violences of the daily lives of the fem queen sex workers. The complexity of their senses of selves and the social realities which structure their experiences on these streets — an intersection of racism, poverty, youth, neoliberal urban policy, policing — cannot be accounted for by a simple resort to "violence against transgender people," even if that is partly true. This matters because reducing murder (or a thrown bottle, or a catcall) to one kind of violence — "racism," "violence against transgender people," "gay bashing" — erases the others. It asserts a one-dimensionality of both the injured and the reasons for injury (see Brown 1995). At a moral level, I agree when Daniel argues that violence is characterized by an excess of evil. But, simultaneously, if we seek an answer to violence, then surely it is important to understand its roots, its complexity, for challenging acts of violence requires far more than simply condemning evil, especially when "violence" can also be found in a journal article or a political position and be understood as assault, rape, or murder. Moreover, in asserting "violence against transgender people," we lose sight of a range of other violences perpetrated at the structural level: neoliberal policies which further disenfranchise the poor and entrench poverty, associated "quality of life" urban policing, the corporatization of public space, and the diminution of the public sphere. By reducing fem queens to their experience as "transgender" and the violences they face as "violence against transgender people," we ignore these broader violences and their own systemic qualities.

Yet, at the same time (and in response to my second question), the value of a category like transgender to make claims against violators is substantial. A vast range of experiences — the violence done against oneself in the past, being subject to the constraints of a binary gender system, having to jump through the hoops set up by medical professionals, social scientific representations, antithetical political positions — all these have potential to become part of a "tool kit" to make claims *against* those practices, positions, and representations. Violence, then, is not only a fact of life but also can be used to narrate one's past in order to explain the present, to characterize the actions of others who should be your allies as no better than the rapists, muggers, doctors, and hecklers who have made your life a horror. That is, in the constitution of "transgender" as an identity category, and a category of political action, the experience of violence becomes available as a theory of the self, where it is assumed that one's attempts to claim a non-ascribed gender are met, almost perforce, by violent opposition. As "transgender" gathers into itself a vast range of identities, so "violence" can become a catch-all for every perceived violation. In this way, all harm or potential harm — whatever its origin or manifestation — can be reread through a framework of violence. And as such, it becomes a powerful tool to appeal to a variety of agencies — grassroots organizations, medical groups, and especially the state — for interventions of different orders.

But the flip side of this dynamic is that to harness the power of this narrative force, one has to narrate oneself through those particular institutionalized frameworks which make sense of the violence, in this case, that of "transgender." Wendy Brown, in addressing feminists' attempts to draw the attention of the state to violence and discrimination against women, asks: "What are the perils of pursuing emancipatory political aims within largely repressive, regulatory, and depoliticizing institutions that themselves carry elements of the regime (e.g., masculine dominance) whose subversion is being sought?" (1995: ix–x). Interventions by the state — and other agencies which have access to resources and forms of social power — require not only an evening out of experience but the assertion of an identifiable source of difference which the state can recognize. And, as I pointed out above, "the state" must itself be understood as a perpetrator of violence, not only in the terms Brown proposes but in its reshaping and restriction of the terms of citizenship.

As I have argued throughout this book, "transgender" is on the one hand potentially inclusive of a vast range of different ways of being in the world, but the insistence that transgender identities lie exclusively in the realm of gender (to the exclusion of sexuality but also race and class and thus of poverty and racism) means that particular — even if potentially radical — understandings of "gender" need to be codified and institutionalized. And once more, my concern is that those people who do not understand themselves through these interpretive and institutionalized practices *come to be unrepresentable in these politics in the terms in which they understand themselves, explain the world, and might experience violence as a result of a complex nexus of these experiences.*

The point here is not to reduce transgender identity to violence but rather to show how, through all these stories, "transgender" is institutionally, narratively, and biographically linked to the experience of violence with complicated, often painful, results. To use one of Cindy's phrases, this is the calculus of pain.[7]

THE CRITICAL EYE

I have argued here that violence, pain, and suffering are neither simple nor precultural facts — they are produced through and drawn into the complexities of daily experience, given meaning, talked about, mounted as claims, and deeply felt. For violence to be understood *as* violence, a story must be told about it, the horror relived but also re-ordered and given narrative form with each telling. Moreover, in addressing that violence, it must be shaped as violence which makes sense in terms of a category of social identification, a category which in turn requires the complexity of violence and its multiple structural logics to be smoothed over. Consequently, the possibilities for ethical and effective action are deeply fraught: it is a complex calculus indeed.

As an anthropologist with commitments to and friendships with many people who participated in my study, I am, moreover, conflicted by the ways in which my own data and conclusions put me in a difficult relationship to the advocacy work I have engaged in. I am thinking again of Vianna-Faye and the Meat Market fem queens who cannot be fully represented through "transgender" both because their understandings of self confound its terms and because it does not account for the structural violences of racism and poverty so central to their experiences. As Moran and Sharpe (2002) point out, the implication of the surveys of violence against transgender-identified people is that transgender-identified people experience violence in structurally equivalent ways, without attention to other factors which can produce moments of violence — poverty, ethnicity, racial identification, immigration status, religion, age — and that they thereby elide the complexity of the lives represented by them. Yet the fem queens who are driven to sex work to survive are the ones most likely to find their way into the list of murdered transgender victims, their lives narrativized and evened out through stories told about them *as* transgender people in the halls of Congress. The use of "transgender" in this activism, then — unintentionally — itself produces and magnifies those elisions.

Ironically then, this analysis of "transgender" enables me as an anthropologist to make my own claim about violence: that the unquestioned inclusion of people like Vianna-Faye or even Brandon Teena into the encompassing category of "transgender" produces a representational colonization of those lives. Given the above analysis, the ways that representation can be seen as violent, I could even write *representational violence,* but again, the slipperiness of "violence" — and the implications for my own and my colleagues' advocacy work — makes this hard to write, so I leave it as an alternative, in italics. Indeed, I am sure that this argument will itself be seen as a form of representational violence, yet another anthropological mischaracterization of transgender experience.

The memory of being in Vianna-Faye's car the last night I saw her alive stays with me. The exposure to violence — however imagined, narrated, or enacted, whether the person is gender variant or not, whether that person is a man or a woman or another gender, whether they are white, black,

Latino/a, Asian, whether they are comfortably off or hustling to make ends meet — is an evident fact of life for many transgender-identified people. My narrative of the intimate details of my last meeting with Vianna-Faye — the number of sugar packets, the warmth of her car, the fear — becomes another condensation of moments and feelings into a narrative of violence, made possible through a variety of institutional fixings: the possibility of turning it into a statistic, a story for a legislator, or an anecdote for a book chapter. My understanding of violence lies in the uneasy ground between two poles: the recognition, on the one hand, of the complexities of acts of violence, their narration, and the often-hidden structural conditions in which they are enacted. On the other is the thought of Vianna-Faye, dead in her nightgown on Christmas morning, knowing that I will never be able to take her chicken soup and eat it with her. It is this dynamic which makes it hard to write this chapter, which makes it difficult to mount an analysis of a political movement that in some moments seems to undermine the goals of social justice it aims to bring about. But it is equally the case that we should keep our critical eyes on this ground if we are to do anything about violence, and as we consider my final question: what is to be done?

For something needs to be done, even if I am sometimes hesitant about what is being done and what should be done.[8] The point of the critical eye is not to prevent us from demanding justice for Vianna-Faye, Brandon Teena, and the many, many other people who are punished (at least in part) for not being men and women as others think they should be. And it must not prevent us from trying to ensure that other people are not harassed, beaten, raped, or murdered for any reason, or from trying to work against poverty, structural injustices, hunger, or the range of other crimes that characterize our world. But as James Ferguson reminds us, in order to address these injustices, we must not only ask "what is to be done" but also ask: who is asking this question? In whose terms is it answered? The point of the critical eye is thus to enable us to think about the terms in which we answer "what is to be done," to consider where the answer comes from, how it can be answered from multiple perspectives, and who has the ability to have their voice heard. It is to these questions that I now turn.

Conclusion

Making Ethnography

Late on a Saturday night, I leave Nancy at Karalyn's bar and go outside to unlock my bicycle. Even though I know it's stupid and dangerous (not to mention illegal), I put on my Walkman headphones, push off into moving traffic, and head south toward the Meat Market. There are few pleasures like cycling through New York on a summer's night, listening to music and feeling the wind in your face. There's a song I like to listen to while I ride, Dire Straits's "Skateaway," a song about a Walkman-wearing woman making movies in her head as she roller skates through the city. She dodges taxi drivers, just for fun, drawing them into a story which is shaped by the DJ's choice of music and her route through the traffic. Like her, I'm listening to my Walkman as I dodge traffic, but I'm not making movies: I'm making ethnography. I imagine the night ahead of me, thinking how fantastic it is that I traverse these places, that 9th Avenue becomes a direct route between here and there, the link between two venues so dissimilar, which are brought together not by a song but by a category, transgender.

Like my trusty bicycle, on these nights transgender is a useful way of getting around, of going from one thing to another, of framing a set of diverse moments and social practices in time and space as an entity. At other times, though, this feeling dissolves into a new story, a fractured sense that I am the starring lead in an ethnographic unity of my own making. And in other moments, it seems to me that whatever I do, however this category works, it is useful to people, myself included. It is useful to be able to map Nancy into this story alongside the social service providers, transactivists, and fem queens. And it is useful not simply for my fieldwork but also for people engaged in social justice activism, for personal identification, for doing something about very bad things in the world.

This mapping may be familiar to you by now: I'm going forty-one blocks south, from Karalyn's at 55th Street to the Meat Market on 14th, from cross-dressers to fem queens, from mostly white to almost exclusively African American and Latina, from flirting (and some sex work) to sex work (and some flirting), from inside to outside, semi-private to very public, yet all encapsulated for me — and simultaneously by me — within the frame of "transgender."

And indeed, there are nights when it works like this. I look back on my notes to the moments when the connections between these dispersed settings and people come together: a long-time cross-dresser tells me about frequenting Sally's, a club that none of the other cross-dressers go to, but which many of the fem queens do; a night when almost all the girls in the Meat Market tell me they know about the GIP; I bump into outreach workers from other agencies and we can talk about people we know in common; a white activist with whom I lobbied in Washington comes and does outreach with me and recognizes one of the African American girls from her days in the clubs; a ball House holds a joint public meeting with the GIP to talk about "transgender issues."

But at other times the promise of transgender seems to crumble: a crossdresser angrily tells me that she does not see herself as "transgender" and that she thinks transexuals are "insane"; a fem queen on the stroll, strung out on drugs, doesn't want condoms, has never heard of the Center or GIP, and says she has no friends, that she wants to die; the same activist who is doing outreach with me denounces GenderPAC for working on intersex issues, arguing that this "confuses the issue" for legislators.

What directed me to attend to transgender as a *category of knowing* rather than as a simple description of a group of people was the fact that my practices as an anthropologist seemed to be part of the ways in which it was solidifying. Cycling around New York, making sense out of diverse social contexts through this category, was also an exercise in the power of language. I was directed to these sites by people who imagined them as belonging to this category, even as the sites I visited and the people I met there found it more or less applicable to themselves, or didn't even know that this was what they were supposed to call themselves. In the end, I found I could not write a book about "the transgender community" because that community — even as it exists, and is real — is at the same time a product of an imagined unity that, upon careful scrutiny, obscures the cultural, historical, and social forces of its origins and consequences of its use.

Yet speaking or writing of transgender brings into being what it presupposes, even if it does not always make sense at all moments. That is, as I argued in chapter 2, there *is* such a thing as a transgender community in a self-evident sense. By bringing together people in town meetings on violence, by claiming certain contexts as transgender spaces, by gathering data on violence against transgender people, or by lobbying the U.S. Congress on transgender issues, a transgender community and transgender identity is produced in a significant, institutionalized way. Such a community, even with limited resources, provides access, information, and possibilities that did not previously exist for some of the most marginalized, marked, and violated people in contemporary U.S. American society. The imagining itself produces a social reality that people draw on — and reproduce — as much as it may be contested by others. Indeed, it is a category like any other social category an anthropologist might study.

My concern throughout this book, though, has been that some people may not be able to benefit from the transformative possibilities of the work done through "transgender." I have argued that this is so because the meanings attached to this category — and to the category homosexuality — reproduce a set of hierarchical relationships along the lines of embodiment, class, race, and age. Moreover, I have argued that "homosexuality" and "transgender" have come to be *ontologized,* that is, given the status of original and transcendent being, and thus have come to describe separate groups of people. But words, language, and categories do more than describe the world — they create it too. While every word we speak is a category, some come to have more power to explain who we are, and thus to limit (as much as enable) the possibilities for our action in the world. Crucially, the limits of "transgender" (as with the limits of "homosexuality") are not simply the failure of categories to account for a complex world. Rather, the reiteration of these categories in a wide range of day-to-day and institutional contexts is *productive* of that failure.

In the end, this is an irresolvable dilemma, for there is only language by which to make sense of ourselves and those with whom we interact as lovers, friends, colleagues, people on the street, or ethnographic informants. The language we use about ourselves and these others can only partially account for the endless stream of our experiences, for in the reduction of experience to language we recreate that experience as something qualitatively different. Throughout this book, I have struggled with this problem in writing about the complexities of four central categories — transgender, homosexuality, gender, and sexuality — while simultaneously invoking them to try to describe experiences and contexts that escape their boundaries, for we have no other words for these things other than the categories themselves.

In identifying these dynamics, I am making a point that is central to poststructuralist arguments about language. Simultaneously, I am therefore setting myself up for two of the most frequently made critiques of critical theoretical and deconstructive methods: first, that in opening up categories for investigation, these approaches evacuate them of meaning; and second, that by doing so (especially with categories of identity that are deeply meaningful to people), they are also, effectively, apolitical — or worse, antipolitical (e.g., Park 2003).

In this final chapter I want to argue against these critiques. First, I will synthesize the various arguments throughout this book and make a case for why I believe the category transgender has helped transform a 150-year-old debate about that-which-we-call gender and sexuality. That is, rather than evacuate transgender or homosexuality of meaning, as some readers might argue I have, I want to show how "transgender" and "homosexuality" have *achieved* a certain institutional meaning in relation to one another. Second, I will argue that this kind of approach should in fact be central both to ethnography and engaged social action. I will make a case for ethnography as a tool for activists, and by doing so I want to argue against certainties, definitions, and final answers. If you take nothing else from this book, I hope to convince you at least that the open question is as important to sustained and effective activism as it is to complex and thorough ethnography.

A POLITICS OF GENDER, SEXUALITY, AND SELF

I wrote in the introduction that I use "imagining" to point to how a particular idea of transgender has been produced and achieved through a diverse set of social practices. In making such an argument, I am drawing on anthropological conceptions which understand culture and meaning making to arise from the exertion of human agency within broader structures of meaning, possibility, and constraint. This understanding of culture has three broad principles: first, culture is not simply located in received wisdom from previous generations but rather arises out of the kinds of situated practices and contexts I have discussed, where individual social actors work both to challenge and reproduce (often simultaneously) ideas about gender variance, transgender identity, democracy, privacy, gender, selfhood, race, class, sexuality, and so on. The second central point is that in such work, differently situated social actors have differing capacities to get things done in the way that they would like them done (what we might refer to as "social power"). The final point is that, whatever their access to resources and whatever their capacities, no single social actor can ever apprehend all the conditions, possibilities, constraints, or outcomes of their action which can produce unintended, as much as intended, consequences (Giddens 1979: 59ff.). To sum up, then, my argument is that over the course of the twentieth century certain social actors in the United States, with relatively more ability to challenge meanings and practices, have (for often very different reasons) actively worked to produce innovative cultural models to distinguish between gender and sexuality, as well as new ways of conceptualizing gender variance and homosexual desire. At the same time, an unintended consequence of this action has been that some people cannot easily be accounted for by these models. Moreover, these models are not entirely new—they resonate with older, historical formations, carrying with them some baggage that is often hard to recognize. Thus, my claim is that the social realities produced through the innovations of transgender are part of the transformation of U.S. American understandings of what gender and sexuality can mean, even as they unintentionally reproduce other social realities, in particular, historically situated structures of class, racial, and gender differences.

I have also noted the different domains in which gender and sexuality came to gain meaning in the twentieth century: medical, social scientific, activist, and social. But it is not simply that "gender" and "sexuality" have come to be seen as distinct in these domains. Rather it is that the *content* of these terms also shifts across different fields and historical time periods. As I argued in chapter 4, sexology, psychiatry, gay and lesbian scholarship, and feminism have all come to an understanding of gender as distinct from biological sex. Within psychiatry, sexology, and gay/lesbian scholarship/

activism, such an understanding has relied further on the conceptualization of the difference between gender and sexuality. That is, "gender" figures in these latter discourses as a set of qualities named in different ways but primarily implying an internal sense of oneself as either a man or a woman. Within feminism, however, while this latter understanding is shared, "gender" also operates as a privileged analytic category — and not simply a social difference — for understanding the relationship between the exertion of gendered agency and the contexts of gendered structures of power.

If the argument of accommodationist gay and lesbian activists is that gay men are unproblematically men who happen to be erotically attracted to other men, this is itself an achievement, as the historical cases discussed in chapter 1 indicate. Indeed, for much of the past 150 years, homosexual men have *not* been seen as "men." Sexological, psychiatric, and other medical frameworks have historically contributed to this dynamic, explaining male-bodied people who are erotically drawn to other male-bodied people as the result of a feminine soul, psyche, biology, or the result of aberrant psychosexual development. But the new possibilities for understanding masculine gender as separable from erotic attraction enables "gender" in this account to stand simply as a neutral social difference. From a feminist perspective, however, in claiming gender-normative masculinity as male-bodied people, gay men have not had to theorize or politicize their gender as men as lesbians have had to do as women. That is, the claims on unproblematic masculinity made by gay men do not engage — and in fact, only serve to reproduce — the gendered structures of difference against which feminists have fought for so long as these claims reduce gender to, simply, a matter of identity.

My argument, then, is that the insistence in mainstream accommodationist gay and lesbian activism that homosexuality is not inflected by gender variance is at root an attempt to argue for the validity of *male* homosexuals as *men* and to erase the stigma that attaches to femininity in male-bodied people. This, in turn, depends on a conceptualization of gender as a form of social difference rather than, from a feminist perspective, a site of social power relations, and is embedded in a structural devaluation of femininity in U.S. society.[1] I hasten to add that I do not mean that individual gay men are necessarily misogynistic (nor do I mean that transgender identification rests on an anti-feminist understanding of gender). My claim is rather about structures of value, the ways that these play out in day-to-day practices, and the effects of institutionalization of such structures as I laid out in chapters 4 and 5.

Let me take these points one by one. I am arguing that the broader structural devaluation of femininity in male-bodied people in the West produces a cultural anxiety for men about the perception of being feminine. As Tyler writes: "It does not follow that because gay men are unafraid of being seen as gay, they are unafraid of being seen as feminine. . . . The fear that homosexuality means a man can be robbed of his virility . . . may animate homophobia outside the gay community and misogyny within it as well as without" (1991: 37). Susan Bordo reads the emphasis on muscularity in contemporary gay male culture as a sign that, whether one is a "top" or a "bottom," one is still masculine by cultivating "[a] body that challenges the cultural gaze that has cast the gay man as soft and effeminate by presenting a surface that nothing can penetrate, granite chiseled according to its owner's specifications" (1999: 58). And Judith Lorber (1994) argues that the stigmatization of male homosexuality must be seen as part of a broader stigmatization of femininity because of a masculinist fear of women encroaching on the public sphere. Lorber argues that the push to be able to identify (male) homosexuals (through studies such as those described by Terry 1995) in all aspects of public life relied on an assumption of visible femininity in male homosexuals. It is precisely this feminization of male homosexuality that is contested by contemporary mainstream gay and lesbian activists (see also McNeal 1999).

As such, the ability of accommodationist gay male activists to deny femininity relies on a simple denial of a particular *gender identity*, a form of radical difference from women/femininity. The model of gender-as-difference is essential to this denial, for a feminist theorization of gender would require gay men to recognize how gender more broadly structures social and political worlds and not simply "identity." While, again, many gay men are concerned about sexism and misogyny, the institutionalization of this understanding of gender-as-difference in political strategies and organizations reproduces its terms as difference-without-power. Likewise, despite the feminist politics of many trans-identified people, transgender as a category itself also reproduces such an understanding of gender because an understanding of gender-as-difference is central to its ontology. Finally, mainstream lesbian political concerns have — ironically — also been subsumed under this logic: in this identity-as-difference system, lesbians can talk about "gender" (as women), but not as ("sexual") lesbians. One fallout of this logic was evident in the Human Rights Campaign's endorsement of New York Republican Senator Alfonse D'Amato in the 1998 Senate race. D'Amato's well-known anti-choice stance on abortion had angered many progressive organizations in New York and nationally, but the endorsement by HRC — defended by that organization as a political tactic — indicates at some level a conception that reproductive rights (the realm of "gender") are not gay or lesbian issues (the realm of "sexuality"). In this case, it is clear why sexuality and gender are not as easily separable for feminists as they are for gay men, for the interlacing concerns of sexuality, reproduction, and gendered power are inseparable. Hence, the use of "gay" as the unmarked category of homosexuality in this book has been quite conscious, for mainstream gay and lesbian politics has been shaped by a concern that is at root a (white, middle-class) gay male concern.

This is not to say that the boundary between lesbians (the "sexual") and transexual men (the "gendered") is not heavily policed, as Halberstam (1998b), Hale (1998), and Henry Rubin (2003) all make clear. Yet there is also evidently a space for the positive eroticization of female masculinity (Halberstam 1998a) in ways that have few if any correlates in gay male culture, as I argued in chapter 4. The rejection of feminine identification for contemporary gay men takes two forms, as evident in the historical accounts by Hekma (1994) and Cole (2000) discussed in chapter 1. First, there is the rejection of the idea that feminine-inflected homosexuality is an appropriate model for contemporary male homosexuality; but second, a rejection of the idea that feminine identification or behavior was *ever* truly desired by historical subjects. In these accounts, femininity was at best simply a strategy to attract gender-normative men in a sexual economy where two gender-normative men having sex was not possible.

It is thus, I would argue, the concern to delink male homosexuality from femininity — more than the lesbian-feminist concern with establishing a stable category of "woman" — which has shaped the politics of gay gender normativity. It is this concern which has in part propelled a radical separation of "gender" and "sexuality" as conceptual categories underpinning different kinds of identities in mainstream LGBT politics, and which has effectively required the birth of a new category — transgender — for those who are not identified primarily in terms of "sexuality." "Gay," in other words, is not naturally about same-sex sexual relations but rather has been actively constructed as such on a model of (male) gender normativity, which impoverishes understandings of systemic gendered structures central to lesbian subjectivities; relies on a rejection of racialized public gender variance/sexuality; and implicitly elides other possible organizations of gendered/sexual experience. In short, the contention that the practice of two men engaging in anal sex is not understandable within an analytical or experiential scheme called "gender" is not a natural fact but a historically produced set of understandings of which practices and identities are seen best to be as sexual, and which are best understood as gendered.

Let me restate my case one more time: I am *not* arguing that gender and sexuality are the "same thing," nor am I advocating a return to an analytic system which sees homosexuality as necessarily linked to cross-gender identification. Indeed, the understanding that gender and sexuality are distinct arenas of social experience has been vital to the recognition that what we call gender and sexuality are *not* causally linked as the dominant cultural model of heteronormative gender implies. Most obviously, the conceptualization of gender and sexuality as separate is useful in that it *does* explain and help describe subjectivities of many gay men and lesbians, as well as many transexual and transgender-identified people. I am therefore not arguing that gay men are "really" feminine because they desire men nor that lesbians are "really" masculine because they desire women. Likewise, I refuse the assertion that transexual women are "really" homosexual men (as Bailey [2003] implies). Finally, I am not claiming that among gay/lesbian/bisexual and transgender-identified people there is not a great deal of resistance to the politics of accommodation I described above. However, the ways in which this theoretical split echoes — and underpins — institutionalized LGBT politics (both accommodationist and radical) is problematic in they are unable to account for the subjectivities I lay out in chapters 2 and 3 in their own terms.

I *am* arguing, therefore, that while there is a common-sense recognition that sexuality and gender are both separable *and* connected categories and experiences, the ways in which "gender" and "sexuality" as cultural and theoretical categories have come to be conceptualized and institutionalized as separate experiences need to be re-opened for investigation. The insistence on this conceptual split — and its ossification in the politics and scholarship which posit "gender" as distinct from "sexuality" — erases "gender" from the realm of (unmarked male) homosexuality, renders lesbians' demands for reproductive rights as a "not-gay" issue, denies the powerful connections among gender, sexuality, publicity, race, and class, and, further, essentializes the experiences gathered under the terms "gender" and "sexuality." That is, even as psychiatry, feminist theory, and the gay and lesbian liberation movement have imagined (from widely differing perspectives) a new world of possibility opened up by conceptualizing gender and sexuality as separate analytic, social, and experiential realms, the effect of this theoretical and political move has, ironically, also been to restrict the analytic and political possibilities of liberatory sexual and gender politics.

RACE, CLASS, PRIVACY

Contemporary gay and lesbian activism and politics do not operate independently of political economy, and to fully understand the power of claims to gender-normative homosexuality, we must look at the broader context of U.S. political-economic developments over the same period. As I outlined in chapter 5, the emergence of the modern gay and lesbian movement in the early 1970s coincided with the rise of neoliberal state and business policies and ideologies, that combination of business activism and attacks on twentieth-century social welfare gains which has transformed global political economies. Central to neoliberal agendas (for they are many, varied, and sometimes contradictory) is the appeal to privatization, privacy, and lack of state intervention in business enterprise (or at least, a lack of regulation, since contemporary corporations rely heavily on state subsidies even as welfare for the poorest citizens is relentlessly attacked [Harvey 2000]). Public institutions are increasingly seen as primarily responsible for the facilitation of private enterprise, even as public space has become increasingly corporatized. Thus, the emergence of the modern gay and lesbian movement (and latterly, the transgender rights movement) has coincided with a remaking of "public" and "private" in U.S. society, a remaking that resonates with the claims of gay and lesbian activists to privacy rights as the key site of activism.

In her book *The Twilight of Equality?* Lisa Duggan coins the term "homonormativity" to capture how politically conservative gay and lesbian scholars and activists explicitly vaunt the power of the liberalized market to achieve civil rights recognitions with a "politics that does not contest dominant heteronormative assumptions and institutions but upholds and sustains them" (2003: 50; see also Chasin 2001, Maskovsky 2002).[2] Duggan critically examines how an appeal to privacy in contemporary gay and lesbian struggles for equality (and simultaneously on the market as the mechanism for achieving recognition) produces homosexuality as implicitly gender normative, white, and middle class. There are deeper historical points of connection between gay and lesbian struggles for recognition and the marketplace, though. As D'Emilio (1983a) has argued, the innovation of homosexuality as a category in the nineteenth century occurred at the same historical moment that new forms of kinship, shaped by transformed market relations, came to dominate American society. D'Emilio argues that the insecurities experienced by heteronormative families as a result of transformed market forces have increasingly been foisted on the figure of the homosexual. The demand for privacy rights and the entry to the discursive and legal space of the family, so central to contemporary gay and lesbian organizing, is thus — to extend D'Emilio's analysis — a demand to no longer be the foil of the market. Yet this activism simultaneously draws on the image of the private market in order to claim the forms of intimacy from which gay men and lesbians have historically been excluded. In other words, mainstream "homonormative" gay and lesbian activism has become increasingly organized around the demand to be "included" as a legitimate niche within a neoliberal ontological economy, in which individual rights are as closely associated with market participation as they are with any theory of civil liberties. As I argued in chapter 5, demands for "inclusion" must always beg the questions: how is that which excludes and that which is to be included formed? What boundaries of the including and excluding groups must be defined in order for "inclusion" to take place?

One of the central boundary drawings in this process has been around that of gender variance. The historical equation of homosexuality with both gender variance and public/commercial sex has been both contested by contemporary gay and lesbian activists as a misrepresentation and countered with a claim that homosexual identity is a private matter of choice and/or inborn traits. In doing so, accommodationist gay and lesbian activists have sought to gain access to the central institution of social and economic life — "the family" — through marriage and parenting rights, refiguring "sexuality" as private, decoupling it from both reproduction and gender variance and from a broader conceptualization of gender/sexuality as productive domains of power relations. This has been made possible precisely because the family is the site where the public and private bleed into one another, and consequently the reason that the issue of gay marriage and family rights has provoked such heated debate in the United States.

The privatization of (homo)sexuality and its distinction from gender variance also thus serves to reproduce the idea of the family (heterosexual or homosexual) as the site of the production of intimacy and sexual love, and of "good sex" as opposed to "bad sex" (see Rubin 1984, Kulick 2005). By placing private homosexual acts in the context of the family, activists are thus attempting to redefine the boundaries of public and private. It should be noted that conservative scholars are just as concerned about this redefinition as left and progressive scholars are, though for quite different reasons. They see the extension of privacy rights and the model of the market as mediator of social relationships as key moves toward an imminent collapse of the social order (e.g., Wood 2003). These perspectives, as well as real contemporary concerns about the state's encroachment on individuals' privacy, should give us pause in simply dismissing "privacy" as a rallying point of neoliberalism. The point is, though, that like gender and sexuality, "private" and "public" are not self-evident realms — they can be mobilized as categories in different ways by different parties and with different meanings and intents. Gay/lesbian privacy claims are equally claims for the participation of gay and lesbian people in *public* life as families, as married couples, as parents, and as consumer-citizens. But this is the very thing that concerns some conservative commentators, and which they contest with their own counter-constructions of private and public. However, what *is* innovative about gay and lesbian activist privacy claims lies in the success in excising the excess of publicity, sexual deviance, gender variance, and street life from the category of homosexuality and insisting on the gender normativity of homosexuality. For all its use to transgender-identified people, then, "transgender" also has the effect of shoring up claims (however contested) about gender-normative, respectable, and privately practiced homosexuality within the tentatively refigured white, middle-class family of the late twentieth and early twenty-first century. To paraphrase Eve Sedgwick (1990), this is an epistemology of the walk-in closet.

BORDERS AND BOUNDARIES, SELF AND OTHER

My third broad point in this book has been about the nature of analytic distinctions, and their implication in the processes described above. The figures of borders or boundaries have animated much of what I have written: those between masculine and feminine, butches and FTMs, public and private, gay and transgender, gender and sexuality. In contemporary social theory, borders have come to stand as a useful—necessary—figure in thinking about the hybridities that result from transnational processes in the context of neoliberalism (e.g., Ortner 1996, Michaelsen and Johnson 1997). Central to these processes is not only the movement of categories of identity and analysis from the West to the non-West but also the simultaneous return of those transformed adoptions through ethnographic and popular texts. Sherry Ortner (1996), in her discussion of the gendered and erotic politics of mountaineering in Nepal, uses the border to query the very categories of apprehension whereby we come to know about the "Other." Ortner makes a claim for the importance of borderlands as a site of recognition of the specifics of "cultures" even as borderland encounters —in this case, between Western and Sherpa men and women—alter the terms of what "culture" can mean.

More importantly, Ortner argues that borderland encounters complicate the very categories of knowing whereby these encounters can be described—how "gender" comes to be transformed by "religion," "nationality," "race," "sexuality," and so on. That is, it is not enough to say that the borders of such categories abut, or that they inflect one another, intersect, are imbricated, overlap, or are mutually constitutive. Rather, the nature of borderlands—physical, historical, epistemological—transforms what these categories can mean or contain in given, local, situated contexts. In short, the locatedness of social practices—in which I include ethnographic and theoretical accounts of other practices—already remakes the categories through which we describe them. This is, again, a feature of language itself, for categories are essential for talk and for representing self and other. My argument is simply that we must constantly attend to the politics of language—not just for its content but for its capacity to constitute the world in particular ways.

As such, my goal has not been to figure out the discrete and absolute borders between a stone butch or a transgender man, or a fem gay man or a transgender woman *but to investigate the history and set of power relations whereby such disputes arise and such definitions are required of people; the political, social, cultural, and economic processes which underlie such power relations; and what effects such requirements have.* Moreover, my analysis does not seek to ignore the complex identities and experiences of contemporary subjects who have far more complicated relationships to gendered and sexual meanings than my analysis above engages: leather men who camp it up, "butches vogueing butch queen vogueing fem," nellie men who body build, dykes in leather who are femmes, transqueers, genderfuckers, femme bois, radical fairies, queers, drag queens for a day, men, women, and others in multiple-partner families, fem queens who enjoy penetrative anal sex, butch bears who wear lingerie, and a vast range of other expressions of self and desire. Rather, I am worried that in the institutionalization of certain understandings of what it means to be gay, lesbian, and transgender — and of the theories of gender and sexuality that underpin them — these identities, expressions, and differences are in danger of falling out of politics, out of "the rich diversity of our community,"[3] even as "LGBT" promises to include them all. I am not suggesting an expansion of the rainbow imaginary of "LGBT" to include more categories. Rather, my concern is how these erasures are complicit in a broader accommodationist politics which both embraces neoliberal market logic and elides a feminist understanding of gender and power, and the consequences of this for progressive politics.

EDUCATING RITA

These concerns travel with me on my bicycle to the streets of the Meat Market, where the girls I meet there are in a multiple bind. They embody all those aspects of variant gender/sexual behavior and identity and of public sexuality that have historically formed the contours of the public imagination of homosexual/gender-variant identity. Simultaneously, they have fallen out of a categorical system where their own understandings of self can be understood in terms of the identity political movements that have arisen since the early 1970s, and which by the 1990s had developed into a discrete politics of "gay and lesbian" and "transgender" movements, neither of which can fully account for them. The primary drive of these movements in terms of the discourses of "privacy" further produces the girls as external to the goals of the movement, even as corporate privacy claims refine the meaning of the public sphere (Chesluk 2004). For, as noted in chapter 3, the work they engage in, and the contexts of street sociality, are not simply "chosen" from a range of choices in a free market economy but are structured by the historical facts of racism and poverty as much as by opprobrium directed at public gender and sexual variance, facts which have themselves only been exacerbated by neoliberal policies in the corporatization of public urban space.

To imagine Rita or Jade or Miss Angel laboring under "false conscious-ness" because they are unable to distinguish their "gendered" and "sexual" identities is thus to assert a modernist telos wherein the recognition of gendered and sexual identification as separate (if related, in some unspec-ified way) is more accurate, more true, more valid. Thus, the Meat Market fem queens like Rita become almost figures of premodernity, people who have not been "educated," who adhere to the "mistaken" belief that homo-sexual identification involves cross-gender identification. They have not joined, in short, in the progress narrative that underpins historical ac-counts of a coming-to-light of this distinction, and as a result they become simultaneously un- (perhaps even anti-) progressive. This narrative, more-over, makes invisible the political-economic structures within which it unfolds and recalls the modernist desire to reshape the personhood of colonized subjects into rational citizens, only this time written onto the Othered streets of neoliberal urban America. In asserting the truth of the distinction between gender and sexuality — rather than recognizing that it is simply one way of carving up how we know about ourselves and others — contemporary critical social theory engages all those aspects of moder-nity that in other guises it critiques: a master narrative, unfolding within a historical teleology, characterized by progress and a coming-to-truth.

If the transgender movement operates on the same trajectory as the mainstream gay and lesbian movement — one that demands of the state certain rights and privileges — then what "exclusions" might follow? If the logic of representation in the "politics of recognition" requires one to present a stable identity — this time consolidated in an understandable and marketable discourse about transgender as an identity based in gender variance — will it necessarily lead to a political movement where, also, whiteness, middle classness, and respectability are assumed? My concern is that the well-intentioned desire to educate Rita into the language of transgender *institutionally* produces expectations of how she should com-port herself in seeking the protection of the state or accessing services. That is, it worries me that transgender itself (because of its institutional life, its implication in agencies of the state, its racial and class entailments) may unintentionally become another tool of "exclusion," even as it prom-ises to "include," to liberate, and to seek redress.

On a broader terrain my argument is not simply about the desire for gay male activists to avoid the stigma of femininity; competing understandings of gender and sexuality; or the racialized and classed implications of identity politics. Rather, underpinning all these dynamics is a longer history of the disaggregation and reintegration of the self in modernity. The distinction between gender and sexuality — to the extent that it has traction — is part of a broader set of discursive and practical technologies of the self. These include others that have obviously been central to the discourses around transgender, such as plastic surgeries, but also far more broadly dispersed practices and discourses of self-help, activism, reinvention of the self, and of "starting over" (Fitzgerald 1986).

These are practices and discourses deeply rooted in U.S. American culture and in the working out of personhood in late modernity, evident as much in the growth of psychiatric diagnostic categories, the assertion of "identity" as a central paradigm in politics, and the elaboration of niche markets for consumption as it is in the construction of "transgender." The point is not to see transgender as a special case, an extreme form, or as exemplary, but as part of the quotidian forms of self-making and self-education in which all modern subjects are imagined to engage. Like all categories, transgender is transformative because of its capacity to refine.

This is *not* the same as saying (as Janice Raymond does) that transgender-identified people "reproduce binary gender" or holding them responsible for patriarchy's power. It is, rather, to argue that all modern subjects are engaged in this same process of disaggregation, reintegration, refinement, and education of the self. The goal is not to identify the perpetrators of fraudulent categorization but to open up the question of how all of us are responsible for — and subject to — the limits and possibilities of self-making in a broader and stratified political-economic context. The goal is to reveal how the categories we live by — must live by — have histories, politics, and economies and produce effects that can be as debilitating for some as they can be liberating for others. The goal is to question how, why, when, and with what effects self-making is other-making. The goal is to recognize how educating Rita is educating ourselves.

ETHNOGRAPHY AS AN ACTIVIST STRATEGY

"Ethnography" ... *is not so much a specific procedure in anthropology as it is a method of being at risk in the face of the practices and discourses into which one enquires.* — DONNA HARAWAY, *Modest_Witness@ Second_Millennium. FemaleMan© _ Meets _ OncoMouse™*

So, what is to be done? It seems unsatisfying — not to mention unethical — to finish a book about the meanings and politics of transgender with the neat assessment that it is a cultural construction which has deep roots in Euro-American culture; that it unintentionally reproduces racist and class-based hierarchies of oppression; that it potentially results in young, poor people of color (the intersection of three of the most vulnerable groups of people in contemporary U.S. society) being further oppressed; and that the notion of a "transgender community" is a political imaginary. As Paisley Currah (2003) notes, drawing on Stuart Hall, exposing contradictions and inconsistencies in social and political systems is not enough. Moreover, inconsistencies and contradictions, which most anthropologists would argue are central to any social system, do not invalidate the formations which contain them.

For again, it is abundantly clear that "transgender" has had tangible and positive effects. Transgender advocacy and activism — hard, barefoot work — has resulted in more sensitive and specific medical services, access to housing, amelioration of discrimination in schools and the workplace, and a host of other gains in the United States and elsewhere. The counting of statistics of violence and the grim tabulation of murders (GenderPAC 1997), the HIV needs assessments (Kammerer et al. 1999), the legislative advocacy (Frye 2000, Currah and Minter 2000), the court cases (Currah 2003, Weiss 2001), as much as the development of a field of knowledge about transgender-identified people (Stryker 2006) and the training of health care professionals (Singer 2005) — all these, and more, have provided immeasurable help to those who understand themselves as, or are understood as, transgender. And, even so, more work needs to be done: more parents will lose custody of their children, more people will be denied housing, more murders will happen. To simply dismiss these efforts and their effects would be worse than unethical. For all the cautions I expressed in chapter 6 about Scheper-Hughes's arguments for the "primacy of the ethical," in the end I agree with her that anthropologists have strong ethical obligations — both in their interactions with their study participants and in presenting their findings — to work against the local realities of violence, discrimination, and suffering that they witness. At the heart of Scheper-Hughes's complaint with contemporary ethnography is the contention that anthropologists who question the terms in which they know about the world (as I have done) produce relativist accounts which

provide no basis for such work. I would argue, though, that critique —
such as the one I have been making in this book — is not unethical in and of
itself, nor does it work against the goals of committed activists. Rather, I
believe that critical analysis is in fact central to the process of committed,
ethical, and effective action.

Anthropology has a checkered history in regard to advocacy and its
impact on public policy formation.[4] Objectively, this seems peculiar, since
anthropology's hallmark relativist perspective would seem to make it a
prime candidate for such interventions. However, within contemporary
anthropology, along with a concern about material conditions and social
power has come a kind of relativism that is qualitatively different from the
"cultural difference" relativism of Franz Boas and his students. Nowadays,
the complexities of an interconnected, globalized world make it hard to
establish with any certainty where "culture" lies. The indeterminacy of
either "tradition" or "modernity" (e.g., Small 1997), the subsuming of the
local into the global and vice versa (e.g., Ortner 1996), the cultural citation
of signs of cosmopolitanism which is simultaneously a reworking of those
signs (e.g., Johnson 1997) are all both social facts *and* the context of
contemporary anthropological fieldwork. The relativism of contemporary
critical anthropology, then, is less focused on describing differences between homogenous "cultures" than it is in revealing the basic difficulty of
how we come to know about "culture" in the first place. In short, analyses
which focus on the indeterminacy of social processes do not often make a
happy fit with the clear-cut and definitional categories of public policy
arenas such as public health or development projects.

But this does not mean that what we come to know is necessarily either
incapable of being acted upon or simple self-absorption. Rather, the impulse to query ways of knowing derives from the very local/global contexts which form the social fields of anthropological investigation. Indeed,
I would argue that without a recognition of and engagement with the
complexity of information flows, competing claims over the truth, and the
frequent indeterminacy of meaning in complex social worlds, claiming a
clear-cut ethical stance will get you into trouble with someone; may, indeed result in you being accused of violence, perhaps even rape. In the end,
however, knowing about how we know about things — including violence,
suffering, and injustice — does not solve the problem for we still have to
decide how to act. Policy interventions, legislative advocacy, and grassroots activism must still engage in the context of institutionalized politics

where the complexities of lived experience exposed by ethnography are reduced, again and again, to simple categories. The question is how we might employ these complexities strategically while maintaining some vision of social justice.

My final point, then, is that in order to have such a vision, we need to attend to differences beyond identity categories or the categories we use to describe the experiences which underpin them. I argue that such a perspective is achievable through doing ethnography. This argument pertains to activism and daily life as much as it does to anthropology. "Ethnography" is, in the end, not a difficult thing to do: at its heart, it involves attentive and ongoing listening. It requires a recognition of other people's perspectives and organizations of their worlds as both historically produced and culturally located but *also* as concrete and real. The stories we hear from people who have suffered are lessons for activists as much as they are for anthropologists, and not simply data — they require that we reshape our frameworks of action, our perspectives, our strategies, and our categories to account for them. That is, being an effective activist also means becoming an anthropologist of sorts. This kind of anthropologist/activist is not simply one who acts on the evidence of suffering but one whose action is underpinned by attention to the complexities of people's shifting alliances, complex politics, and the contradictions of social life and social action. It requires a recognition of hanging questions and the difficulties of knowing, as much as the documentation of the evidence of suffering. Donna Haraway (who provides the epigraph for this section) writes that ethnography entails an epistemological and political "being at risk," a risk that involves the possibility that one's frameworks can be shattered, diffracted. "To be at risk," she adds, "is not the same thing as identifying with the subjects of study; quite the contrary. . . . Not limited to a specific discipline, an ethnographic attitude is a mode of practical and theoretical attention, a way of remaining mindful and accountable. Such a method is not about 'taking sides' in a predetermined way. But it is about risks, purposes, and hopes — one's own and others' — embedded in knowledge projects" (1997: 190–91).

Throughout this book, I have risked pointing to the problems of forming a body of knowledge around the figure of "transgender," even as I have recognized its social and political uses. My point is that this risk *enables* rather than prevents attending to the real, embodied risks that transgender-identified people face on a day-to-day basis. In order to take this risk, I have suggested that we should attend to a central question in contemporary social theory: what is the relationship between gender and sexuality? By putting those terms in quotation marks for much of this book, I am suggesting that they should receive ethnographic and critical attention as categories. Rather than accept uncritically that "gender" and "sexuality" (back in quotation marks again) are separable human experiences, I think we should take a risk and ask other kinds of questions, such as: For whom is this the case? Where? When? With what effects? From whose perspective? What political effects does such an argument produce beyond the liberatory possibilities of such a formulation? How did this argument take shape in particular, situated contexts? What does "gender" mean in any particular context? How does "gender identity" articulate with broader structures of power and value? When is "sexuality" about sexual practice, and what constitutes the sexual? What practices are being talked about? When might it be code for something else — such as morality or identity or gender-variant expression? Or vice versa? When might the distinction not make sense? When might the distinction be valuable? The point of asking such questions is not simply to develop new theoretical paradigms, or simply to ask new questions, but to think ethnographically about the ongoing effects of social theories and the ways they are part of a dialogue with the daily practices of situated social actors. And, as Haraway suggests, these kinds of questions are not restricted to anthropological analyses; they are democratic questions.

Let me give an example which concretizes these questions in daily practice. The work of Ben Singer — an activist, teacher, scholar, and transman living and working in Philadelphia — demonstrates the possibilities of living ethnographically as an approach to the fundamental questions I raise here. An ethnographer himself, he was also the co-designer and founding director of the Trans-health Information Project (TIP) in Philadelphia. Singer recognizes the power of transgender as a category of analysis and action, and he uses this category to organize his teaching in academic contexts as well as in trainings of health care professionals on transgender issues. At the same time, his ethnographic research among public health officials and activists showed him that the terms of "transgender," as it is being institutionalized, mean that in order to receive services, those who don't understand themselves through its terms have to learn to represent themselves as such. His work with TIP mirrored many of my own ethnographic experiences, as it brought him in contact with mostly young, frequently poor people of color who, while understood in institutional terms as "transgender," professed understandings of self that exceeded or directly contested its terms. Like myself, he has also struggled with how to name and talk about his participants, but unlike me, Singer has been in the business of direct service provision and training. In a program that serves "transgender" populations, and in trainings where he is to educate health care professionals on "transgender issues," Singer thus faces on a daily basis the kinds of fundamental political and theoretical issues of how to act, what kinds of questions to raise, and how — on his feet — to know when to raise a question and when to assert the importance of the collectivity of trans-gender. In a training for health care professionals, Ben explains the "um-brella" model of transgender and then tries to explain when it can fail to do all the work that it promises (Singer 2005). He explains the differences that are faced by people of different embodiments, different politics, different capacities to articulate their desires and selves, and how they may not be best served by the assumptions that have come to travel with "transgender." And he places these questions in a broader context of the political econo-mies of health care provision in the contemporary United States. Sometimes it works, sometimes it doesn't, but Ben presses on.

And so do thousands of others on a daily basis, in the range of interlock-ing social activisms that characterize contemporary American life. Raising questions about the categories of progressive political organizing — partic-ularly in a context when, as is currently the case, such organizing seems so under fire — may seem to be self-defeating. But in the end it is crucial because otherwise the progressive impulse can be erased by the power of institutionalization and the capacity of institutions to abruptly cut off the question. This perspective is increasingly common in contemporary eth-nography as anthropologists struggle to find ways to both actively incorpo-rate advocacy positions and critical perspectives on that advocacy in their ethnographies. Anthropologists such as Fortun (2001) and Lyon-Callo (2004) author their work from the position of on-the-ground social actors, making their advocacy work a central topic but also a methodology and critical object itself. Fortun describes — and enacts in her writing — the multiply positioned ways in which she advocates on behalf of Bhopal's gas victims, noting the choices, strategies, and half-victories of both ethnogra-phy and advocacy. Lyon-Callo's long-term activism in the homeless-shelter-ing industry in Massachusetts employs both his ethnographic fieldwork and his ethnographic writing to raise questions for shelter staff, homeless guests, and policymakers about the neoliberal modes of governance that elide the structural causes of homelessness in favor of individual pathology. These texts (and others) demonstrate the possibilities for anthropological advocacy, the symbiosis of ethnography and activism, and the importance of maintaining open questions. In Fortun's words, this is "advocacy without the guarantees of teleology" (2001: 16).

But it seems to me that ethnographic texts are like unfit athletes, trying to keep up with a crowd of marathon runners who are intent on the ribbon, for the ethnographer and her subjects keep on running after ethnography becomes bound — as this one is — in time and space. Ethnographies inevitably fall behind, and even as they attempt to open up spaces and resist codification they still become fixed in time and part of history. But the image of the race also captures the sense that, for many ethnographic subjects, there is indeed something to win, something solid and meaningful and tangible. This is a tension that characterizes the process of ethnography, and which has permeated this book: the impulse to open up transgender for both theoretical and political purposes, and the recognition that in some cases, the work of many of my activist informants aims to do just the opposite. But I would argue that effective advocacy and ethnography must engage in precisely the kinds of deconstructive methodologies that so many critics have condemned as apolitical. That is, in order to understand and act on local manifestations of violence or to engage in a politics of social change, all those features of contemporary social analysis often gathered under the umbrella of "postmodernism" — the focus on multiple, shifting identities; the borderless nature of political discourses and practices; the investigation of what power is — are as vital to committed, ethical, and effective advocacy as they are to ethnography.

Yet the anthropologist himself may still be trying to keep up in the race beyond the life of written ethnography. That is, there is an important distinction to be made here between ethnography as a written product, ethnography as a methodology, and the ethnographer who produces/practices it. If as I argue ethnography (as methodology and an orientation to daily life) can be broadly used, then ethnographers — anthropologists and others — can exploit the kinds of openings and questions raised in its practice to continue in the race, keeping the questions open, even as written ethnography becomes fixed. The focus on the writing of texts which has absorbed anthropology for some decades now obscures the fact that anthropologists and their subjects have lives beyond what is written, and that the techniques of critical ethnography are social practices that continue to act on and in the domains of daily life. It is here that, I suggest, ethnography as a practice has the best chances of being simultaneously thoughtfully critical, ethical, and transformative. We may not be able to produce final answers (indeed, we should aim not to), but we can continue to expose questions productively in ways that engage with the concerns of one's study participants, political constituents, and fellow activists, even if we do not agree on what the finish line looks like — or even if there is one.

CYCLING

Having said all that, I'm back on my bicycle again, but the geography has changed. Almost all the sites that I have written about in this book have moved or transformed. Riki has moved from Manhattan to split hir time between Florida and Washington, D.C., where s/he is still the executive director of GenderPAC, and Rosalyne now lives in Los Angeles, where she recently finished her own book (Blumenstein 2003). I got to see Riki at the Center some years back for a GenderPAC benefit screening of the film *Boys Don't Cry* about the murder of Brandon Teena. Afterwards, about thirty of us gathered on the sidewalk with candles to remember Fitzroy Green, another murdered transgender-identified person whose murderer had been found "not guilty." I walked home with Melissa who, like me, misses our evenings doing outreach together in the Meat Market.

Karalyn's bar on 10th Avenue closed down shortly before my fieldwork ended and morphed into a weekend party at a midtown restaurant, though Tranny Chaser continued to operate in its old venue until recently. The Meat Market is now thoroughly gentrified: an elegant boutique occupies the space where Dizzy Izzy's Bagels used to feed and water truckers, fem queens, and bar-goers, and the loading dock where I used to sit with Rita, Sybil, India, and the other girls has been removed to make way for an upscale restaurant. The girls still work this neighborhood, but with increased pressure from police and residents it is harder all the time.

And the discourses and practices around transgender have shifted too. This book is a snapshot of a moment in a rapidly changing field of meanings. At the balls, transgender is increasingly gaining currency. A current study sponsored by the Centers for Disease Control and Prevention has, indeed, made the balls the primary site for its first study of HIV and TB transmission in the "transgender community." The New York City Human Rights Commission has begun to publicize the inclusion of "gender identity and expression" in the city's human rights ordinance, the bill that my colleagues in NYAGRA worked so hard to have passed. The postcard which publicizes the law includes a long list—longer even than the one I made in chapter 1—of people who are protected by such language (see figures 6a and b in chapter 5), giving notice that discrimination against transgender-identified people in New York will not be tolerated.

At the same time, "transgender" has already come under critique by those who have found its terms to be too constraining, too institutionalized already. Even as it promised an inclusivity and radical transformative potential in the early to mid-1990s, the very processes of institutionalization I have discussed in this book have made it untenable to those whose understandings of self exceed its institutionalized meanings. For many (and particularly younger) people identified as transgender, the term genderqueer has emerged in the early years of the twenty-first century (see Nestle, Howell, and Wilchins 2002), encompassing a call for a complex politics of identification that evades the necessity of boundary policing (see also Hale 1998). This sounds, indeed, very much like early 1990s uses of transgender itself. Though it is too early to tell what the relationship between this category and transgender will be, it is evident that the ways in which transgender has been increasingly absorbed by the institutions of the medical profession, the academy, the media, and bodies of the state have curtailed its transformative potential. As the meanings around genderqueer evolve, it will be essential to think about how this category works not only against the solidity of identity categories but against the solidity of the broader categories of social experience which it describes: gender, sexuality, sex, race, class, and so on.

Yet we cannot abandon transgender nor do I think that we should, for it is useful, both politically and personally. Despite all my concerns, I am above all hopeful for the possibilities of the activism that I have described and for the vision of those who resist these smoothings-over, who attempt to work beyond the categorical imperatives of identity politics. For the point is that everyone in this study "knows what they are," even those who, like Sherry, claim not to, for when they claim not to know, it is in terms of categories which cannot account for the fullness of their experiences. Both Nora and Jade know what they are: in Nora's case a heterosexual woman of transexual/transgender experience, and in Jade's, a hard daddy who is a woman, a mother, and who thinks like a guy. Riki knows what s/he is, but refuses to name it precisely because s/he is alert to the failures of naming "what I am" through categories, even if they are life-saving ways of knowing the self for others. And I, too, know what I am, a knowledge enabled by a particular set of discourses and political developments in the West over the past 150 years: a gay man, whose gender identity is experienced (if not always read) as masculine and whose sexual desire can be subsumed as private and non-negotiable. But only some of these knowledges become validated in a system which confers "identity" upon those who express that knowledge in terms of an identity-based politics which in turn relies on a range of stratifications and elided injustices.

If, in the end, the use of transgender enables Rita, Miss Angel, Jade, or the many others I have discussed in this book to make their lives better, to give them access to hormones, to housing, and recourse to the courts, I could only be delighted. And if this new form of imagining helps them to reorganize their understandings of themselves, I would not be manifestly distressed, for things change (and sometimes, even for the better). But our imaginations should not be limited by these goals, or their implications. If we imagine the world transformed through transgender, then the challenge is to let that imagination expand to incorporate the broad vision of social justice that we need to continue in the race.

Notes

INTRODUCTION

1. Most of the names in this book are pseudonyms, though I have retained the real names of those people who have agreed to let me use them or who are well-known public figures. I have not indicated, however, which are pseudonyms and which are actual names. My use of the term "transgender-identified" will be explained in the latter part of this chapter. In the meantime, it is enough to say that I use this construction to mark the ways in which people both take on the category transgender as something meaningful about themselves, as well as the sense of being identified by others as belonging to a category, even if it is not used by the people so identified.

2. I discuss the origins and histories of transgender in chapter 1.

3. I use "mapping" here both as a way of bringing together a rag-tag assortment of ethnographic anecdotes by means of a bicycle and a category, and also as a way of discussing sets of interrelated conceptual themes. While scholars have critiqued the metaphor of the map for social analysis for its tendency to imply fixity (e.g., Bourdieu 1977), I use it here in a very specific sense that I owe to Deleuze and Guattari (1987). In their terms, mappings are not concrete *forms* of description but rather subversive *practices* which draw connections between things in ways that may seem at first counterintuitive. I thank Tom Boellstorff for helping me clarify the points in this note.

4. As with many of the places I write of in this section and in the chapters to follow, THE clinic and its host, CHP — now the Callan-Lorde Center — have moved. One of the interesting features of the bars, clubs, and even social service agencies that serve the transgender community is the rapid shift in location, personnel, and organization. I write of places like THE Clinic in the ethnographic present, but the reader should be aware that most of the places I discuss in the following paragraphs — and chapters — are no longer extant. The Lesbian and Gay Community Services Center is still on 13th Street, but owing to extensive renovations to the building, it moved to Little West 12th Street in September 1998 and relocated to 13th Street in June 2001, when it was renamed "The Lesbian, Gay, Bisexual, and Transgender Community Center." I will deal with this move and renaming in chapter 5.

5. "Transition" is a complicated idea, one which often refers to someone's physical transition, through sex reassignment surgery, from one gender position to another. But transition does not necessarily require or imply surgery. One can begin transition by taking hormones, or transition by adopting one's desired gender in one's workplace or at home through more mundane gendered technologies of clothing. The paths to transition are as varied and complex as the lives that undergo this shift.

6. That is, Andrew is a person who was born female but identifies as a man and has taken steps toward physical transition. He also identifies as a gay man. See H. Rubin (2003) for a discussion of gay-identified transmen.

7. While some of those who participated in its founding would have characterized GenderPAC as a coalition of transgender groups, Riki would contest this idea. At the time of writing, GenderPAC — and Riki's leadership — have become a contentious issue among transgender-identified activists. I discuss these issues in chapters 5 and 6.

8. I discuss the use of non-standard pronouns such as "hir" later in this chapter.

9. In 2003, HRC finally agreed to include "gender identity and expression" in ENDA. However, the bill's legislative sponsors refused to consider the inclusion of language which would protect transgender-identified people, and despite its commitment to including such language, HRC still supported the bill as it was originally drafted. However, as this book was going to press in April 2007, ENDA was reintroduced, this time including both sexual orientation and gender identity as protected categories in its language. See chapters 5 and 6.

10. See note 4 above. Karalyn's, too, has closed down and opened up in another venue in the East 20s.

11. I use "transvestite" to describe Nancy as this is what she calls herself and her sex partners rather than "cross-dresser."

12. Compare this to the claims reported by Boellstorff (2004: 167) and Kulick (1998: 6). I elaborate on the similarities between Rita's "I know what I am" and the claims of ethnographic subjects in other contexts in chapter 4. For the time being, it is enough to note here that one of Boellstorff's Indonesian study participants says something remarkably similar to Rita: "I was born a man, and when I die I will be buried as a man, because that's what I am" (2004: 167).

13. Bereft of the traditional unifying concepts of culture and community, anthropologists have needed to find new ways of describing the objects they study. So, for example, Rayna Rapp, in her long-term study of the meanings of and practices around amniocentesis, defines her object of study as a "complex cultural object" that cannot be located in any one place (1999: 12–13). Emily Martin (1994), in her work on cultural ideas about immunity that spans laboratories, workplaces, and management training courses, writes that she and her graduate students "wanted our fieldwork to fetch us up in what have been called *implosions,* places where different elements of the system come into energetic contact and collapse in on themselves" (11, emphasis in original). And James Ferguson, who examines the decaying promises of modernity in the Zambian Copperbelt, argues that his analytic object, far from being a place or a group of people, is "a mode of conceptualizing, narrating, and experiencing socioeconomic change" (1999: 21).

14. Safer sex outreach refers to the direct intervention programs that many AIDS organizations have developed where agency outreach workers go to venues frequented by people at risk for HIV/AIDS to distribute safer sex supplies (condoms, dental dams, lubricants, and so on), information on how to use them, and how to contact the agency. My role as a safer sex outreach worker with the GIP was facilitated by Nora Molina, who helped me immeasurably in teaching me how to approach people around these issues.

15. George Marcus captures this dynamic beautifully: "The basic condition that defines the altered mise-en-scène for which complicity rather than rapport is a more appropriate figure is an awareness of existential doubleness on the part of *both* anthropologist and subject; this derives from having a sense of being *here* where major transformations are under way that are tied to things happening simultaneously *elsewhere,* but not having a certainty or authoritative representation of what those connections are. . . . Social actors are con-

fronted with the same kind of impasses that academics uncomfortably experience these days, and this affinity suggests the particular salience of the figure of complicity" (1998: 118, emphasis in original).

16. Part of the reason for this is the particular constellation of social spaces I was able to access as an anthropologist. In New York City during 1996 and 1997, when I did the bulk of my research, there was no consistent social space or organized venue in which FTMs or female-bodied masculine people congregated as a group. In many of the contexts in which I worked—the drag balls I discuss in chapter 2, for example—there were certainly female-bodied butches (identified as "transgender" by the organization for which I worked), some of whom I got to speak to, but the networks I was developing were heavily biased in favor of the male-bodied fem queens and butch queens whom I also met in other venues. Likewise, I worked with and interviewed several transmen who were GIP clients or peer counselors, but both the client base and staff of GIP were primarily transgender- and transsexual-identified women and male crossdressers. Some activists argue that these absences speak to broader social processes where transgender-identified women and male-bodied feminine people, who were socialized as male, are more able to claim public spaces, or have benefited from male socialization prior to transition by having had more secure employment and so on. This claim itself is controversial because for many of the transexual women and male-bodied feminine people with whom I worked, their public expression of femininity was anything but easy. They see in this claim an ignorance of the ways in which their male socialization was deeply complicated by childhood and adolescent expressions of femininity which were met by a good deal of punitive response in the very public arenas that some FTMs argue they are more capable of claiming.

17. While there is an important historical and theoretical/pragmatic overlap between the broad array of social and discursive formations that have arisen through these two terms, there are also conceptual and political problems in their relationship (Stryker 1998). Frequently, "queer" is used as a synonym for the lumpier "LGBT" as an attempt to stress the commonalities of experience across particular identity formations, though this move is itself contested by transgender-identified people who identify as heterosexual and not at all "queer," which for them implies homosexuality. Likewise, because of the centrality of poststructuralist conceptions of the contingent subject to queer theory, queer also undermines the notion of fixed subjectivity and identity which are so central to many transgender (as well as lesbian and gay) identities. While some in the early 1990s (and indeed in the present) used transgender in ways

that resonated more powerfully with the discourses of queerness (e.g., Boswell 1991), transgender has been institutionalized in significant ways that undercut the kinds of political and intellectual analyses made available by "queer" as a term.

18. Another category that people may be looking for—and will not find—in this book is that of bisexuality. As a "sexual orientation," "bisexual" is often listed alongside "gay" and "lesbian" in lists of identities, but, as bisexual scholars and activists have pointed out, there is a lack of theorization of bisexuality in discussions of sexual identity and desire, though the reasons are somewhat different from those I posit for transgender. While, as I will discuss in chapter 5, bisexual and transgender activists have worked side-by-side to address what they see as exclusions from lesbian and gay organizations and politics, bisexuals did not figure largely in my research. Like FTMs and transgender men, bisexual people may see in this a central omission that undermines my arguments. Rather than conflate bisexual with lesbian and gay identity and desire, I specifically do not include "bisexual" when I write of "lesbian and gay" organizations, discourses, and movements. By this exclusion I hope, at the very least, not to invoke bisexuality without theorizing it.

19. Since the end of my fieldwork, the prefix "trans" has come to stand by itself in many contexts, partly to avoid precisely the categorical issues that arise in using "transgender." While I am interested in this usage (and while I believe many of the same issues are at stake), my focus will be on "transgender" in particular.

1. IMAGINING TRANSGENDER

1. Here I draw on dissertation research by Robert Hill at the University of Michigan which he very generously shared with me. Hill's research into early transvestite publications at the Kinsey Institute (and especially Prince's *Transvestia* magazine) reveals only a few instances over many years in which Prince used varieties of this term in her writings. As early as the December 1969 issue of *Transvestia* (#60), Prince created a category—"transgenderal"—for transvestites who lived full time as women but who did not intend to have SRS. However, Hill finds no evidence of her use of this term—or variations of it— again for almost a decade, despite discussing this group of people in her writings. Moreover, Hill's research shows evidence of another early pioneer, Ariadne Kane, using the term in print, identifying as a "transgenderist" (in the sense of a "third way" between transexual and transvestite) in a 1976 re-

printed interview in the magazine *Hose and Heel* (later renamed the *Journal of Male Feminism*). Hill further notes that in the early editions of this journal, the editors wrote that they had explicitly rejected "transgenderism" as an organizing category for their organization and journal because, they argued, it reinstantiated binary gender and ignored the lessons of feminism. Hill writes that Kane and Prince were friends and speculates that whoever originated it, Kane embraced the term, using it more often than Prince. "Transgenderal" or "transgenderist" does not appear in Prince's 1971 book, *How to Be a Woman though Male,* with "transgenderist" appearing for the first time in Prince's writings in a 1978 paper entitled "The 'Transcendents' or 'Trans' People" published in *Transvestia* (#95), two years after the Kane interview mentioned above. Other than a second use of this term in the following issue of *Transvestia* (#96), and once more in 1981 (#104), Hill has been unable to find any other published use of "transgenderist" by Prince. Moreover, a 1980 publication by an organization called the Human Outreach and Achievement Institute defines "transgenderist" as a term which had been used in the 1970s to bridge the transvestite/transexual gap but which had been superseded by "androgyne" by 1980. It appears then that Prince's usage of the term was patchy at best, that it was used by Prince later than most authors acknowledge, and that other people and organizations were engaged in the working out of its meanings from the late 1960s to the early 1980s. It is also clear from this data that while the "third way" meaning of transgender was in circulation in the 1970s, it did not gain traction over other categories (like "androgyne"), nor was it used in the politicized and collective sense that it gained in the early 1990s (Hill, personal communication, March 21 and August 3, 2005; see Hill 2007 for a more detailed account of this history. See also Ekins and King 2005, 2006 and note 2 below).

2. Jason Cromwell (personal communication) notes that he first heard the use of "transgender" as a collective term as early as 1984 on the West Coast, but I have found no textual record of such usage prior to the early 1990s. In the United Kingdom, the sociologist Richard Ekins established the Trans-Gender Archive at the University of Ulster in 1986, using "trans-gender" explicitly as a collective category (Richard Ekins, personal communication). The Oxford English Dictionary definition, to which Ekins contributed, offers several earlier uses of "transgender," some dating from the 1980s, though none of them imply the collectivity of later uses. Ekins and Dave King, in their more recent work on transgender (2005, 2006), further note various uses of "transgender" and "trans.people" (*sic*) as collective umbrella terms in the mid-1970s in the UK (2006: 3). Likewise, the Merriam-Webster dictionary's definition

provides a date of 1979 for the first appearance of this word in print in the United States (the dictionary, however, has no record of the document on which this dating was based). The definition in Merriam-Webster, though, does not explicitly capture this particular sense of transgender: "exhibiting the appearance and behavioral characteristics of the opposite sex." The OED's current definition is more qualified and comprehensive (no doubt reflecting Ekins's involvement in its writing): "Of, relating to, or designating a person whose identity does not conform unambiguously to conventional notions of male or female gender, but combines or moves between these; transgendered. Although often used (esp. among participants in transgender lifestyles) as a generic and inclusive term which deliberately avoids categorizations such as transsexual or transvestite, in wider use transgender is sometimes used synonymously with these more specific terms." It is clear though that prior to the early 1990s, at least in the United States, this collective meaning had not coalesced in a significant, institutional form.

3. As Califia notes, "cross-dresser" and "transvestite" are usually read as indexing male-bodied people (2003 [1997]: 199–200).

4. It is important to note that Hirschfeld's coinage of "transvestite" in 1910 incorporated many kinds of cross-gender behavior and identity, including people who lived full time as a non-ascribed gender. The contemporary meanings of the term "transvestite" — indexing heterosexual male erotic cross-dressing — is a more recent and medicalized phenomenon.

5. On the other hand, Freud was central in shifting the debates toward psychological causes, where homosexuality was seen as a result of arrested psychosexual development that could not be accounted for by simple reference to biology. As Terry notes, though, these different causal arguments often intersected. She notes how Freud himself vacillated between somatic and psychological arguments for the etiology of homosexuality (1995: 136–37).

6. Manalansan (2003) notes that Stonewall's significance can be read from an immigrant perspective as well. His gay Filipino immigrant informants tended to dismiss Stonewall as an event, primarily because "coming out" as a trope is not central to their understandings of self (30–35).

7. I am grateful to Lee Brown for helping to identify the published letters and reports I discuss in this section.

8. I located these quotations from microfilms at the New York Public Library. The following quotation appears to be from the same issue as the previously

quoted article, but may be from a flier that was inserted into the newspaper since it is on an unnumbered page.

9. In contrast, Rosario (1996) argues that sexology — and historians' readings of sexology — conflate homosexuality and transexuality from the beginning, and condemns scholars like Hekma for proposing a teleological framework in which "inverts" naturally become masculine gay men. Rosario makes precisely the opposite (and quite as teleological) claim: that accounts of the falsity of gender variance ignore the historical evidence of distinct and persistent forms of transexualism across time, even though it was not named until the 1950s. Yet both positions rely on an assumption of a distinct difference in identificatory projects on the part these historical subjects.

10. This is the case referred to by Jeff, the letter writer to the *Gay Liberator,* cited above.

11. Male transvestism ("transvestitic fetishism") was already included in the pages of the second edition of the DSM and remains in the most recent, fourth edition text revision (APA 2000). I do not have space to elaborate on this issue here, but it is worth noting that for all that cross-dressers or transvestites are included (in many accounts) in "transgender" alongside transexuals and others, transvestism and transexuality have been kept categorically separate in the pages of the DSM, a separation itself animated by a distinction between gender and sexuality. Transvestites are seen to have a disorder in the realm of psychosexual development, whereas transexuals and others with "gender identity disorder" are understood to be suffering from a gendered disorder (though how these disorders relate to one another varies across the editions).

12. However, the view that transexuals are in fact homosexual people who have reread their desire as being "trapped in the wrong body" has continued to attract proponents even as SRS and the category of GID have become accepted practice and diagnosis. For example, in a recent and controversial book, J. Michael Bailey (2003) argues that transexual women (he does not deal with transexual men) are really extremely feminine gay men, or else are men who are erotically drawn to the idea of being women. That is, he places sexuality at the heart of the gendered identification of transexual women, arguing that far from being separate, sexual orientation and gender identity are part of the same psychodynamic package. This flies in the face (as he recognizes) of most contemporary clinical and social theory which argues that gender and sexuality are *separate* and *separable* aspects of human experience. Some readers may detect in my argument a similarity to Bailey's position. If I am arguing that

"gender" and "sexuality" are not naturally separate, then it may appear that I am supporting his argument that (some) transexual women are "really" very feminine gay men. However, there is an important distinction I want to draw here. Bailey's argument relies upon a *psychodynamic* argument, positing a link between femininity (gender) and same-sex desire (sexuality) in a developmental schema which leads, for various reasons, to some feminine men becoming gay, and others transexual women. My argument is quite different. I am making a *semiotic* and *historical* argument, positing that the very categories of "gender" and "sexuality" themselves can, at different moments in history, contain different elements. See chapter 4 for a further discussion of Bailey's work.

13. The recognition by medical professionals that transexual patients were presenting textbook cases and developing ideal medical profiles in order to meet the requirements of surgery was not long in coming (e.g., K. MacKenzie 1978; see also Meyerowitz 2002: 161ff.).

14. Indeed, Butler argues that this methodological carving up of sexuality and gender depends on a denial of the crucial analysis of sexuality from a feminist perspective (see Blackwood 2002) and, moreover, ignores the vital work within feminism that has complicated gender and sexuality with analyses of race, class, and culture. Part of the reason for Rubin's centrality in the founding of a field of lesbian and gay studies, Butler argues, flows from her attempts to separate sexuality from kinship. This resonates with a Foucauldian perspective in which a regime of "sexuality" was seen to replace a regime of "kinship" as the focus of the state's attention in the late nineteenth century. But while it is certainly true that kinship is not determining of sexuality, "it would be equally mistaken to claim their radical separability" (1994: 14). Butler also queries whether the claim for the separation of kinship/gender from sexuality is valid cross-culturally, a question I take on in chapter 4 (see also Jolly and Manderson 1997, Collier and Yanagisako 1987).

15. Another example is in the debates in the gay and lesbian press over public sexuality and HIV transmission. Some prominent gay writers have publicly denounced publicly visible and/or promiscuous sexuality, indicating that there is an ambivalence within the gay (male) community in terms of how to negotiate the meanings of sex and the realm in which it should be practiced (see Bawer 1993, Rotello 1997). This conception of "gay" erases not only the differently gendered person, therefore, but also the person who does not "do" their sexuality, the realm of "homosexuality," in an acceptably private way.

16. This passage from a 1998 Gay and Lesbian Alliance Against Defamation (GLAAD) news release about media coverage of a gay pride parade is telling: "many newspaper and television outlets chose to focus on stereotypes that have come to signify Pride to many mainstream media: black leather, drag queens, motorcycle-riding lesbians, and exotically dressed and/or minimally-clad young men. Certainly, these are accurate images so long as they are placed within the broader context of the rich diversity of our community. But when the media's representations of Pride are solely or almost entirely the more flamboyant aspects of our community, it paints an inaccurate picture" (GLAAD 1998). GLAAD certainly takes care not to condemn the "flamboyant aspects of our community," but at the same time, like historians who are concerned to deny a desire for femininity on the part of historical male-bodied "homosexual" subjects, and like the homophile leaders of the 1950s or the letter writers to *The Advocate* in the early 1970s, it sees "flamboyance" — "overt," public gayness in which gender transgression and public sexuality abound — as simply unrepresentative of "gay people." One can hardly imagine GLAAD issuing a press release about blanket media coverage of gender-normative, monogamous gay and lesbian couples because there were no drag queens, leather men, or dykes on bikes represented.

2. MAKING COMMUNITY

1. There are also some Asian-Pacific Islanders and Asian Americans at the balls too, though their interpretations of drag and the significance of "realness" (see below) are different from those of the other ball-goers (see Manalansan 2003). Manalansan makes the point that drag "realness" is reread for Filipino gay men (as he calls them) at the balls through yet another trope, that of mimicry, which a salient interpretive frame for drag in the Philippines (137–38).

2. Livingstone's *Paris Is Burning* has generated a cottage industry of critique about race, power, gender, and performativity at the balls. On the whole, these discussions tend to fall into the somewhat tedious (at this point) debate over whether drag is "transformative" or "hegemonic." As with my treatment of drag more generally, I do not intend to enter these debates as my concern is not with the meanings of drag qua drag but rather with an analysis of specific forms of drag in relation to the category transgender. See Butler (1993), Harper (1994), hooks (1992), McCarthy Brown (2001), Prosser (1998), and Reddy (1998) for some differing views of *Paris Is Burning* and the place of gender, race, and class in the ball scene.

3. Needle exchange is a hotly contested social service focused on getting intravenous drug users to use clean needles to inject drugs, thereby reducing their risk of exposure to HIV by not sharing needles. The focus is on "harm reduction," a model of contemporary social service outreach to drug users and others engaging in risky (and illegal) behaviors. PHP's Transgender Initiative is focused on the provision of clean needles to transgender-identified people who inject black market hormones.

4. Contrary to Butler's (1993) description of the balls from her viewing of *Paris Is Burning,* there are indeed categories for "realness" (at least in the balls of the late 1990s), though her broader point, that realness is "a standard that is used to judge any given performance within the established categories" (129) holds true for much of what happens at a ball.

5. The use of "cunt" here is one that readers may find objectionable and, indeed, gives weight to those feminist critiques of "drag" as derisive of women. At the same time, though, as will become apparent, the stakes of looking "cunty" are high indeed and exceed the boundaries of derision and parody. Beyond the walls of the ballroom, fem queens mostly live full time in a feminine gender and have a good deal invested — at the level of personal safety — in looking "cunt."

6. As I didn't know this person, nor did I get to question him/her about his/her identity, I have resorted to the "him/her," "s/he" pronoun form in order to reflect my own uncertainty, not his/hers.

7. There are a few exceptions: the first is a non-transexual woman who attends most CDI events. Her motives and interests, though, are not clearly understood, since she generally remains silent during these events. However, her presentation of self is always as a woman, and she does not cross-dress as a man in these settings. Second, there are a few members who initially identified as cross-dressers but have subsequently surgically transitioned and identify as women but still retain the social links with CDI, where they are welcomed and supported.

8. The New York Court is part of the national drag Court system, which was established in San Francisco in the 1960s, and is one of about sixty in the country, though this Court has some historical and organizational peculiarities which set it somewhat apart from the others.

9. The Imperial Court of New York had one transexual woman as a member during my research, and three male-bodied members that I know of who have used the term "transgender" about themselves in interviews with me or in print. However, these three men still primarily identify as gay men.

10. The quote is: *"For the master's tools will never dismantle the master's house.* They may allow us temporarily to beat him at his own game, but they will never enable us to bring about genuine change" (Lorde 1984: 112, emphasis in original).

11. However, as Halberstam notes, in these contexts "fluidity" does not refer to the experience of individual social actors as much as it does to the range of possibilities that individuals have in making sense of their selves and experiences.

3. "I KNOW WHAT I AM"

1. Rosalyne explains that this phrase — drawing on similar constructions such as "person of African descent" — foregrounds her identity as a woman first and foremost while acknowledging her transexual/transgender history.

2. The majority of the people I discuss were ascribed male at birth. The one extended case of a female-bodied person — Jade — that I discuss below further complicates the gay/transgender distinction, but there are clear differences between Jade's experience and those of the male-bodied feminine people I am discussing. I must stress that I do not intend to simply conflate Jade's experience with the experiences of the other (male-bodied feminine) people I discuss. Rather, I want to point to the place where many kinds of differences — gender, sexuality, class, race, age — become smoothed out through the assumption of common transgender identification and experience.

3. During my fieldwork from 1996 through 1998, the Meat Market was still an active semi-industrial space. Nowadays, it is better known for its art galleries, boutiques, and upscale bars and restaurants which have replaced most of the meat industry in the eastern blocks of the district, pushing the sex-work industry into the as-yet-undeveloped area between Washington Street and the Hudson River. The development of the Hudson River Park and the Christopher Street Piers bordering the Meat Market to the west has accelerated the process of gentrification. The descriptions which follow draw on my experience in the late 1990s.

4. Tamara corrected me when I referred to him as "she" to one of his friends, indicating that when dressed as a masculine person, he preferred masculine pronouns.

5. In many ways, this set of meanings around hardness, softness, and penetration are similar to those that Kulick (1998) discusses for Brazilian *travestis.*

The majority of the girls in the Meat Market do not desire genital surgeries (at least in their response to my questions). Like Kulick's informants, the fem queens often turn to unlicensed practitioners for body modifications; one of them, India, told me of her plans to have breast and hip silicone injections from a person in Brooklyn who did such procedures in her apartment, a procedure I later attended.

6. I have adapted this from Henry Goldschmidt's (2006) phrase "visual economy of race," itself adapted from Wiegman (1995).

7. The choice of the feminine pronoun here is one I agonized over, and it speaks both to the power of binary gender and the assumptions underlying the categories "gay" and "transgender" I am analyzing. As the following interview excerpts make clear, Jade does identify as masculine in many ways, but she also insists that she is a woman. Consequently, I use Jade's own gendering of herself, as I have with all the people I discuss in this study.

8. I use a pseudonym for the center's name.

9. Given my argument, one might imagine that Nora would have said "gender" rather than "sexuality" here. At the same time, however, her use of "sexuality" indicates the slippage between these categories in talk and practice and points to the gaps produced by needing to talk about erotic desire and gendered practices in discrete categories.

10. Again, my use of "her" and "she" to describe Sherry is a conscious decision, based not necessarily on Sherry's understandings of herself (which, as I discuss below, are not easily understood in terms of binary gender) but rather on the fact that I interacted with Sherry mainly in her feminine persona.

PART 3 INTRODUCTION: THE TRANSEXUAL, THE ANTHROPOLOGIST, AND THE RABBI

1. It seems unlikely that the man was a rabbi, though he displayed signifiers of Orthodox Judaism in hairstyle and clothing. Also, his appearance on this evening was not a casual or mistaken visit as he was a regular attendee at Tranny Chaser.

4. THE MAKING OF A FIELD

1. Other non-transgender-identified authors, while they might not find transgenderism/transexuality objectionable, are taken to task for seeing trans-

gender/transexual people as mere theoretical figures through which to elaborate ideas about the social construction of gender and sexuality. Garber (1992), for example, is critiqued for considering the (male) transvestite primarily as a figure of "thirdness" which elaborates broader cultural concerns about crossing boundaries (Cohen 1995, Halberstam 1998a, Towle and Morgan 2002). Hausman's (1995) claim that transexual identities must be read through their relationship to technology is critiqued for its lack of attention to transexual agency and the differences between FTMs and MTFs (Halberstam 1998a, Rubin 1998). And scholarship which elaborates on Judith Butler's (1990) famous invocation of "drag" as a possible site for the disruption of gendered norms has also drawn fire for ignoring the lived realities of transgender-identified peoples' lives even as it valorizes gender variant practices (Wilchins 1997).

2. Apart from one brief commentary in a Chicago gay newspaper (Varnell 2003), I have not been able to find any other critique of Bailey's work from non-transgender gay men.

3. This also points to the unmarked nature of certain kinds of masculinity: it does not need to be explained — at least, in male-bodied people.

4. "Berdache" is a contested term. Derived from a French word for "catamite" or "kept boy," it reduces complex and varied social roles and identities across precolonial North America to prostitution and male homosexuality and erases the experiences of female-bodied people (Cromwell 1999, Jacobs et al. 1997b, Lang 1998). The term "Two Spirit" has been offered as an alternative (Jacobs et al. 1997a: 2ff.), though this coinage, arising from contemporary Native American self-identified Two Spirit people, likewise produces a discursive problem in talking about such historical individuals (see Jacobs et al. 1997a: 3). In this section, though, I will stick to "berdache" in quotation marks, because this category itself is what I'm interested in. The quotation marks (which authors like Lang and Jacobs et al. also use) are to indicate my recognition of its pejorative meanings, as well as its problems.

5. In contrast to Califia, Lang (1998) — who is not transgender-identified — argues that Williams "largely escaped the temptation" of equating "berdache" with modern, Western homosexuals. Rather, Lang writes, Williams delineates an ambiguous gender status for "berdache" which is in her opinion "the most sensitive representation up to now of 'berdaches' in their own cultural context" (43). In order to understand Williams's position, though, it is necessary to go back to an earlier work, Harriet Whitehead's "The Bow and the Burdenstrap" (1981). In this chapter, Whitehead argues from a feminist perspective

"that each of the different homosexualities in the world rests on a different cultural construction of gender" (Löfström 1992: 22), and that it is gendered occupation, rather than sexual object choice, which defines "berdache" status. However, Whitehead has been critiqued in turn by Williams, but also by Evelyn Blackwood (1984), for making *sexuality* "disappear" and writing of "Berdache" only in terms of gender, where sexual object choice becomes a pragmatic choice in order to gain prestige (see Löfström 1992: 22).

6. While some contemporary transgender-identified people (and some scholars, such as Garber [1992] and Bolin [1994]) have made a case for transexuality, transvestism, or transgenderism as a "third" of some kind, "thirdness" as a trope for understanding modern Western identities — transexuality, transgenderism, or homosexuality — is not tremendously popular in academic framings.

7. This heading is modeled on the title of Sherry Ortner's "Is Female to Male as Nature Is to Culture?" (1974), though its analysis is closer to her later work (1996).

8. Donham notes that there is still diversity in gender identification among black South Africans, but for all this, there is also an imagined sameness to the experience of gayness among black and white South Africans (though see Gevisser and Cameron 1994, Stein 2003).

9. I thank Tom Boellstorff for this observation.

10. Indeed, this observation is also made by Gayle Rubin in "Thinking Sex" (1984: 307), the chapter which is often credited with the move to analytically separate gender and sexuality, as I discussed in chapter 1.

5. THE LOGIC OF INCLUSION

1. As Joseph (2002b) and Butler (1994) argue in different contexts, the danger of analogy as a mode of argumentation is that it effaces complexity through producing a categorical solidity to the objects it compares.

2. One sign of the transgender community's success at organizing was evident from an e-mail I received while doing the final revisions for this book, announcing the intention of a market research company to conduct surveys of "transgender consumers."

3. Central to the market-driven model of citizenship is the broadly held assumption of both the whiteness and relative wealth of gay and lesbian commu-

nities, an assumption challenged by both empirical work (Badgett 1998) and ethnography (e.g., Amory 1996, Manalansan 2003, Maskovsky 2002).

4. See Park (2003) for a defense of identity-based politics contra Wilchins.

5. Broad (2002) draws on Melucci's (1996) concept of identization, which attempts to capture the sense in which collective identity is processual and not static, the product of ongoing self-reflexive and constructed understandings of self on the part of social actors. Broad's experience with transactivists who actively deconstructed "transgender" as a category of social action was mirrored by my own. Most of the activists with whom I worked recognized the complexities of racial, class, sexual, and other experience and identification that exceeded "transgender" as a category of action. However, to reiterate, unlike Broad I am more concerned with how what she calls "fracturings" of transgender identity come up against, and are generally absorbed by, another process, that of institutionalization. Thus, even as Broad's transactivist participants recognized that sexual, gendered, racial, and class identities/experiences intersected and reshaped what transgender identity could be in a complex "politics of difference," I argue that despite the differences and complexities in transgender politics, the logic of identity-based claims often silences that complexity, reducing the panoply of political arguments made by transgender-identified activists to the "recognition" model. Phelan's (2001) analysis of "inclusion" politics provides another critical insight into these politics. Phelan argues that the inclusion of bisexual and transgender people into lesbian and gay politics through the acronym "LGBT" simply incorporates that difference without attending to the cross-cutting identifications among such groups. Phelan also notes that the politics of contemporary accommodationist lesbian and gay groups depends on a gender normativity and gender binary and effectively argues that by the "inclusion" of the "B" and the "T," the containment of difference—rather than an elaboration of the complexities of identity—is achieved. Phelan's argument is close to my own, but while she recognizes how contemporary gay and lesbian identity depends on a produced and productive distinction between gender and sexuality, she yet characterizes bisexual and transgender people as distinct groups. Phelan's response is to argue that gay and lesbian people can learn from the complexity of bisexual and transgender people's experience to enrich their politics. My question remains: how is it that these groups have been produced—and institutionalized—as distinct in the first place?

6. In August 2006, the organizers of the festival changed their policy, allowing transgender-identified women to purchase tickets. However, paradoxically,

organizers also released a statement asking transwomen not to purchase tickets, restating their intention that the Festival was for "womyn who were born womyn and have lived their entire life experience as womyn," and claiming that transexual women who did purchase tickets would be disrespecting the Festival organizers' intentions. While transactivists have hailed this as a significant shift in policy, they also decry the half-measure this change represents.

7. I use the name Brandon Teena here, but as I discuss in chapter 6, it is not entirely clear how this person identified. While I use this name and male pronouns for him, Hale (1998) argues that to assert a masculine gender for Brandon is complicated by his history and experience.

8. My descriptions of the Center refer to the 13th Street space as it was during my fieldwork in 1996–98. The physical space and layout of the building have been significantly altered since its renovation and renaming as the "Lesbian, Gay, Bisexual, and Transgender Community Center" in June 2002. I return to the Center's moves and renaming in the latter part of this chapter.

9. Warren is referring to Raymond's *Transsexual Empire* (1994 [1979]), discussed in chapter 4.

10. STA — Survivors of Transsexuality Anonymous — was initially purely volunteer driven. STA built on a twelve-step recovery model borrowed from Alcoholics Anonymous. It is important to note that STA did not aim to "cure" people of their transsexuality; rather, the aim was to provide a safe and peer-led therapeutic space where people could work through issues of shame, social ostracism, and so on that often accompany coming out as transsexual.

11. Warren is referring to a form of in-your-face direct activism employed by many grassroots organizations, a tactic which involves tying up a target's phone lines in order to draw attention to activists' claims and demands.

12. Social workers at other agencies told me that the Center's perceived whiteness was one reason their clients of color were reluctant to go there. Another reason was age: clients of some youth projects, for example, found that the makeup of support groups at GIP was of people in their thirties, forties, and fifties, and that they shared little in common. However, in the imagined community of transgender in New York, age is often a code word for race as well. In my analysis of the intake records of the Gender Identity Project over eight years (Valentine n.d.), age and race were significantly correlated, where white clients tend to be older than clients of color. Indeed, while almost half of the Gender Identity Project's clients were people of color in the late 1990s, the

single biggest group of clients has historically been middle-aged, middle-class, white transexual women whose goal was surgical transition. Emilia Lombardi's more recent study (2005) supports the findings of my study of GIP intake data, which indicate that African American MTF transgender-identified people transition at an earlier age than white MTFs. While race and age did not correlate in any significant way for FTM clients in my study, this could be partly due to another important and telling statistic: the vast majority of GIP clients were MTF transexual and transgender-identified people, perhaps also a reason that the telephone zaps Warren recalls did not appear to engage transexual men as targets.

13. The bill was revised as the Local Law Enforcement Enhancement Act in 2000, was re-introduced in May 2003 as the Local Law Enforcement Enhancement Act (S. 966) and again as the Local Law Enforcement Hate Crimes Prevention Act in March 2007. See GenderPAC (n.d.).

14. The text of the release cannot be found on the HRC website.

15. This legislation had been lobbied for by NYAGRA, on whose board I served at the time.

6. THE CALCULUS OF PAIN

1. Riki Anne Wilchins, who was central to GenderPAC's founding, maintains that s/he never intended to start a "transgender organization" and that hir vision had always been for an organization that moved beyond identity categories, a point s/he made frequently during the founding meeting in November 1996.

2. I assume that Jillian was referring to the (minimal) funding that the GIP receives from various state and local health agencies, primarily from HIV/AIDS funds.

3. Much contemporary ethnography of groups identified as "transgender" or as gender variant has shown much more sensitivity to these issues. Kulick (1998) stresses the contexts of violence and negative social representations of Brazilian travesti sex workers as a central element of their lives. Johnson (1997) argues that ideas about gays/bantut in the Southern Philippines are formed as much through a discourse about violence as they are through a framework of gender. See also Klein (1998).

4. The issue of representation and its links to violence are further evident in the attempts by transgender activists, like gay activists before them in the 1970s,

to have "gender identity disorder" (GID) removed from the DSM. As with that activism, transgender activists argue that the presence of GID in DSM authorizes violence and discrimination against transgender-identified people by stigmatizing gender variance. However, some contemporary transgender-identified writers, like Vivian Namaste (2002), argue that those who work toward this goal are in effect doing harm themselves, giving rise to the possibility that should GID be removed from the DSM, the (already few) opportunities for claiming insurance reimbursement for surgeries and other treatments would be cut off: "So here we have a case of some transgendered activists, influenced by social constructionist theory, who argue that they are the cutting edge of social change. Yet they are involved in political work which is deeply conservative." Here, too, representation, political positions, and harm or violence become realigned as different actors with different stakes mount competing claims.

5. The full text of the statement appears in Wilchins (1997: 59–62).

6. I have made editorial changes to spelling and punctuation. The ellipses in square brackets are mine; those in the text are Cindy's.

7. Even when transgender activism is focused on other issues, violence is often rhetorically and narratively brought into play. As I mentioned in chapter 5, in early 2002, the New York Association for Gender Rights Advocacy (NYAGRA), of which I was a board member at the time, successfully led a campaign to introduce and pass a bill in the New York City Council which would include "gender identity and expression" (and therefore, transgender-identified people) as a protected category in the city's Human Rights Ordinance. While much of the focus of the campaign was on discrimination in housing, employment, and public accommodations, these concerns were linked to practices of violence both in NYAGRA's own data collection (through our survey which gathered information on "discrimination and violence") and the narratives of transgender-identified people who gave testimony at the two public hearings preceding the bill's passage. Indeed, the context of this bill's passage gave very different kinds of individuals — sex workers, activists, homeless people, professionals — the ability to draw on that "tool kit" which brings together transgender experience and the experience of violence, representations and practices, and agencies of the state with individual histories.

8. Judith Butler, in *Excitable Speech*, is similarly hesitant at some moments. Even as she argues against the idea of hate speech legislation, she writes: "this is not to say that subjects ought not to be prosecuted for their injurious speech;

I think that there are probably occasions when they should" (1997a: 50), though she, like me, is unable to give hard and fast answers as to what those occasions might be.

CONCLUSION

1. See Murray (1997) for a counter-argument, in which he claims that *gender* is the "master discourse" through which gay male sexuality has been investigated. On the one hand, I would agree with Murray that, historically, relatively little attention has been paid to *sexuality,* or perhaps more correctly, sexual behavior in accounts of gay male lives (and, I would add, of lesbian lives either). I believe that Murray's arguments fail because he assumes a categorically clear distinction between gender and sexuality, one which I am attempting to problematize here.

2. Duggan's term is a creative adaptation of Warner's (1993) concept of "heteronormativity."

3. See note 16 in chapter 1.

4. American anthropology, from some perspectives, was born in the mode of critique and advocacy, animated by Boasian concerns with overturning racist and primitivizing evolutionism (Baker 1998). On the other hand, anthropology has been critiqued for its implication in colonialism (Asad 1973), spying (Price 2000), and even war (Wakin 1992). On a broader terrain, feminist, neo-Marxist, and other critical accounts take anthropology to task for producing objectivist and nonmaterialist accounts of exotic others with little recognition of the effects of colonialism and modernization on their subjects. Despite this, the public engagement of anthropologists across the span of the twentieth century speaks to an ongoing spirit of advocacy within the discipline, even among those who from the perspective of the present seem to have been most deeply implicated in colonial systems (Ferguson 1999). Yet, as Robins (1986), Fetterman (1993) and others have pointed out, historically, anthropology has had relatively little impact in the formation of public policy aimed at eradicating injustices.

Works Cited

Adam, Barry D. 1995. *The Rise of a Gay and Lesbian Movement*. Rev. ed. New York: Twayne Publishers.

Alarcón, Norma. 1990. "The Theoretical Subject(s) of *This Bridge Called My Back* and Anglo-American Feminism." In *Making Face, Making Soul/Haciendo Caras: Creative and Critical Perspectives by Feminists of Color*, edited by Gloria Anzaldúa, 356–69. San Francisco: Aunt Lute.

Altman, Dennis. 1993. [1971]. *Homosexual: Oppression and Liberation*. New York: New York University Press.

American Psychiatric Association. 1980. *Diagnostic and Statistical Manual of Mental Disorders*. 3rd ed. Washington, D.C.: American Psychiatric Association.

——. 2000. *Diagnostic and Statistical Manual of Mental Disorders*. 4th ed. text revision. Washington, D.C.: American Psychiatric Association.

Amory, Deborah P. 1996. "Club Q: Dancing with (A) Difference." In *Inventing Lesbian Cultures in America*, edited by Ellen Lewin, 145–60. Boston: Beacon Books.

Anderson, Benedict. 1991. [1983]. *Imagined Communities: Reflections on the Origin and Spread of Nationalism*. London: Verso.

Anonymous. 1972a. "Full Civil Rights." *Gay Liberator*, October, 1.

——. 1972b. "Gay Pride Week '72, June 17–25." *Fag Rag*, Summer, n.p.

——. 1972c. "Transvestites." *Fag Rag*, Summer, 4.

Asad, Talal, ed. 1973. *Anthropology and the Colonial Encounter*. New York: Humanities Press.

Axel, Brian Keith. 2001. *The Nation's Tortured Body: Violence, Representation, and the Formation of a Sikh "Diaspora."* Durham, N.C.: Duke University Press.

Badgett, M. V. Lee. 1998. *Income Inflation: The Myth of Affluence among Gay, Lesbian, and Bisexual Americans.* New York: Policy Institute of the National Gay and Lesbian Task Force and the Institute for Gay and Lesbian Strategic Studies.

Bailey, J. Michael. 2003. *The Man Who Would Be Queen: The Science of Gender-Bending and Transsexualism.* Washington, D.C.: Joseph Henry Press.

Baker, Lee D. 1998. *From Savage to Negro: Anthropology and the Construction of Race, 1896–1954.* Berkeley: University of California Press.

Baker, Roger. 1994. *Drag: A History of Female Impersonation in the Performing Arts.* New York: New York University Press.

Bawer, Bruce. 1993. *A Place at the Table: The Gay Individual in American Society.* New York: Poseidon Press.

Bayer, Ronald. 1987. "Politics, Science, and the Problem of Psychiatric Nomenclature: A Case Study of the American Psychiatric Association Referendum on Homosexuality." In *Scientific Controversies: Case Studies in the Resolution and Closure of Disputes in Science and Technology,* edited by H. Tristam Engelhardt Jr. and Arthur L. Caplan, 381–400. Cambridge: Cambridge University Press.

Beauvoir, Simone de. 1989 [1952]. *The Second Sex.* Translated by H. M. Parshley. Introduction by Deidre Bair. New York: Vintage Books.

Benjamin, Harry. 1966. *The Transsexual Phenomenon.* New York: Julian Press.

Berlant, Lauren, and Michael Warner. 1998. "Sex in Public." *Critical Inquiry* 24: 547–66.

Besnier, Niko. 2002. "Transgenderism, Locality, and the Miss Galaxy Beauty Pageant in Tonga." *American Ethnologist* 29 (3): 534–66.

Bieber, Irving. 1987. "On Arriving at the American Psychiatric Association Decision on Homosexuality." In *Scientific Controversies: Case Studies in the Resolution and Closure of Disputes in Science and Technology,* edited by H. Tristam Engelhardt and Arthur L. Caplan, 417–36. Cambridge: Cambridge University Press.

Billings, Dwight B., and Thomas Urban. 1982. "The Socio-Medical Construction of Transsexualism: an Interpretation and Critique." *Social Problems* 29 (3): 266–82.

Blackwood, Evelyn. 1984. "Sexuality and Gender in Certain Native American Tribes: The Case of Cross-Gender Females." *Signs* 10 (1): 27–42.

———. 1995. "Falling in Love with An-Other Lesbian: Reflections on Identity in Fieldwork." In *Taboo: Sex, Identity, and Erotic Subjectivity in Anthropological Fieldwork,* edited by Don Kulick and Margaret Willson, 51–75. New York: Routledge.

———. 2002. "Reading Sexualities across Cultures: Anthropology and Theories of Sexuality." In *Out in Theory: The Emergence of Lesbian and Gay Anthropology,* edited by Ellen Lewin and William L. Leap, 69–92. Urbana: University of Illinois Press.

Blumenstein, Rosalyne. 2003. *Branded T.* Bloomington, Ind.: Authorhouse.

Boas, Franz. 1889. "On Alternating Sounds." *American Anthropologist* 2 (1): 47–54.

Boellstorff, Tom. 2004. "Playing Back the Nation: *Waria,* Indonesian Transvestites." *Cultural Anthropology* 19 (2): 159–95.

———. 2005. *The Gay Archipelago: Sexuality and Nation in Indonesia.* Princeton, N.J.: Princeton University Press.

Bolin, Anne. 1988. *In Search of Eve: Transsexual Rites of Passage.* South Hadley, Mass.: Bergin and Garvey.

———. 1994. "Transcending and Transgendering: Male-to-Female Transsexuals, Dichotomy, and Diversity." In *Third Sex, Third Gender: Beyond Sexual Dimorphism in Culture and History,* edited by Gilbert Herdt, 447–85. New York: Zone Books.

Bordo, Susan. 1999. *The Male Body: A New Look at Men in Public and in Private.* New York: Farrar, Straus and Giroux.

Bornstein, Kate. 1994. *Gender Outlaw: On Men, Women, and the Rest of Us.* New York: Vintage.

———. 1998. *My Gender Workbook: How to Become a Real Man, a Real Woman, the Real You, or Something Else Entirely.* New York: Routledge.

Boswell, Holly. 1991. "The Transgender Alternative." *Chrysalis Quarterly* 1 (2): 29–31.

Bourdieu, Pierre. 1977. *Outline of a Theory of Practice.* Translated by Richard Nice. Cambridge: Cambridge University Press.

Boyd, Nan Alamilla. 2003. *Wide-Open Town: A History of Queer San Francisco to 1965.* Berkeley: University of California Press.

Boykin, Keith. 1996. *One More River to Cross: Black and Gay in America.* New York: Anchor Books.

Brake, Mike. 1976. "I May Be Queer, but at Least I Am a Man: Male Hegemony and Ascribed versus Achieved Gender." In *Sexual Divisions and Society: Process and Change,* edited by Diana Leonard Barker and Sheila Allen, 174–98. London: Tavistock.

Bravmann, Scott. 1995. "Queer Fictions of Stonewall: Race, Riots, and the Crisis in Representation." *Perversions* 6: 47–61.

Broad, Kendal. L. 2002. "Fracturing Transgender: Intersectional Constructions and Identization." In *Gendered Sexualities,* edited by Patricia Gagné and Richard Tewksbury, 235–66. Amsterdam: JAI Press.

Brown, Wendy. 1995. *States of Injury: Power and Freedom in Late Modernity.* Princeton, N.J.: Princeton University Press.

Butler, Judith. 1990. *Gender Trouble: Feminism and the Subversion of Identity.* New York: Routledge.

———. 1993. *Bodies That Matter: On the Discursive Limits of "Sex."* New York: Routledge.

———. 1994. "Against Proper Objects: Introduction." *Differences* 6 (2–3): 1–26.

———. 1997a. *Excitable Speech: A Politics of the Performative.* New York: Routledge.

———. 1997b. "Merely Cultural." *Social Text* 52–53:265–89.

Califia, Patrick. 2003. [1997]. *Sex Changes: The Politics of Transgenderism.* San Francisco: Cleis Press.

Callender, Charles, and Lee Kochems. 1983. "The North American Berdache." *Current Anthropology* 24:443–70.

Cameron, Loren. 1996. *Body Alchemy: Transsexual Portraits.* Pittsburgh: Cleis Press.

Cartwright, Donna. 2000. "Remembering Falls City: The Resurgence of Transgender Activism." *Against the Current* 15 (5): 24–28.

———. 2001. "Whither GPAC? Reflections at My Time of Resignation." *Transgender Tapestry* 93:56–58.

Chase, Cheryl. 1998. "Hermaphrodites with Attitude: Mapping the Emergence of Intersex Political Activism." *GLQ* 4 (2): 189–211.

Chasin, Alexandra. 2001. *Selling Out: The Gay and Lesbian Movement Goes to Market.* New York: Palgrave Macmillan.

Chauncey, George. 1994. *Gay New York: Gender, Urban Culture, and the Makings of the Gay Male World.* New York: Basic Books.

———. 2000. "The Queer History and Politics of Lesbian and Gay Studies." In *Queer Frontiers: Millennial Geographies, Genders, and Generations,* edited by Joseph A. Boone, Martin Dupuis, Martin Meeker, Karin Quimby, Cindy Sarver, Debra Silverman, and Rosemary Weatherston, 298–315. Madison: University of Wisconsin Press.

Chesluk, Benjamin. 2004. "Visible Signs of a City Out of Control: Community Policing in New York City." *Cultural Anthropology* 19 (2): 250–75.

Cohen, Lawrence. 1995. "The Pleasures of Castration: The Postoperative Status of Hijras, Jankhas, and Academics." In *Sexual Nature, Sexual Culture*, edited by Paul R. Abramson and Steven D. Pinkerton, 276–304. Chicago: University of Chicago Press.

Cole, Shaun. 2000. *"Don We Now Our Gay Apparel": Gay Men's Dress in the Twentieth Century*. Oxford: Berg.

Collier, Jane F., and Sylvia J. Yanagisako, eds. 1987. *Gender and Kinship: Essays toward a Unified Analysis*. Stanford, Calif.: Stanford University Press.

Conrad, Peter. 1994. "Wellness as Virtue: Morality and the Pursuit of Health." *Culture, Medicine, and Psychiatry* 18:385–401.

Conway, Lynn. N.d. "An Investigation into the Publication of J. Michael Bailey's Book on Transsexualism by the National Academies." http://ai.eecs.umich.edu/people/conway/ts/lynnsreviewofbaileysbook.html (accessed April 16, 2006).

County, Jayne, with Rupert Smith. 1995. *Man Enough to Be a Woman*. London: Serpent's Tail.

Crenshaw, Kimberle. 1991. "Mapping the Margins: Intersectionality, Identity Politics, and Violence Against Women of Color." *Stanford Law Review* 43 (6): 1241–99.

Cromwell, Jason. 1999. *Transmen and FTMs: Identities, Bodies, Genders, and Sexualities*. Urbana: University of Illinois Press.

Currah, Paisley. 2003. "The Transgender Rights Imaginary." *Georgetown Journal of Gender and the Law* 4 (2): 705–20.

Currah, Paisley, and Shannon Minter. 2000. *Transgender Equality: A Handbook for Activists and Policymakers*. Washington, D.C.: Policy Institute of the National Gay and Lesbian Task Force and the National Center for Lesbian Rights.

Currante, Donald. 1973. "Fags Destroy." *The Advocate* 115:36, 40.

Daniel, E. Valentine. 1996. *Charred Lullabies: Chapters in an Anthropography of Violence*. Princeton, N.J.: Princeton University Press.

Davis, Mike. 1992. [1990]. *City of Quartz: Excavating the Future in Los Angeles*. London: Verso.

D'Emilio, John. 1983a. "Capitalism and Gay Identity." In *Powers of Desire: The Politics of Sexuality*, edited by Ann Snitow, Christine Stansell, and Sharon Thompson, 100–113. New York: Monthly Review Press.

———. 1983b. *Sexual Politics, Sexual Communities: The Making of a Homosexual Minority in the United States, 1940–1970*. Chicago: University of Chicago Press.

———. 2002. *The World Turned: Essays on Gay History, Politics, and Culture.* Durham, N.C.: Duke University Press.

De Motier, Beren. 1998. "The Transgender Craze." *New York Blade News,* June 26, 30.

Deleuze, Gilles, and Félix Guattari. 1987. *A Thousand Plateaus: Capitalism and Schizophrenia.* Translated and with a foreword by Brian Massumi. Minneapolis: University of Minnesota Press.

DeMello, Margo. 2000. *Bodies of Inscription: A Cultural History of the Modern Tattoo Community.* Durham, N.C.: Duke University Press.

Devereux, George. 1937. "Institutionalized Homosexuality of the Mohave Indians." *Human Biology* 9:498–527.

Devor, Aaron H., and Nicholas Matte. 2004. "One Inc. and Reed Erickson: The Uneasy Collaboration of Gay and Trans Activism, 1964–2003." GLQ 10 (2): 179–209.

Devor, Holly. 1997. FTM: *Female-to-Male Transsexuals in Society.* Bloomington: Indiana University Press.

Docter, Richard F. 1988. *Transvestites and Transsexuals: Toward a Theory of Cross Gender Behavior.* New York: Plenum.

Donham, Donald L. 1998. "Freeing South African: The 'Modernization' of Male-Male Sexuality in Soweto." *Cultural Anthropology* 13 (1): 3–21.

Douglas, Mary. 1992. [1966]. *Purity and Danger: An Analysis of Concepts of Pollution and Taboo.* London: Pelican Books.

Duberman, Martin Bauml. 1993. *Stonewall.* New York: Dutton.

Duggan, Lisa. 2003. *The Twilight of Equality? Neoliberalism, Cultural Politics and the Attack on Democracy.* Boston: Beacon Books.

Duggan, Lisa, and Nan D. Hunter. 1995. *Sex Wars: Sexual Dissent and Political Culture.* New York: Routledge.

Dunne, John Gregory. 1997. "The Humboldt Murders." *New Yorker,* January 13, 44–62.

Eckert, Penelope, and Sally McConnell-Ginet. 1992. "Think Practically and Look Locally: Language and Gender as Community-Based Practice." *Annual Review of Anthropology* 21:461–90.

Edelman, Marc. 2001. "Social Movements: Changing Paradigms and Forms of Politics." *Annual Review of Anthropology* 30:285–317.

Editors of *Gay Liberator.* 1973. "Drag/TV/TS: And a Response." *Gay Liberator* 31:6.

Ekins, Richard. 1997. *Male Femaling: A Grounded Approach to Cross-Dressing and Sex-Changing.* London: Routledge.

Ekins, Richard, and Dave King. 1999. "Towards a Sociology of Transgendered Bodies." *Sociological Review* 47 (3): 580–602.

————. 2006. *The Transgender Phenomenon*. London: Sage.

Ekins, Richard, and Dave King, eds. 1996. *Blending Genders: Social Aspects of Cross-Dressing and Sex-Changing*. New York: Routledge.

————. 2005. *Virginia Prince: Pioneer of Transgendering*. New York: Haworth.

Elliot, Patricia, and Katrina Roen. 1998. "Transgenderism and the Question of Embodiment: Promising Queer Politics?" *GLQ* 4 (2): 231–62.

Ellis, Havelock. 1927. *Studies in the Psychology of Sex,* vol. 7. New York: Random House.

Elliston, Deborah. 2002. "Anthropology's Queer Future: Feminist Lessons from Tahiti and its Islands." *In Out in Theory: The Emergence of Lesbian and Gay Anthropology,* edited by Ellen Lewin and William L. Leap, 287–315. Urbana: University of Illinois Press.

Epprecht, Marc. 1998. "The 'Unsaying' of Indigenous Homosexualities in Zimbabwe: Mapping a Blind Spot in an African Masculinity." *Journal of Southern African Studies* 24 (4): 631–51.

Epstein, Stephen. 1987. "Gay Politics, Ethnic Identity: The Limits of Social Construction." *Socialist Review* 17 (3–4): 9–54.

Faderman, Lillian. 1991. *Odd Girls and Twilight Lovers: A History of Lesbian Life in Twentieth-Century America*. New York: Columbia University Press.

Feder, Ellen. 1997. "Disciplining the Family: The Case of Gender Identity Disorder." *Philosophical Studies* 85:195–211.

Feinberg, Leslie. 1992. *Transgender Liberation: A Movement Whose Time Has Come*. New York: World View Forum.

————. 1993. *Stone Butch Blues: A Novel*. Ithaca, N.Y.: Firebrand Books.

————. 1996. *Transgender Warriors: Making History from Joan of Arc to Dennis Rodman*. Boston: Beacon Books.

————. 1998. *Trans Liberation: Beyond Pink or Blue*. Boston: Beacon Books.

Feldman, Allen. 1991. *Formations of Violence: The Narrative of the Body and Political Terror in Northern Ireland*. Chicago: University of Chicago Press.

Ferguson, James. 1999. *Expectations of Modernity: Myths and Meanings of Urban Life on the Zambian Copperbelt*. Berkeley: University of California Press.

Ferguson, Roderick A. 2005. "Of Our Normative Strivings: African American Studies and the Histories of Sexuality." *Social Text* 84–85:85–100.

Fetterman, David M., ed. 1993. *Speaking the Language of Power: Communication, Collaboration, and Advocacy (Translating Ethnography into Action)*. Washington, D.C.: Falmer Press.

Fitzgerald, Frances. 1986. *Cities on a Hill: A Journey through Contemporary American Cultures*. New York: Simon and Schuster.

Fortun, Kim. 2001. *Advocacy after Bhopal: Environmentalism, Disaster, New Global Orders.* Chicago: University of Chicago Press.

Foucault, Michel. 1983. "The Subject and Power." In *Michel Foucault: Beyond Structuralism and Hermeneutics,* edited by Hubert L. Dreyfus and Paul Rabinow, 208–26. New York: Pantheon Books.

——. 1990. [1978]. *The History of Sexuality.* Volume 1: *An Introduction.* Translated by Robert Hurley. New York: Vintage.

Fox, Richard, and Orin Starn. 1997. Introduction to *Between Resistance and Revolution: Cultural Politics and Social Protest,* edited by Richard Fox and Orin Starn, 1–16. New Brunswick, N.J.: Rutgers University Press.

Fraser, Nancy. 1997. *Justice Interruptus: Critical Reflections on the "Postsocialist" Condition.* New York: Routledge.

Freedman, Estelle B. 1989. " 'Uncontrolled Desires': The Response to the Sexual Psychopath, 1920–1960." In *Passion and Power: Sexuality in History,* edited by Kathy Peiss and Christina Simmons, 199–225. Philadelphia: Temple University Press.

Freedman, Estelle B., and John D'Emilio. 1990. "Problems Encountered in Writing the History of Sexuality: Sources, Theory, and Interpretation." *Journal of Sex Research* 27 (4): 481–95.

Frye, Phyllis Randolph. 2000. "Facing Discrimination, Organizing for Freedom: The Transgender Community." In *Creating Change: Sexuality, Public Policy, and Civil Rights,* edited by John D'Emilio, William B. Turner, and Urvashi Vaid, 451–68. New York: St. Martin's Press.

Gagné, Patricia, and Richard Tewksbury. 2002. *Gendered Sexualities.* New York: JAI Press.

Gamson, Joshua. 1995. "Must Identity Movements Self-Destruct? A Queer Dilemma." *Social Problems* 42 (3): 390–407.

Garber, Marjorie. 1992. *Vested Interests: Cross-Dressing and Cultural Anxiety.* New York: Routledge.

GenderPAC. 1997. *The First National Study on Transviolence.* Waltham, Mass.: GenderPAC.

——. n.d. "About the Hate Crimes Prevention Act." http://www.gpac.org/violence/lleeainfo.html (accessed April 16, 2006).

Gevisser, Mark, and Edwin Cameron, eds. 1994. *Defiant Desire: Gay and Lesbian Lives in South Africa.* Johannesburg: Raven Press.

Giddens, Anthony. 1979. *Central Problems in Social Theory: Action, Structure, and Contradiction in Social Analysis.* Berkeley: University of California Press.

——. 1990. *The Consequences of Modernity.* Stanford, Calif.: Stanford University Press.

Ginsburg, Faye D. 1989. *Contested Lives: The Abortion Debate in an American Community.* Berkeley: University of California Press.

GLAAD (Gay and Lesbian Alliance against Defamation). 1998. "GLAADalert Special Analysis: Media Mixed for Pride '98." http://www.glaad.org/action/al _ archive _ detail.php?id=1755 (accessed April 16, 2006).

Gluckman, Amy, and Betsy Reed. 1997. Introduction to *Homo Economics: Capitalism, Community, and Gay Life,* edited by Amy Gluckman and Betsy Reed, xi–xxxi. New York: Routledge.

Goldberg, Carey. 1996. "Shunning 'He' and 'She,' They Fight for Respect." *New York Times,* September 8, 24.

———. 1999. " 'People of Size' Gather to Promote Fat Acceptance." *New York Times,* July 29, A12.

Goldschmidt, Henry. 2006. *Race and Religion Among the Chosen Peoples of Crown Heights.* New Brunswick, N.J.: Rutgers University Press.

Goleman, Daniel. 1994. "Revamping Psychiatrists' Bible." *New York Times,* April 19, C1, Cll.

Gregory, Steven. 1998. *Black Corona: Race and the Politics of Place in an Urban Community.* Princeton, N.J.: Princeton University Press.

Gupta, Akhil, and James Ferguson, eds. 1997. *Anthropological Locations: Boundaries and Grounds of a Field Science.* Berkeley: University of California Press.

Halberstam, Judith. 1997. "Mackdaddy, Superfly, Rapper: Gender, Race, and Masculinity in the Drag King Scene." *Social Text* 52–53: 104–31.

———. 1998a. *Female Masculinity.* Durham, N.C.: Duke University Press.

———. 1998b. "Transgender Butch: Butch/FTM Border Wars and the Masculine Continuum." *GLQ* 4 (2): 287–310.

———. 2000. Book Review of *Second Skins: The Body Narratives of Transsexuality,* by Jay Prosser, *Trans Liberation: Beyond Pink or Blue,* by Leslie Feinberg, and *FTM: Female-to-Male Transsexuals in Society,* by Holly Devor. *Signs* 26 (1): 313–18.

———. 2003. "The Brandon Teena Archive." In *Queer Studies: An Interdisciplinary Reader,* edited by Robert J. Corber and Stephen Valocchi, 159–69. Malden, Mass.: Blackwell.

Halberstam, Judith, and Del La Grace Volcano. 1999. *The Drag King Book.* New York: Serpent's Tail.

Hale, C. Jacob. n.d. "Suggested Rules for Non-Transsexuals Writing about Transsexuals, Transsexuality, Transsexualism, or Trans———." http://www.sandystone.com/hale.rules.html (accessed April 16, 2006).

———. 1998. "Consuming the Living, Dis (re)membering the Dead in the Butch/FTM Borderlands." *GLQ* 4 (2): 311–48.

Halperin, David. 1990. *One Hundred Years of Homosexuality, and Other Essays on Greek Love.* New York: Routledge.

Haraway, Donna. 1997. *Modest_Witness@Second_Millennium. FemaleMan© _Meets_OncoMouse™: Feminism and Technoscience.* New York: Routledge.

Harper, Philip Brian. 1994. " 'The Subversive Edge': *Paris Is Burning,* Social Critique, and the Limits of Subjective Agency." *Diacritics* 24 (2–3): 90–103.

Harvey, David. 1993. "Class Relations, Social Justice, and the Politics of Difference." In *Place and the Politics of Identity,* edited by Michael Keith and Steve Pile, 41–66. New York: Routledge.

———. 2000. *Spaces of Hope.* Berkeley: University of California Press.

Hausman, Bernice L. 1995. *Changing Sex: Transsexualism, Technology, and the Idea of Gender.* Durham, N.C.: Duke University Press.

———. 2001. "Recent Transgender Theory (Review Essay)." *Feminist Studies* 27 (2): 465–90.

Hekma, Gert. 1994. " 'A Female Soul in a Male Body': Sexual Inversion as Gender Inversion in Nineteenth-Century Sexology." In *Third Sex, Third Gender: Beyond Sexual Dimorphism in Culture and History*, edited by Gilbert H. Herdt, 213–39. New York: Zone Books.

Helms, Monica. 2000. "The Death of GenderPAC: A Personal Opinion." http://www.ntac.org/news/01/01/02gpac.html (accessed April 16, 2006).

Herdt, Gilbert H., ed. 1994. *Third Sex, Third Gender: Beyond Sexual Dimorphism in Culture and History.* New York: Zone Books.

Hill, Robert. 2007. " 'As a Man, I Exist; As a Woman—I Live': Heterosexual Transvestism and the Contours of Gender and Sexuality in Postwar America." Ph.D. dissertation, Program in American Culture, University of Michigan.

Hirschfeld, Magnus. 1991. [1910]. *Transvestites: The Erotic Drive to Cross Dress.* Translated by Michael A. Lombardi-Nash. Introduction by Vern Bullough. Buffalo: Prometheus Books.

hooks, bell. 1992. "Is Paris Burning?" *Black Looks: Race and Representation.* Boston: South End Press.

Horowitz, Craig. 1998. "It Shakes a Village." *New York,* November 9, 28–33, 88.

In Your Face. 1998. "HRC Board Passes Resolution to Support Trans-Issues." http://legalminds.lp.findlaw.com/list/queerlaw-edit/msg02637.html (accessed April 16, 2006).

Ingstad, Benedicte, and Susan Reynolds Whyte, eds. 1995. *Disability and Culture.* Berkeley: University of California Press.

Jackson, Jonathan David. 2002. "The Social World of Vogueing." *Journal for the Anthropological Study of Human Movement* 12 (2): 26–42.

Jacobs, Andrew. 2004. "For Young Gays on the Streets, Survival Comes before Pride." *New York Times*, June 27, 24, 29.

Jacobs, Sue-Ellen, Wesley Thomas, and Sabine Lang. 1997a. Introduction to *Two-Spirit People: Native American Gender Identity, Sexuality, and Spirituality*, edited by Sue-Ellen Jacobs, Wesley Thomas, and Sabine Lang, 1–18. Urbana: University of Illinois Press..

——, eds. 1997b. *Two-Spirit People: Native American Gender Identity, Sexuality, and Spirituality*. Urbana: University of Illinois Press.

Jeffreys, Sheila. 1996. "Heterosexuality and the Desire for Gender." In *Theorizing Heterosexuality: Telling it Straight*, edited by Diane Richardson, 75–90. Oxford: Oxford University Press.

Johnson, Mark. 1997. *Beauty and Power: Transgendering and Cultural Transformation in the Southern Philippines*. New York: Berg.

Jolly, Margaret, and Lenore Manderson. 1997. "Introduction: Sites of Desire/Economies of Pleasure in Asia and the Pacific." In *Sites of Desire, Economies of Pleasure: Sexualities in Asia and the Pacific*, edited by Lenore Manderson and Margaret Jolly, 1–26. Chicago: University of Chicago Press.

Joseph, Miranda. 2002a. *Against the Romance of Community*. Minneapolis: University of Minnesota Press.

——. 2002b. "Family Affairs: The Discourse of Global/Localization." In *Queer Globalizations: Citizenship and the Afterlife of Colonialism*, edited by Arnaldo Cruz-Malave and Martin F. Manalansan IV, 71–99. New York: New York University Press.

Kammerer, Nina, Theresa Mason, and Margaret Connors. 1999. "Transgender Health and Social Service Needs in the Context of HIV Risk." *International Journal of Transgenderism* 3 (1, 2). http://www.symposion.com/ijt/hiv_risk/kammerer.htm (accessed April 16, 2006).

Katz, Jonathan Ned. 1976. *Gay American History: Lesbians and Gay Men in the USA*. New York: Thomas Y. Crowell.

Kennedy, Elizabeth L., and Madeline D. Davis. 1993. *Boots of Leather, Slippers of Gold: The History of a Lesbian Community*. New York: Routledge.

King, Dave. 1993. *The Transvestite and the Transsexual: Public Categories and Private Identities*. Aldershot, U.K.: Avebury.

Kinsey, Alfred C., Wardell B. Pomeroy, and Clyde E. Martin. 1948. *Sexual Behavior in the Human Male*. Philadelphia: W. B. Saunders.

Kirk, Marshall, and Hunter Madsen. 1989. *After the Ball: How America Will Conquer its Fear and Hatred of Gays in the 90s*. New York: Doubleday.

Klein, Charles H. 1998. "From One 'Battle' to Another: The Making of a *Travesti* Political Movement in a Brazilian City." *Sexualities* 1 (3): 327–42.

Kleinberg, Seymour. 1978. "Where Have All the Sissies Gone?" *Christopher Street,* March, 4–12.

Kleinman, Arthur, and Joan Kleinman. 1996. "The Appeal of Experience, the Dismay of Images: Cultural Appropriations of Suffering in Our Times." *Daedalus* 125 (1): 1–23.

Knopp, Lawrence. 1992. "Sexuality and the Spatial Dynamics of Capitalism." *Environment and Planning D, Society and Space* 10:651–69.

Knox, Sara Louise. 1998. *Murder: A Tale of Modern American Life*. Durham, N.C.: Duke University Press.

Krohn-Hansen, Christian. 1994. "The Anthropology of Violent Interaction." *Journal of Anthropological Research* 50:367–81.

Kulick, Don. 1998. *Travesti: Sex, Gender, and Culture among Brazilian Transgendered Prostitutes*. Chicago: University of Chicago Press.

———. 2003. "No." *Language and Communication* 23 (2): 139–51.

———. 2005. "Four Hundred Thousand Swedish Perverts." *GLQ* 11 (2): 205–35.

Kulick, Don and Anne Meneley, eds. 2005. *Fat: The Anthropology of an Obsession*. New York: Penguin.

Laclau, Ernesto, and Chantal Mouffe. 2001. [1985]. *Hegemony and Socialist Strategy: Towards a Radical Democratic Politics*. 2nd ed. London: Verso.

Lancaster, Roger. 1992. *Life Is Hard: Machismo, Danger, and the Intimacy of Power*. Berkeley: University of California Press.

Lang, Sabine. 1998. *Men as Women, Women as Men: Changing Gender in Native American Cultures*. Translated by John L. Vantine. Austin: University of Texas Press.

Levine, Martin P. 1998. *Gay Macho: The Life and Death of the Homosexual Clone*. New York: New York University Press.

Likosky, Stephan. 1992. *Coming Out: An Anthology of International Gay and Lesbian Writings*. New York: Pantheon Books.

Löfström, Jan. 1992. "Sexuality at Stake: The Essentialist and Constructionist Approaches to Sexuality in Anthropology." *Suomen Antropologi* 17 (3): 13–27.

Lombardi, Emilio L. 1995. "History Repeats Itself: The Transgender Movement in Relation to the Homosexual Rights Movement." *Journal of Gender Studies* 17:73–83.

Lombardi, Emilia L. 2005. "Findings from a Federally Funded Trans Study." Paper delivered at the Trans Politics, Social Change, and Justice Conference, CUNY, New York, May 6–7.

Lombardi-Nash, Michael. n.d. "Karl Heinrich Ulrichs." http://www.angelfire
.com/fl3/celebration2000 (accessed April 16, 2006).

Lorber, Judith. 1994. *Paradoxes of Gender.* New Haven, Conn.: Yale University Press.

Lorde, Audre. 1984. *Sister Outsider.* Trumansburg, N.Y.: Crossing Press.

Lothstein, Leslie Martin. 1983. *Female-to-Male Transsexualism: Historical, Clinical and Theoretical Issues.* Boston: Routledge and Kegan Paul.

Lyon-Callo, Vincent. 2004. *Inequality, Poverty, and Neoliberal Governance: Activist Ethnography in the Homeless Sheltering Industry.* Orchard Park, N.Y.: Broadview Press.

MacKenzie, Gordene Olga. 1994. *Transgender Nation.* Bowling Green, Ohio: Bowling Green State University Popular Press.

MacKenzie, K. Roy. 1978. "Gender Dysphoria Syndrome: Towards Standardized Diagnostic Criteria." *Archives of Sexual Behavior* 7 (4): 251–62.

Manalansan, Martin F., IV. 1997. "In the Shadows of Stonewall: Examining Gay Transnational Politics and the Diasporic Dilemma." In *The Politics of Culture in the Shadow of Capital,* edited by Lisa Lowe and David Lloyd, 485–505. Durham, N.C.: Duke University Press.

———. 2003. *Global Divas: Filipino Gay Men in the Diaspora.* Durham, N.C.: Duke University Press.

Mantilla, Karla. 2000. "Men in Ewe's Clothing: The Stealth Politics of the Transgender Movement." *Off Our Backs* 30 (4): 5, 8–9, 12.

Marcus, Eric. 1999. "Stonewall Revisited." Independent Gay Forum, March 7. http://www.indegayforum.org/authors/marcus/marcus56.html (accessed April 16, 2006).

Marcus, George. 1998. *Ethnography through Thick and Thin.* Princeton, N.J.: Princeton University Press.

Martin, Biddy. 1994. "Sexualities without Genders and Other Queer Utopias." *Diacritics* 24 (2–3): 104–21.

Martin, Emily. 1994. *Flexible Bodies: Tracking Immunity in American Culture from the Days of Polio to the Age of AIDS.* Boston: Beacon Books.

Maskovsky, Jeff. 2002. "Do We All 'Reek of Consumption'? Consumption and the Erasure of Poverty in Lesbian and Gay Studies." In *Out in Theory: The Emergence of Lesbian and Gay Anthropology,* edited by Ellen Lewin and William L. Leap, 264–86. Urbana: University of Illinois Press.

Mass, Lawrence. 1990. *Dialogues of the Sexual Revolution.* Volume 1: *Homosexuality and Sexuality.* New York: Harrington Park Press.

McCall, Leslie. 2005. "The Complexity of Intersectionality." *Signs* 30 (3): 1771–1800.

McCarthy Brown, Karen. 2001. "Mimesis in the Face of Fear: Femme Queens, Butch Queens, and Gender Play in the Houses of Greater Newark." In *Passing: Identity and Interpretation in Sexuality, Race, and Religion,* edited by María Carla Sánchez and Linda Schlossberg, 208–27. New York: New York University Press.

McLean, Hugh, and Linda Ngcobo. 1994. " 'Abangibhamayo Bathi Ngimnandi' (Those Who Fuck Me Say I'm Tasty): Gay Sexuality in Reef Townships." In *Defiant Desire: Gay and Lesbian Lives in South Africa,* edited by Mark Gevisser and Edwin Cameron, 158–85. Johannesburg: Raven Press.

McNeal, Keith E. 1999. "Behind the Make-Up: Gender Ambivalence and the Double-Bind of Gay Selfhood in Drag Performance." *Ethos* 27 (3): 344–78.

McNeill, Sandra. 1982. "Transsexualism . . . Can Men Turn Men into Women?" In *On the Problem of Men: Two Feminist Conferences,* edited by Scarlet Friedman and Elizabeth Sarah, 83–87. London: Women's Press.

Melucci, Alberto. 1996. *Challenging Codes: Collective Action in the Information Age.* Cambridge: Cambridge University Press.

Members of the Gay and Lesbian Historical Society of Northern California. 1998. "MTF Transgender Activism in the Tenderloin and Beyond, 1966–1975: Commentary and Interview with Elliot Blackstone." *GLQ* 4 (2): 349–72.

Meyerowitz, Joanne. 1998. "Sex Change and the Popular Press: Historical Notes on Transsexuality in the United States." *GLQ* 4 (2): 159–87.

———. 2002. *How Sex Changed: A History of Transsexuality in the United States.* Cambridge, Mass.: Harvard University Press.

Michaelsen, Scott, and David E. Johnson, eds. 1997. *Border Theory: The Limits of Cultural Politics.* Minneapolis: University of Minnesota Press.

Millot, Catharine. 1990. *Horsexe: Essay on Transsexuality.* New York: Autonomedia.

Minkowitz, Donna. 1994. "Love Hurts." *Village Voice,* April 19, 24–30.

Monro, Surya, and Lorna Warren. 2004. "Transgendering Citizenship." *Sexualities* 7 (3): 345–62.

Moraga, Cherrie, and Gloria Anzaldúa, eds. 1981. *This Bridge Called My Back: Writings by Radical Women of Color.* Watertown, Mass.: Persephone Press.

Moran, Leslie J., and Andrew N. Sharpe. 2002. "Policing the Transgender/Violence Relation." *Current Issues in Criminal Justice* 13 (3): 269–85.

More, Kate, and Stephen Whittle, eds. 1999. *Reclaiming Genders: Transsexual Grammars at the Fin De Siecle.* London: Cassell.

Morris, Ken, and Kay Brown. n.d. "The Alan Lucill Hart Story." http://www.transhistory.org/history/th_alan_hart.html (accessed July 27, 2004).

Mumford, Kevin J. 1997. *Interzones: Black/White Sex Districts in Chicago and New York in the Early Twentieth Century*. New York: Columbia University Press.

Murray, Stephen O. 1997. "Explaining Away Same-Sex Sexualities When They Obtrude on Anthropologists' Notice at All." *Anthropology Today* 13 (3): 2–5.

Namaste, Viviane K. 2000. *Invisible Lives: The Erasure of Transsexual and Transgendered People*. Chicago: University of Chicago Press.

———. 2002. "Addressing the Politics of Social Erasure: Making the Lives of Transsexual People Visible. An Interview with Viviane Namaste." *New Socialist* 39. http://www.newsocialist.org/magazine/39/article04.html (accessed April 16, 2006).

Nanda, Serena. 1990. *Neither Man nor Woman: The Hijras of India*. Belmont, Calif.: Wadsworth.

Nelson, James. 1998. "The Silence of the Bioethicists: Ethical and Political Aspects of Managing Gender Dysphoria." *GLQ* 4 (2): 213–30.

Nestle, Joan, Clare Howell, and Riki Wilchins, eds. 2002. *Genderqueer: Voices from beyond the Sexual Binary*. Los Angeles: Alyson Books.

Newton, Esther. 1979. [1972]. *Mother Camp: Female Impersonators in America*. Chicago: University of Chicago Press.

———. 1993. *Cherry Grove, Fire Island: Sixty Years in America's First Gay and Lesbian Town*. Boston: Beacon Press.

O'Hartigan, Margaret Deirdre. 2002. "Alan Hart." In *The Phallus Palace: Female to Male Transsexuals*, edited by Dean Kotula and William E. Parker, 157–66. Los Angeles: Alyson Books.

Oetomo, Dédé. 2000. "Masculinity in Indonesia: Genders, Sexualities, and Identities in a Changing Society." In *Framing the Sexual Subject: The Politics of Gender, Sexuality, and Power,* edited by Richard Parker, Regina Maria Barbosa, and Peter Aggleton, 46–59. Berkeley: University of California Press.

Ortner, Sherry B. 1974. "Is Female to Male as Nature Is to Culture?" In *Women, Culture, and Society,* edited by Michelle Rosaldo and Louise Lamphere, 67–87. Stanford, Calif.: Stanford University Press.

———. 1996. *Making Gender: The Politics and Erotics of Culture*. Boston: Beacon Press.

Park, Pauline. 2003. "GenderPAC, the Transgender Rights Movement, and the Perils of a Post-Identity Politics Paradigm." *Georgetown Journal of Gender and the Law* 4 (2): 747–65.

Pettiway, Leon E. 1997. *Honey, Honey, Miss Thang: Being Black, Gay, and on the Streets*. Philadelphia: Temple University Press.

Phelan, Shane. 2001. *Sexual Strangers: Gays, Lesbians, and Dilemmas of Citizenship*. Philadelphia: Temple University Press.

Plummer, Ken. 1992. "Speaking its Name: Inventing a Lesbian and Gay Studies." In *Modern Homosexualities: Fragments of Gay and Lesbian Experiences*, edited by Ken Plummer, 3–25. New York: Routledge.

Price, David. 2000. "Anthropologists as Spies." *The Nation* 271 (16): 24–27.

Prieur, Annick. 1998. *Mema's House, Mexico City: On Transvestites, Queens, and Machos*. Chicago: University of Chicago Press.

Prince, Virginia. 1971. *How to Be a Woman though Male*. Los Angeles: Chevalier Publications.

Prosser, Jay. 1998. *Second Skins: The Body Narratives of Transsexuality*. New York: Columbia University Press.

Raffo, Susan, ed. 1997. *Queerly Classed: Gay Men and Lesbians Write about Class*. Boston: South End Press.

Rapp, Rayna. 1999. *Testing Women, Testing the Fetus: The Social Impact of Amniocentesis in America*. New York: Routledge.

Raymond, Janice. 1994. [1979]. *The Transsexual Empire: The Making of the She-Male*. Boston: Beacon Press.

——. 1996. "The Politics of Transgenderism." In *Blending Genders*, edited by Richard Ekins and Dave King, 215–23.

Rechy, John. 2000. "The Outlaw Sensibility in the Arts: From Drag and Leather to Prose, the Mythology of Stonewall, and a Defense of Stereotypes." In *Queer Frontiers: Millennial Geographies, Genders, and Generations*, edited by Joseph A. Boone, Martin Dupuis, Martin Meeker, Karin Quimby, Cindy Sarver, Debra Silverman, Rosemary Weatherston, 124–32. Madison: University of Wisconsin Press.

Reddy, Chandan C. 1998. "Home, Houses, Nonidentity: Paris Is Burning." In *Burning Down the House: Recycling Domesticity*, edited by Rosemary Marangoly George, 355–79. Boulder, Colo.: Westview Press.

Riches, David. 1986. "The Phenomenon of Violence." In *The Anthropology of Violence*, edited by David Riches, 1–27. New York: Blackwell.

Robertson, Jennifer. 1998. *Takarazuka: Sexual Politics and Popular Culture in Modern Japan*. Berkeley: University of California Press.

Robins, Edward. 1986. "The Strategy of Development and the Role of the Anthropologist." In *Practicing Development Anthropology*, edited by Edward C. Green, 10–21. Boulder, Colo.: Westview Press.

Roen, K. 2002. " 'Either/Or' and 'Both/Neither': Discursive Tensions in Transgender Politics." *Signs* 27 (2): 501–22.

Rosario, Vernon A. II. 1996. "Trans (Homo) Sexuality? Double Inversion,

Psychiatric Confusion, and Hetero-Hegemony." In *Queer Studies: A Lesbian, Gay, Bisexual, and Transgender Anthology,* edited by Brett Beemyn and Mickey Eliason, 35–51. New York: New York University Press.

Roscoe, Will. 1991. *The Zuni Man-Woman.* Albuquerque: University of New Mexico Press.

Rotello, Gabriel. 1997. *Sexual Ecology: AIDS and the Destiny of Gay Men.* New York: Dutton.

Rubin, Gayle. 1984. "Thinking Sex: Notes for a Radical Theory of the Politics of Sexuality." In *Pleasure and Danger: Exploring Female Sexuality,* edited by Carole Vance, 267–319. Boston: Routledge and Kegan Paul.

———.1992. "Of Catamites and Kings: Reflections on Butch, Gender, and Boundaries." In *The Persistent Desire: A Femme-Butch Reader,* edited by Joan Nestle, 466-82. Boston: Alyson Books.

———. 2002. "Studying Sexual Subcultures: Excavating Ethnography of Gay Communities in Urban North American." In *Out in Theory: The Emergence of Lesbian and Gay Anthropology,* edited by Ellen Lewin and William L. Leap, 17–68. Urbana: University of Illinois Press.

Rubin, Henry. 1998. "Phenomenology as Method in Trans Studies." GLQ 4 (2): 263–81.

———. 2003. *Self-Made Men: Identity and Embodiment among Transsexual Men.* Nashville, Tenn.: Vanderbilt University Press.

Rutherford, Jonathan. 1990. "The Third Space: An Interview with Homi Bhabha." In *Identity: Community, Culture, Difference,* edited by Jonathan Rutherford, 207–21. London: Lawrence and Wishart.

Scheper-Hughes, Nancy. 1995. "The Primacy of the Ethical: Propositions for a Militant Anthropology." *Current Anthropology* 36 (3): 409–40.

Scott, Joan W. 1986. "Gender: A Useful Category of Historical Analysis." *American Historical Review* 91 (5): 1053–75.

———. 1993. "The Evidence of Experience." In *The Lesbian and Gay Studies Reader,* edited by Henry Abelove, Michèle Aina Barale, and David M. Halperin, 397–415. New York: Routledge.

Sedgwick, Eve Kosofsky. 1990. *Epistemology of the Closet.* Berkeley: University of California Press.

———. 1993. "How to Bring Your Kids up Gay." In *Fear of a Queer Planet,* edited by Michael Warner, 69–81. Minneapolis: University of Minnesota Press.

Seidman, Steven. 1993. "Identity Politics in a 'Postmodern' Gay Culture: Some Historical and Conceptual Notes." In *Fear of a Queer Planet,* edited by Michael Warner, 105–42. Minneapolis: University of Minnesota Press.

Sender, Katherine. 2004. *Business, Not Politics: The Making of the Gay Market.* New York: Columbia University Press.

Silverman, Victor, and Susan Stryker. 2005. *Screaming Queens: The Riot at Compton's Cafeteria.* Film. USA. Frameline Distribution.

Sinfield, Alan. 2004. "The Challenge of Transgender, the Moment of Stonewall, and Neil Bartlett." *GLQ* 10 (2): 267–72.

Singer, Ben. 2005. "Sex/Gender Categorization in Trans Surveys 1996–2005: A Brief Meta-Analysis." Paper delivered at the Trans Politics, Social Change, and Justice Conference, CUNY, New York, May 6–7.

Sinnott, Megan. 2004. *Toms and Dees: Transgender Identity and Female Same-Sex Relationships in Thailand.* Honolulu: University of Hawaii Press.

Small, Cathy. 1997. *Voyages: From Tongan Villages to American Suburbs.* Ithaca, N.Y.: Cornell University Press.

Stein, David. 2003. "Where Are SA's Black Gays?" http://www.mambaonline .com/feature/feature _ blackgay.htm (accessed February 24, 2003).

Stoller, Robert. 1968. *Sex and Gender: The Development of Masculinity and Femininity.* New York: Science House.

———. 1975. *Sex and Gender.* Volume II: *The Transsexual Experiment.* New York: Jason Aronson.

Stone, Sandy. 1991. "The Empire Strikes Back: A Posttranssexual Manifesto." In *Body Guards: The Cultural Politics of Gender Ambiguity,* edited by Julia Epstein and Kristina Straub, 280–304. New York: Routledge.

Stryker, Susan. 1998. "The Transgender Issue: An Introduction." *GLQ* 4 (2): 145–58.

———. 2006. "(De)Subjugated Knowledges: An Introduction to Transgender Studies." In *The Transgender Studies Reader,* edited by Susan Stryker and Stephen Whittle, 1–17.

Stryker, Susan, and Stephen Whittle, eds. 2006. *The Transgender Studies Reader.* New York: Routledge.

Sullivan, Andrew. 1995. *Virtually Normal: An Argument about Homosexuality.* New York: Alfred A. Knopf.

Taylor, Charles. 1992. *Multiculturalism and the Politics of Recognition: An Essay.* With commentary by Amy Gutmann. Princeton, N.J.: Princeton University Press.

Taylor, Melanie A. 1998. " 'The Masculine Soul Heaving in the Female Bosom': Theories of Inversion and *The Well of Loneliness.*" *Journal of Gender Studies* 7 (3): 287–96.

Terry, Jennifer. 1995. "Anxious Slippages between 'Us' and 'Them': A Brief History of the Scientific Search for Homosexual Bodies." In *Deviant Bodies:*

Critical Perspectives on Difference in Science and Popular Culture, edited by Jennifer Terry and Jacqueline Urla, 129–69. Bloomington: Indiana University Press.

Towle, Evan B., and Lynn M. Morgan. 2002. "Romancing the Transgender Native: Rethinking the Use of the 'Third Gender' Concept." *GLQ* 8 (4): 469–97.

Tsing, Anna Lowenhaupt. 1993. *In the Realm of the Diamond Queen: Marginality in an Out-of-the-Way Place.* Princeton, N.J.: Princeton University Press.

Tyler, Carole-Anne. 1991. "Boys Will Be Girls: The Politics of Gay Drag." In *Inside/Out: Lesbian Theories, Gay Theories,* edited by Diane Fuss, 32–70. Ann Arbor: University of Michigan Press.

Ulrichs, Karl Heinrich. 1994. *The Riddle of "Man-Manly" Love: The Pioneering Work on Male Homosexuality.* Volume 1. Translated by Michael A. Lomardi-Nash. Introduction by Vern L. Bullough. Buffalo, N.Y.: Prometheus Books.

U.S. Congress. House. 1999. *The Hate Crimes Prevention Act of 1999.* HR 1082. 106th Cong., 1st sess.

Vaid, Urvashi. 1995. *Virtual Equality: The Mainstreaming of Gay and Lesbian Liberation.* New York: Doubleday.

Valentine, David. n.d. "Gender Identity Project: Report on Intake Statistics, 1989–April 1997." Unpublished Report.

———. 2004. "Transgender Histories, Identities, and Politics." Course syllabus. http://www.geocities.com/davidvalentine2002/syllabi (accessed April 16, 2006).

———. 2006. " 'I Went to Bed with My Own Kind Once': The Erasure of Desire in the Name of Visibility." In *The Transgender Studies Reader,* edited by Susan Stryker and Stephen Whittle, 397–409.

Valentine, David, and Riki Anne Wilchins. 1997. "One Percent on the Burn Chart: Gender, Genitals, and Hermaphrodites with Attitude." *Social Text* 52–53: 215–22.

Valerio, Max Wolf. n.d. "Why I'm Not 'Transgender.' " http://content.gay.com/channels/home/trans_stories/valerio_max.html (accessed January 30, 2005).

Vance, Carole. 1990. "Negotiating Sex and Gender in the Attorney General's Commission on Pornography." In *Uncertain Terms: Negotiating Gender in American Culture,* edited by Faye D. Ginsburg and Anna Lowenhaupt Tsing, 118–34. Boston: Beacon Press.

———. 1991. "Anthropology Rediscovers Sexuality: A Theoretical Comment." *Social Science and Medicine* 33 (8): 875–84.

———. 1992. "More Danger, More Pleasure: A Decade after the Barnard Sexuality Conference." In *Pleasure and Danger: Exploring Female Sexuality,* 2nd ed., edited by Carole Vance, xvi–xxxix. London: Pandora Press.

Varnell, Paul. 2003. "Bailey on Gay Femininity." *Chicago Free Press,* July 23.

Wakin, Eric. 1992. *Anthropology Goes to War: Professional Ethics and Counterinsurgency in Thailand.* Madison: University of Wisconsin, Center for Southeast Asian Studies.

Warner, Michael. 1993. Introduction to *Fear of a Queer Planet: Queer Politics and Social Theory,* edited by Michael Warner, vii–xxxi. Minneapolis: University of Minnesota Press.

———. 1999. *The Trouble with Normal: Sex, Politics, and the Ethics of Queer Life.* New York: Free Press.

Weeks, Jeffrey. 1981. *Sex, Politics, and Society: The Regulation of Sexuality since 1800.* London: Longman.

———. 1985. *Sexuality and its Discontents: Meanings, Myths, and Modern Sexualities.* Boston: Routledge and Kegan Paul.

Weiss, Jillian T. 2001. "A Review of Lesbian, Gay, Bisexual, and Transgender Legal Issues." *Tulane Law School Journal of Law and Sexuality* 10:123–86.

West, Candace, and Don Zimmerman. 1987. "Doing Gender." *Gender and Society* 1 (2): 125–51.

Weston, Kath. 1993. "Lesbian/Gay Studies in the House of Anthropology." *Annual Review of Anthropology* 22:339–69.

Whitehead, Harriet. 1981. "The Bow and the Burden Strap: A New Look at Institutionalized Homosexuality in Native North America." In *Sexual Meanings: The Cultural Construction of Gender and Sexuality,* edited by Sherry B. Ortner and Harriet Whitehead , 80–113. Cambridge: Cambridge University Press.

Whorf, Benjamin Lee. 1956. [1939]. "The Relation of Habitual Thought and Behavior to Language." In *Language, Thought, and Reality: Selected Writings of Benjamin Lee Whorf,* edited by John B. Carroll, 134–59. Cambridge: MIT Press.

Wiegman, Robyn. 1995. *American Anatomies: Theorizing Race and Gender.* Durham, N.C.: Duke University Press.

Wieringa, Saskia, and Evelyn Blackwood. 1999. Introduction to *Female Desires: Same-Sex Relations and Transgender Practices across Cultures,* edited by Evelyn Blackwood and Saskia Wieringa, 1–38. New York: Columbia University Press.

Wikan, Unni. 1977. "Man Becomes Woman: Transsexualism in Oman as a Key to Gender Roles." *Man* 12:304–19.

———. 1991. "The Xanith: A Third Gender Role?" *Behind the Veil in Arabia: Women in Oman.* Chicago: University of Chicago Press.

Wilchins, Riki Anne. 1997. *Read My Lips: Sexual Subversion and the End of Gender.* Ithaca, N.Y.: Firebrand Books.

———. 2002. "Deconstructing Trans." In *Genderqueer: Voices from beyond the Sexual Binary,* edited by Joan Nestle, Clare Howell, and Riki Wilchins, 55–63. Los Angeles: Alyson Books.

Williams, Walter L. 1986. *The Spirit and the Flesh: Sexual Diversity in American Indian Culture.* Boston: Beacon Press.

Wilson, Mitchell. 1993. "DSM-III and the Transformation of American Psychiatry: A History." *American Journal of Psychiatry* 150:399–410.

Wilson, Robin. 2003a. " 'Dr. Sex': A Human-Sexuality Expert Creates Controversy with a New Book on Gay Men and Transsexuals." *Chronicle of Higher Education* 49 (41): A8.

———. 2003b. "Transsexual 'Subjects' Complain about Professor's Research Methods." *Chronicle of Higher Education* 49 (46): A10.

Wood, Peter. 2003. "Sex and Consequence: An Anthropologist Vindicates the Traditional Family." *American Conservative,* July 28. http://www.amconmag.com/2003/07_28_03/cover.html (accessed April 16, 2006).

Yudkin, Marcia. 1978. "Transsexualism and Women: A Critical Perspective." *Feminist Studies* 4 (3): 97–106.

Index

Activism and advocacy: diversity and inclusion as modes of, 18, 37, 173–78, 180–203, 214, 265 n. 16; gay liberation, 54–56; hate crimes and, 192–95, 212–16; lesbian feminist, 45–48, 50, 56, 58–59, 184, 217–18; manifestations of transgender, 172, 173–203 passim, 210–20, 244–45, 274 n. 4, 275 n. 7; origins of transgender, 35–36, 101–2, 179–81; privacy as claim of, 18–19, 55–56, 62–64, 240–44. *See also* Ethnography: as activist strategy; National Gay and Lesbian Task Force; Stonewall rebellion, disputes over origins of; Violence

Bailey, J. Michael, 149–50, 152–53, 264 n. 12

Berdache, 153–56, 270 nn. 4–5
Bisexuality, 187–90, 261 n. 18
Body/embodiment, 27, 36, 80, 88–89, 97, 112–13, 145, 218–19, 220–23, 268 n. 5
Butches. *See* FTMs and female-bodied masculine people
Butch queens up in drags. *See* MTFs and male-bodied feminine people

Class. *See* Intersectionality
Community, theories of, 72–73, 98–99, 101–4. *See also* Transgender: as community, understandings of
Crossdressers International (CDI), 85–86
Culture, anthropological theories of, 72–73, 234–35, 242–44, 259 n. 13

Diagnostic and Statistical Manual of Mental Disorders (DSM): gender identity disorder in, 55, 274 n. 4; homosexuality in, 54–56

Diversity. *See* Activism and advocacy: diversity and inclusion as modes of

Drag, 12–13, 73–74, 84, 87–104

Employment Non-Discrimination Act (ENDA). *See* GenderPAC: relationship with HRC of

Ethics. *See* Ethnography: ethical practice and

Ethnography: as activist strategy, 246–53, 276 n. 4; ethical practice and, 21–22, 205–6, 208–12, 215–17, 220–23, 226–30, 247–53; as practice, 13–14, 19–20, 231–33, 259 n. 15; transgender and texts of, 150–66

Feinberg, Leslie, 29–30, 64, 148

Feminism. *See* Activism and advocacy: lesbian feminist; Gender: feminist accounts of; Sexuality: feminist accounts of

FTMs and female-bodied masculine people, 45–46, 50–51, 99–100, 151–57, 163–64, 223–26; absence of in text, 23–24, 74, 260 n. 16; butch/FTM border wars, 50–51, 151–53, 170–71; butches, 80–84, 110, 120–23; relationship to transgender of, 34, 145, 148. *See also* Lesbian identity

Gay identity, modes of, 11, 15, 80–84, 92–94, 97, 100–101, 115–19, 121–22, 126–27, 129–33, 143–44, 162, 202, 235–42. *See also* Homosexuality

Gender: as analytic category, 15, 57–62, 100, 132–33, 150–51, 154–66, 169–72, 264 n. 12, 235–40, 242–44, 276 n. 1; feminist accounts of, 46–47, 58–60, 170–72, 236–40. *See also* Sexology; Sexuality

Gender identity disorder, in DSM, 55, 274 n. 4

Gender Identity Project (GIP), 20–21, 71–72, 182–87

GenderPAC: disputes around, 214–16; relationship with HRC of, 8–9, 189, 192–95, 200–201, 212–15

Genderqueer, 136, 254

Gender variance. *See* Transgender: genealogies of; Transgender: meanings of

HIV: public sex and, 265 n. 15; safer-sex outreach and, 259 n. 14. *See also* Social service provision

Homonormativity, 133, 240–42

Homosexuality: in DSM, 54–56; genealogies of, 14–15, 29–31, 40–45, 48–52, 132–33, 238, 241–42; meanings of, 4–5, 22–23, 45, 48–54, 82, 84, 88, 92–94, 97, 114–19, 121–23, 126–27, 130–33, 150–51, 157–66, 200–203, 233–40; unmarked male, 237–38. *See also* Gay identity; Lesbian identity

House balls, 75–84, 266 n. 2, 267 nn. 4–5

Human Rights Campaign (HRC), 8–

9, 189, 192–95, 200–201,
212–15

Identity and identification, 25–26,
105–37 passim, 223–28, 234–
40, 245–46, 271 n. 5. *See also*
Personhood
Identity politics. *See* Activism and
advocacy: diversity and inclusion
as modes of
Imperial court, 90–94, 267 n. 8,
Intersectionality: as mode of analysis, 17, 61, 94–98, 100, 131–32,
178–87, 191, 197, 199–203,
240–42; race and class experience
of transgendered people and, 17–
18, 43–44, 48, 60, 63–64, 95–98,
105–6, 110–11, 132–34, 159–60,
176–79, 185–203, 224–26, 240–
42, 266 n. 1, 273 n. 12

Language: anthropological
approaches to, 31, 233–34; use of
in text, 25–27. *See also* Transgender: representation of
transgender-identified people
Lesbian and Gay Community Services Center: described, 182–83;
as ethnographic site, 7, 20–21,
173, 182–83, 187; move and
renaming of, 101–2, 195–96,
199–200, 258 n. 4
Lesbian identity: meanings of, 16,
45–48, 52; modes of, 45–48,
237–38. *See also* Activism and
advocacy: lesbian feminist; FTMs
and female-bodied masculine people; Homosexuality
LGBT/queer studies. *See* Queer;

Transgender: LGBT/queer studies
and

Meat market, 10–11, 101–2, 109–
13, 207–8, 244, 268 n. 3
Media, role of in inscribing categories, 48–51, 186
MTFs and male-bodied feminine people: butch queens up in drags, 81–
84; cross-dressers, 9–10, 85–89;
fem queens, 1–5, 11, 101–2, 105–
6, 109–19, 244–46; treatment of
historical and ethnographic subjects, 41–43, 45, 48–52, 152–66,
171–72

National Gay and Lesbian Task
Force (NGLTF), 175; Creating
Change conference and, 187–
92
New social movements, 177–80,
215. *See also* Activism and
advocacy
New York Association for Gender
Rights Advocacy (NYAGRA), 196–
98, 275 n. 7

Passing women. *See* FTMs and
female-bodied masculine people.
Personhood, 18–19, 118–19, 234–
40. *See also* Identity and
identification
Prince, Virginia, 32, 261 n. 1
Privacy. *See* Activism and advocacy:
privacy as claim of
Prostitution. *See* Sex work
Psychiatry, 54–56, 58–59. *See also*
Gender identity disorder, in DSM;
Homosexuality: in DSM

Queer, as analytic category, 24, 260 n. 17. *See also* Transgender: LGBT/queer studies and

Race. *See* Intersectionality
Raymond, Janice, 149, 184, 217–19
Rivera, Sylvia, 45, 54

Sexology, understandings of gender and sexuality in, 41–42, 57, 59, 149, 235–36, 263 n. 4
Sexuality: as analytic category, 15, 57–62, 100–101, 132–33, 150–51, 154–66, 169–72, 235–44, 264 n. 12, 275 n. 1; feminist accounts of, 60, 236–40, 265 n. 14
Sex work, 10–11, 101–2, 109–13, 195–99
Social service provision, 3–5, 71–72, 105–6, 113–14, 118, 125, 142–44, 182–87, 216–17
Stonewall rebellion, disputes over origins of, 43–45, 195–200

Teena, Brandon, 181, 218–19, 223–26
Third gender, 153–58, 269 n. 1, 271 n. 6

Transexuality: debates over, 71, 217–20, 274 n. 4; genealogies of, 57–58; meanings of, 68–51; spelling of, 25. *See also* Transgender
Transgender: as collective, spectrum, or umbrella, 14, 33, 37–40, 71–72, 99, 102, 125, 186, 201–3; as community, understandings of, 20, 71–73, 94–104, 232–33;

genealogies of, 29–35, 261 n. 1, 262 n. 2; institutionalization of, 14, 33–34, 100–101, 132–33, 167–72, 186–87, 190, 194–95, 201–3, 228–34, 254; LGBT/queer studies and, 24, 145–47, 172; meanings of, 4–6, 7–14, 32–35, 37–40, 84, 99–100, 105–6, 147, 159–61, 169–74, 224–27, 233–40, 243–44, 253–55; representation of transgender-identified people, 22–26, 112, 147–48, 268 n. 2, 269 n. 7, 269 n. 10; resistance to and critiques of, 8–9, 34, 93–94, 99, 207, 224–26; transgender studies, 143–72 passim. *See also* FTMs and female-bodied masculine people; Gender identity disorder; MTFs and male-bodied feminine people; Transexuality; Transvestism
Transsexuality. *See* Transexuality
Transvestism: genealogies of, 48–51; relationship of to transexuality, 264 n. 11. *See also* MTFs and male-bodied feminine people: cross-dressers; Transgender

Violence: anthropological approaches to, 206, 208–12, 215–16, 226–28; exposure of transgender-identified people to, 101–2, 205–8, 213, 215–20, 223–30; representation and, 204–6, 209–30

Wilchins, Riki Anne, 8, 184, 192–94, 204–5, 218–23, 274 n. 1

David Valentine is an assistant professor

of anthropology at the University of Minnesota.

Library of Congress Cataloging-in-Publication Data

Valentine, David, 1966–

Imagining transgender: an ethnography of a category /

David Valentine. p. cm.

Includes bibliographical references and index.

ISBN 978-0-8223-3853-6 (cloth: alk. paper)

ISBN 978-0-8223-3869-7 (pbk.: alk. paper)

1. Transsexualism. 2. Transsexuals — Social conditions. 3. Gender identity.

4. Transsexualism — Research. 5. Anthropology.

I. Title. HQ77.7V35 2007

306.76'8 — dc22

2007006304

47350281R00190

Made in the USA
Middletown, DE
22 August 2017